"This man is a ge

MW00529260

"The perfect blend of insightful scholarship, pop-culture savvy, and bloody good fun. Highly recommended!" —Jonathan Maberry, *New York Times* best-selling author of *Kagen the Damned*

STRANGER THINGS PSYCHOLOGY: LIFE UPSIDE DOWN

"Look into the psyche of *Stranger Things* and get ready to see the show in a whole new way, uncovering new insights and perspective into the characters, the '80s, and ourselves. Be ready to have your perception turned . . . Upside Down. I really liked it." —Gail Z. Martin, author of the *Deadly Curiosities* series

"Stellar anthology . . . eye-opening . . . The entries mix genuine appreciation with measured critique, taking seriously the complex issues powering the show's plot, without undercutting its overall entertainment value. Fans looking to delve deeper into the show will devour this." —Publishers Weekly

BATMAN AND PSYCHOLOGY: A DARK AND STORMY KNIGHT

"Marvelous!" —Adam West

"Scholarly and insightful . . . His professional credentials, mixed with his love for comic books and the character of Batman, create a fascinating, entertaining, and educational read." —Michael Uslan, *Batman* film series originator and executive producer

"It is a terrific book." —Dennis O'Neil, *Batman* comic book writer/editor

"A modern classic." —Mark D. White, author of *Batman and Ethics*

"If you ever wanted to really know if Bruce Wayne is nuts, then this is the book for you. Perhaps some incarnations of Batman are more crazy than others! Great read and tremendously insightful into the psyche of The Dark Knight." —Batman-on-Film.com

"An intriguing read and a fascinating book." —eXpert Comics

"Easily one of my top 10 favorite books of any genre. Super work!"
—Chad Ellsworth, author of *Building Up without Tearing Down*

"Possibly the most fascinating book I have ever read." —Chelsea Campbell, author of the *Renegade X* series

DOCTOR WHO PSYCHOLOGY
(1ST EDITION, WITH 2ND EDITION COMING SOON!)

"This book is a must-read for every Whovian!" —Night Owl Reviews

"These hyperintelligent superfans deliver intriguing insights…"
—Midlife Crisis Crossover

"This is a must-read for Who fans. The diverse range of topics will have you wanting to watch all the Doctors over again." —The Beguiled Child

"A cracking read. They know their *Who* inside and out, and the science is impeccable . . . This is an exceptional example of what must now be regarded as a legitimate genre." —*The Psychologist*, British Psychological Society

SPIDER-MAN
PSYCHOLOGY

Also by Travis Langley

Stranger Things Psychology: Life Upside Down
Batman and Psychology: A Dark and Stormy Knight
The Joker Psychology: Evil Clowns and the Women Who Love Them
Black Panther Psychology: Hidden Kingdoms
Westworld Psychology: Violent Delights
Daredevil Psychology: The Devil You Know
Supernatural Psychology: Roads Less Traveled
Star Trek Psychology: The Mental Frontier
Wonder Woman Psychology: Lassoing the Truth
Doctor Who Psychology: A Madman with a Box
Game of Thrones Psychology: The Mind is Dark and Full of Terrors
Captain America vs. Iron Man: Freedom, Security, Psychology
Star Wars Psychology: Dark Side of the Mind
The Walking Dead Psychology: Psych of the Living Dead

Also by Alex Langley

100 Greatest Graphic Novels
Make a Nerdy Living
The Geek Handbook series
Kill the Freshman

SPIDER-MAN

PSYCHOLOGY

UNTANGLING WEBS

EDITED BY
TRAVIS LANGLEY
AUTHOR OF *BATMAN AND PSYCHOLOGY*

CO-EDITED BY
ALEX LANGLEY

WILEY

JOHN WILEY & SONS, INC.
AN IMPRINT OF TURNER PUBLISHING COMPANY
Nashville, Tennessee
www.turnerpublishing.com

WILEY

Spider-Man Psychology: Untangling Webs

Cover design by M.S. Corley
Book design by William Ruoto

Library of Congress Cataloging-in-Publication Data
Names: Langley, Travis, 1964- editor. | Langley, Alex, editor.
Title: Spider-Man psychology : untangling webs / Travis Langley, editor ; Alex Langley, co-editor.
Description: Nashville, Tennessee : John Wiley & Sons, [2023] | Series: Popular culture psychology | Includes bibliographical references and index.
Identifiers: LCCN 2022055644 (print) | LCCN 2022055645 (ebook) | ISBN 9781684429332 (paperback) | ISBN 9781684429349 (hardcover) | ISBN 9781684429356 (epub)
Subjects: LCSH: Spider-Man (Fictitious character)—Psychology. | Psychology in comics. | Spider-Man films—Psychological aspects. | Identity (Psychology) in motion pictures. | LCGFT: Comics criticism. | Film criticism.
Classification: LCC PN6728.S6 S74 2023 (print) | LCC PN6728.S6 (ebook) | DDC 741.5/973—dc23/eng/20221130
LC record available at https://lccn.loc.gov/2022055644
LC ebook record available at https://lccn.loc.gov/2022055645

Printed in the United States of America

Contents

About Team Spidey-Psych

Editor

Travis Langley, PhD, series/volume editor and distinguished professor of psychology at Henderson State University, has been a child abuse investigator, courtroom expert, and *Wheel of Fortune* game show champion. A popular keynote speaker for the American Psychological Association, Amazon, and other organizations, he speaks at events throughout the world, discussing heroism and the power of story in people's lives. The *New York Times*, *Wall Street Journal*, *Saturday Evening Post*, CNN, MTV, and hundreds of other outlets have interviewed him and covered his work. He appears as an expert interviewee in documentary programs such as *Necessary Evil*, *Legends of the Knight*, *Superheroes Decoded*, *Pharma Bro*, *AMC Visionaries: Robert Kirkman's Secret History of Comics*, and Hulu's *Batman & Bill*.

He ranks among the most popular psychologists online. Just look for Travis Langley as **@Superherologist** or **@DrTravisLangley**.

Co-Editor

Alex Langley, MS, is the author of *Make a Nerdy Living*, *100 Greatest Graphic Novels*, and The Geek Handbook series as well as the graphic novel *Kill the Freshman*. He also wrote chapters for several Popular Culture Psychology books, most recently *Stranger Things Psychology: Life Upside Down*. Online, he has covered retro and modern gaming for

Arcade Sushi, edited content for web celebrity @ActionChick Katrina Hill at ActionFlickChick .com, served as gaming editor at Nerdspan.com, and co-created the YouTube web series *Geeks and Gamers Anonymous*. He regularly speaks on nerdy topics and shares writing advice at fan conventions such as Wonder-Con, Fan Expo, and San Diego Comic-Con International. His published works also include academic papers, and he likes your hair like that. Social media: **@RocketLlama**.

Interior Illustrator

Jeffrey Henderson is an award-winning writer, illustrator, filmmaker, actor, and musician. A renowned storyboard artist, his major film and TV credits include *The Dark Knight*, *Black Adam*, *The Boys*, *Ms. Marvel*, *Jungle Cruise*, *Uncharted*, *Fargo*, and *Inception*, to name just a few. He wrote, directed, and starred in the LucasFilm Fan Film Award-winning short film *Star Wars: The Sable Corsair*, and has contributed vocal performances, songs, and music to a number of film, TV, and video game projects. Henderson worked with director Sam Raimi on multiple projects such as *Oz the Great and Powerful*, *Spider-Man 3*, and the legendary, unproduced *Spider-Man 4*. You can find some of Henderson's storyboards and concept art for those films online.

Find him online at **planethenderson.com** and everywhere on social media as **@PlanetHenderson**.

Other contributor biographies appear at the ends of their respective chapters.

Keep up with these books through the Popular Culture Psychology page at **Facebook.com/ThePsychGeeks**.

Acknowledgments

Our Amazing Friends

I
Travis Langley, Editor

Once upon a time, Danny Fingeroth's book *Superman on the Couch: What Superheroes Really Tell Us about Ourselves and Our Society*,[1] made me think, "I want to write this kind of book," before we ever met. Over the years in which I've known this author,[2] educator, Spider-Man group editor, public speaker, convention panel organizer, and legendary figure, Danny has become a valued friend. In addition to providing this book's foreword, he has helped me in several ways. Among them, he has proven to be a valuable resource by answering questions, whether convolutedly complicated or as simple as "Is it Spider-sense or spider-sense? And what about Spidey-sense?"[3] (Comic book text had consistently appeared in ALL CAPS, after all.)

Tom DeFalco, John Semper Jr., and others also helped answer odd questions. They and other comics pros have joined us in panel discussions partly or primarily about Marvel's spider-heroes and sinister foes: Brian Michael Bendis, Paul Benjamin, Amy Chu, Victor Dandridge Jr., Jo Duffy, Mark Evanier, Michael Eury, Dean Haspiel, Arie Kaplan, Scott Larson, Fred Van Lente, Ron Marz, Bryan Q. Miller, Jose Molina, Ann Nocenti, Denny O'Neil, Carl Potts, Christopher Priest, Jim Salicrup, J. J. Sedelmaier, Gail Simone, Louise Simonson, R. Sikoryak, Michael Uslan, Len Wein, Renee Witterstaetter,

Marv Wolfman, and Emmy-winner Joe Wos—several of whom I met through Danny. I was honored to hear the now-departed Denny O'Neil and Len Wein call me friend, and we miss them often. One of my Zoom conversations with Jonathan Butler (writer and executive producer on *The Flash*) inadvertently handed me an insight for chapter 14: When I talked about how Spider-Man's story involves straying from his core values then getting a hard lesson that reconnects him with them, I meant the origin but it sounded like I meant *Spider-Man: No Way Home*, which made me realize it's true there too. It's true in many stories.

Danny's observation in *Superman on the Couch* that "it has been decades since psychiatry or psychology has taken a look at such questions about superheroes"[4] stayed with me when I attended San Diego Comic-Con for the first time. There, I met comics scholars through the Comics Arts Conference (CAC, Comic-Con's educational conference-within-the-con), watched fans bustling about in a con environment that celebrated their nerdy passions, and knew I had to become part of it all. Peter Coogan and Randy Duncan founded the CAC, which Kate McClancy now chairs and I help organize. Because I met comic book creators, filmmakers, and many of this book's contributors through comic cons, I thank the organizers at Comic-Con International (Eddie Ibrahim, Gary Sassaman, Cathy Dalton, Jackie Estrada, Sue Lord, Karen Mayugba, Adam Neese, Amy Ramirez, Chris Sturhan), Fan Expo (Kevin Boyd, Tajshen Campbell, Mike Gregorek, Peter Katz, Bruce MacIntosh, Jerry Milani, Brittany Rivera, Betty Waypa, Alex Wer), Lubbock-Con (DeNae Cortez), and other conventions and related events.

In addition to my regular load teaching on the psychology of mental illness, social behavior, and crime, each spring I normally add something different, usually a media-related class using film or literature as a lens through which to examine the science of real human behavior—including one course on Marvel heroes after Stan Lee suggested it to me. I remain grateful to all the students whose participation in those courses challenge me and prod me to carry on. I thank our faculty writers group members (Angela Boswell, Andrew Burt, Maryjane Dunn, Martin Halpern, William Henshaw,

Michael Taylor, Shannon Wittig) for reviewing portions of this material. Latrena Beasley, Sandra D. Johnson, Connie Testa, and other staffers provide invaluable service.

My literary agent Evan Gregory, Bibi Lewis, and others at the Ethan Ellenberg Literary Agency handle many essential tasks and details. From Turner Publishing, I thank acquisitions editor Ryan Smernoff, top man Todd Bottorff, and other helpful folks such as Claire Ong, Tim Holtz, and Makala Marsee. Connie Santisteban joins us again, this time on both line and copy editing. Without them and with our previous works' countless readers and listeners, these new books could not exist.

Chapter contributors want to recognize supportive people from their lives: Lisa Barker, Chris Burk, Carlyjo Bybee, Dawn Cisewski, Dan Cohen, Albert Dieu, Marjorie Hanft, Grace Hann, Sharon Manning, Dustin McGinnis, Todd Poch, Andrea Schwartz, Howard Schwartz, Sandra Siegel, Caroline Greco and Ava Stover, Michael Thibodeaux, Jeremy and Andie Tucker, Cay Williams, Travis Williams, Ann Yeoman, and Amanda, Jim, Sue, and Evan Wesselmann. Brittney Brownfield, Hannah Espinoza, Scott Jordan, Harpreet Malla, Leandra Parris, Billy San Juan, Patrick O'Connor, Yoni Sobin, Lynn Zubernis, and other psych geeks not writing for this one helped us contemplate Spider-Man supervillains through convention panels. While Elizabeth 방실 Smith may not have written chapter text, she made important points about the superhero Silk. To all these names, I add Spencer, Nicholas, my parents Lynda and Travis Sr., and Rebecca M. Langley, who is my wife, my best friend, and my Black Cat (not a cat burglar but a cat lover who wears a lot of black) whose company and support I treasure beyond measure. Much as I'd love to mention everyone who has joined us when pondering spidery topics on social media, there are too many to list but not too many to appreciate. We owe you such gratitude.

Jeffrey Henderson provided this book's interior artwork. As his bio shows, Jeff's work includes working as storyboard illustrator on Sam Raimi's motion picture *Spider-Man 3* and Raimi's unfilmed *Spider-Man 4*. When your friend who worked on Spider-Man movies volunteers to help on your Spider-Man book, you cheer and welcome him aboard. Thank you, Jeff. Thank you also, Jenna Busch, for bringing this project to Jeff's attention, helping with communication and coordination, assisting, contributing on all Popular Culture Psychology books so far, transcribing Stan Lee's introductions for us twice, and being a true friend. Along those lines, I similarly thank Janina Scarlet, the only person other than myself who has written in every Popular Culture Psychology anthology up through this one. She won't be free to work on the next new one because, among other things, she has books of her own to write. I could not be happier for her success.

When I told our regular Popular Culture Psychology contributors this book would need a co-editor, Alex Langley surprised me as the one who inquired. I flatly told him that the fact that he's my son would make it harder to sell me on the idea, but he made a strong case, shared his vision for the book, and has authored his own stack of books including a graphic novel and *The Geek Handbook* series. With his wife, he extensively researched and authored *100 Greatest Graphic Novels*, so he carries comics expertise. When I ran this by other contributors, they resoundingly endorsed Alex as co-editor and called him the perfect person for the spot.

To explain my part of the book's dedication: First, Eric Bailey and I have been discussing superheroes and other nerdiness together for centuries, starting when we met as students in his first week at Hendrix College. A funny, fun, and fine friend, Eric has been the best traveling companion to many fan conventions, and some of those trips turn into true adventures. It was a joy to introduce him to Adam West and to make sure Eric got to meet and spend time with Stan Lee. Everyone to whom I introduce Eric enjoys his company, even the one who also calls him evil because of how much that person drank while trying to keep up with Eric when we were all in New Orleans for a fan convention. Here's Eric's description of what Spider-Man means to him:

> *I related to Peter Parker as an awkward teen. Anxious, filled with self-doubt at times, never having enough money, navigating girls and problems and adversaries, I grew up with Peter. He became more than a*

childhood fantasy. He was like a true friend who has been with me all my life. To this day, I know when I am down or just want to have some fun and play or maybe even save my world, I can always count on the help of my friendly neighborhood Spider-Man.

I had expected to dedicate a book to Michael French while he was alive to see it instead of making it "and in memory of" my younger, closest cousin. (His sisters Melynda and Michelle rock too.) When we were kids playing with his action figures and robots and Godzilla, we were creating stories about heroes. Because my comics came from a store that sold only DC titles, Michael owned the first Marvels I ever read. For a while, he was the only person with whom I could discuss some of that. Out of our many conversations about heroes both fictional and real, I distinctly recall discussing a story in which Spidey and the Human Torch show Sandman kindness at Christmas.[5] We shared our anticipation for an upcoming *Spider-Man* movie and our dismay over the TV show's dearth of supervillains.[6] The superheroes' principles stayed with Michael for life: He believed people need to stand up, do the right thing, oppose injustice, and look out for others. Though he later loved Star Wars more (and it was Indiana Jones who

Michael French (center) with wife, daughters, and cousin. (I have no idea what the thing is that we were all looking at.)

inspired his archaeology career), I remember his Star Trek comics and toys. I can hear Michael quoting Spock: "I have been and always shall be your friend."[7]

For giving us Spider-Man, we all owe creators Stan Lee and Steve Ditko, along with anyone who might have inspired them in the first place, plus Jack Kirby, the Romitas, and countless other comics creators, filmmakers, actors, and more who have kept the stories going all these decades. Steve Ditko, with his quirky style and inventive imagination, set the pace for Peter Parker, gave faces to his supporting cast, and generated one great villain after another. In addition to Stan Lee's place in Spider-Man history and Marvel Universe development, Stan also contributed the forewords to two of our previous Popular Culture Psychology books.[8] Jenna Busch, who co-hosted his program *Cocktails with Stan*, fondly remembers "all the Spider-Man stories he would tell me between episodes of our show." As Stan said regarding one world's Peter Parker in *Into the Spider-Verse*, "I'm going to miss him."[9]

Finally, we thank all of you for joining us as we climb the walls and spin psychological tales about Marvel tales, examining the amazing, spectacular, astonishing, superior (ahem), friendly neighborhood Spider-Man. Spidey-sense is tingling. It's time to swing.

II
Alex Langley, Co-Editor

Thank you to Katrina, with whom life is always a great big bang-up, and to my son, Spencer, a truly terrific kid whose enthusiasm for discovery shows me new joys and helps me rediscover old ones. Thanks to my brother, Nicholas, and my parents, Rebecca and Travis (hey, that's the other guy whose name is on this book!), for being the best family anyone could ask for.

Thanks to my found family: Tim Yarbrough, Stephen "Ricardo Gigante" Huckabee, Iseulle Kim, Carly Cate, Marko Head, Renee Couey, and Sarah "Fiz" Fuller. Thanks to the creative wonderful weirdos who adopted me like a patchy-furred stray: Molly, Annie, Sam, Za, Cassie, Ben, Laurie, Rimz, Kim, Ian, Febe, Lisa, Laura, Jenn, Nush, Mike, Dan, Regina, Russ, Clay, Payton, and everyone else who's ever held a pen in our crit group. The timer's always running, and you all help me outrun it. Thanks to the many incredible psychologists, experts, and nerds extraordinaire whose words grace this book. Thanks to Slott, Zdarsky, Bendis, Bagley, Romita, and so, so, so many others, and thanks, of course, to Steve and Stan.

Alex Langley, *Spider-Man Psychology* co-editor (left), shares a moment with Stan "the Man" Lee, Spider-Man co-creator (right), after hours during Comic-Con.

Foreword

"He Must Be a Neurotic of Some Sort!" Spidey and Me . . . and You!

Danny Fingeroth

It was the luck of the draw that I became professionally involved with Spider-Man—my own personal irradiated spider-bite.

I was an assistant editor at Marvel Comics and was in line for promotion to full editor when the next slot came open. Tom DeFalco, who had been editing the Spider-titles, was promoted to executive editor, and I became Spider-editor (with a Spidey-emblazoned business card proclaiming that title) and took over his books.

I don't know if I had great power, but I sure had great responsibility.

I had been a fan of Spider-Man from the beginning—missed *Amazing Fantasy* #15 when it appeared but bought *The Amazing Spider-Man* #1 off the stands. I enjoyed the character, especially the first few years of Lee/Ditko/Romita. Never missed an issue. But I was a hardcore Fantastic Four fan. For personal reasons—perhaps neurotic, but your DSM may vary—I also preferred Iron Man and Daredevil to Spidey. There were elements of their origins and themes that resonated with me more deeply than did Peter Parker's endless highs and lows.

And then I was handed the Spider-Man line to edit: *Amazing. Spectacular. Marvel Team-Up* featuring Spider-Man and [your name here].

Suddenly, like Peter Parker, I had been dropped into a world that didn't always understand me and that I didn't always understand. While I'd edited comics before under the watchful eyes of my mentors—Larry Lieber, Louise Simonson, and Jim Shooter—I always had them there to backstop me. Now, just like that, I was on my own. And, just like that, I suddenly had a much deeper understanding of, and connection to, the ever-amazing Spider-Man.

Now my decisions affected what went into the Spider-Man books. I'm not sure if it was more frightening when writers and artists listened to my dictates or when they *didn't*. (Did I mention that I edited Stan Lee, himself, on Spidey a bunch of times?) Either way, like Peter Parker, I learned—or *re*learned, but in a specific context—one of the foundational lessons of life, as crystallized by Jim Shooter: *Actions have consequences.* Like Peter Parker, I wondered what I was really accomplishing, why I was doing what I was doing, wondering if I was just a self-centered glory hound, and so on. (Maybe I was identifying a little too much with Spider-Man . . .)

But, aside from asking myself these questions, in my new position I dove into a deep study of Peter Parker and his web-slinging alter ego. I discovered the person under the mask whose attributes, positive and negative, were front-loaded into the character by Stan Lee and Steve Ditko. I discovered that there was more to Spider-Man than I'd realized as both a kid and as a comics professional. I realized that "With great power there must also come great responsibility" was more than just a dramatic line that Stan came up with—or borrowed from any number of possible sources—to give an intense ending to a new "long underwear character's" origin (a character that, contrary to myth, seems to have definitely been intended to be an ongoing character in an ongoing series). I realized that, with that credo, Stan and Steve had distilled the essence, the *raison d'être*, of all superhero fiction.

You're given great power. Or *any* power. How will you use it? And what kind of responsibility do you have regarding *how* you use it? You didn't ask for it. Or maybe you did, and it's not what you thought it would be. But there you are. And no matter what decision you make, *someone's* going to be unhappy about it (maybe even you).

One of the great spider-experts, comic book writer and former Marvel editor-in chief Tom DeFalco, once gave me some acute insight into Spider-Man. I said to him: "Tom, can you please clarify something for me about Spider-Man? He sometimes says he's Spider-Man because he feels like he has to atone for Uncle Ben's death. Sometimes he says he wants to make sure no one ever suffers like he did (an impossible goal). Sometimes he says he does it because he needs to earn money to help Aunt May. Sometimes he says it's because he likes sticking it to Jonah Jameson when he sells him photos of Spider-Man taken *by* Spider-Man. Sometimes he says he does it because it's just plain *fun* to be Spider-Man. So, which is it? Why do you think he *really* does it?"

To this profound question, Tom replied: "The guy doesn't have a clue. Peter tells himself that there are all sorts of reasons for him being Spider-Man, but ultimately, he really doesn't know *why* he does it. He just *does* it."

And so, Peter Parker, this regular guy superhero, is truly just like us. Or just like me, anyway. But I bet like you too. We tell ourselves we know the reasons we do what we do. We each have our own origin stories, our own triumphs and tragedies, and we think we know why we act and react the way we do. But let's face it:

We don't have a clue.

In 1963's *Amazing Spider-Man* #4, people on a New York street are discussing Spider-Man just a few feet away from Peter Parker, who can't help but overhear them.

Peter Parker overhears New Yorkers on the street discussing Spider-Man and his motives in *The Amazing Spider-Man* #4 (1963). Art by Steve Ditko.

"What would make a guy wear a goofy costume and run around chasin' crooks?" asks one man.

"I dunno!" his friend replies, making the universal swirling gesture with his index finger, indicating Spider-Man is more than a bit off. "He must be a *neurotic* of some sort! Probably has delusions of grandeur!"

Having heard that evaluation, Peter asks himself, "Can they be *right*? Am I *really* some kind of a crack-pot, wasting my time seeking fame and glory? Am I more interested in the adventure of being *Spider-Man* than I am in helping people?? Why do I do it? Why don't I give the whole thing up?"

Who among us has not been so judged by others? So judged by ourselves? There's a little bit of Peter Parker in all of us. The insightful contributors to *Spider-Man Psychology* will tell you about that and lots, lots more. Sure, you have obligations to deal with before you have time to delve into the book. But take the time—give it a read. Your responsibilities can wait.

What's the worst that could happen . . .?

Webs away!

Danny Fingeroth was the Group Editor of Marvel's Spider-Man comics line in the 1980s and 1990s and consulted on what would become the first Sam Raimi *Spider-Man* movie. He was the writer of *Web of Spider-Man* and *Deadly Foes of Spider-Man*. His non-comics books include *Superman on the Couch: What Superheroes Really Tell Us about Ourselves and Our Society*, *Disguised as Clark Kent: Jews, Comics, and the Creation of the Superhero*, and most recently, *A Marvelous Life: The Amazing Story of Stan Lee*, the definitive biography of the co-creator of the Marvel Universe. All three books have been published as audiobooks with narration by the author. Danny is currently working on a prose biography of Jack Ruby (the man who shot Lee Harvey Oswald on live television), a confounding psychological puzzle in his own right. For more information, visit **dannyfingeroth.com**.

Introduction

"A Really Tough Life" and "the Real Pain"

Travis Langley

 "I've never studied psychology officially, but all around us, everything in the world involves psychology," Spider-Man co-creator Stan Lee said when introducing one of our previous books. "The way you behave with people. The image you want to leave of yourself with other people. Your association with other people. Everything you do is linked with psychology. That's what I wanted to bring to our superheroes."[1]

Stan often recounted how, having grown weary of telling the same shallow comic book stories over and over, he followed his wife Joan's advice and told one the way he wanted. Since he was considering quitting anyway, why not risk getting fired? Instead of costing him his job, though, *Fantastic Four* #1 became a fantastic hit.[2] These untraditional heroes would break the old superhero tropes to build new ones. They squabble, mope, divulge their secret identities, declare bankruptcy, repeatedly disband and reunite, and by no means exemplify perfect mental health.[3] Humanity remolded the superhuman. Mundanity transformed the fantastic. Following up on the FF's success, Lee and artist co-creators, especially Jack Kirby, built a universe on a foundation of human worries.[4] Other troubled heroes would follow, the pinnacle of which would prove to be Spider-Man.

In their inversion of superhero tropes, Lee and artist Steve Ditko found the sweet spot with a teenager who would be the hero, not the sidekick, whose spider motif would put people on edge. Angst would fill him and guilt would fuel him. He would alternately love and loathe being Spider-Man,[5] and his pain would color not only one fictional universe, not only one multiverse, but superhero storytelling across all media platforms. Giving him hassles that echoed young adults' everyday lives would reconfigure the superhero story as a whole. As comic book writer John Ostrander put it, "Marvel came along in the '60s and introduced a psychological realism—the heroes had neuroses, psychological problems, issues that they needed to work out."[6]

Over time, Spider-Man would become one of the three most famous superheroes alongside Batman and Superman: the bug, the bat, and the baby from another planet, three orphan boys.[7] Many creators, commenters, and even characters have contemplated why parental loss befalls all these great superheroes.[8] I once asked Stan Lee about that. While he mulled it over, artist John Romita Jr. sitting beside him weighed in.

ROMITA: Excellent question. Why are they all orphans? You wanted to protect the family. You didn't want anybody to have leverage against them.

LEE: *(shaking his head)* No, I'm trying to think if they are all orphans. The Fantastic Four—I don't know who their parents were, come to think of it.

ROMITA: Well, Peter Parker was an orphan because his parents were murdered.

LEE: Peter Parker's parents had to be murdered so that I could give him an aunt to live with, and I wanted him to be an orphan. I wanted Peter Parker to have a really tough life.

After contemplating other superheroes, Stan said that except for Spider-Man and Daredevil, whose status as orphans figured prominently in their origins, "I just didn't think about it." This issue came up again after Stan was gone, when Danny Fingeroth and I convened a group of comic book writers for a Comic-Con panel, "Neurotic Superheroes and the Writers Who Love Them." At one point, we wound up comparing Spider-Man with Batman and Superman in terms of their mental health and popularity.[9]

BRIAN MICHAEL BENDIS (*ULTIMATE SPIDER-MAN* CO-CREATOR): The thing that connects these three heroes: They're all orphans.

BRYAN Q. MILLER (*SMALLVILLE, BATGIRL* WRITER): All the best heroes are.

BENDIS: Two of my children are adopted. They're orphans and know it and wear it, and you see on a day-to-day basis how they process that. A big part of why people connect to these characters so much is because no matter where you are in your own process, they're telling the truth.

LANGLEY: I had a conversation with Stan once about why his heroes were orphans. He said, "I just didn't think about it."

BENDIS: Every time Stan says, "I didn't mean it," I think that's the real stuff. I think that was where his pain was, that's where his trauma was. Maybe he did not want to look you in the eye and share it like that, but he shared it in every issue. You can't make that stuff up. That's his real pain.

Orphanhood is by no means all that Spidey shares with his renowned predecessors. Guilt-ridden Bruce Wayne and Peter Parker feel driven by loved ones' brutal, all-too-ordinary murders. In costume, both embody spooky little animals that many people fear.[10] Nebbishy-looking Clark Kent and Peter Parker work for metropolitan newspapers, regularly covering stories on crime. As superheroes, both possess incredible superpowers. Unlike Bruce or Clark, though, Peter has to worry about making his rent. He has inherited neither family wealth nor Kryptonian technology, and he cannot crush lumps of coal to make diamonds with his bare hand. From his fictional public, Spider-Man gets far less respect.

Peter Parker shares more in common with Superman's creators than with Superman. When pining for attractive girls "who either didn't know I existed or didn't care," writer Jerry Siegel recalled from his own youth, "it occurred to me: What if I was really terrific? What if I had something going for me, like jumping over buildings or throwing cars around, or something like that?"[11] So he and Joe Schuster, his artist friend even less lucky in love, created the god-like champion who only pretends to be a mild-mannered sap. As opposed to two nerdy kids who created the superpowered adult, Stan Lee and Steve Ditko created the nerdy kid who at first only calls himself "Man." Right before the spider bites Pete, a girl rejects him for Flash Thompson, Flash and friends ride off while mocking the bookworm, and Peter sobs, "Someday I'll show them!"[12]

The creators ignited Spider-Man's fire off the flint of their own humanity. Stan and Steve imbued Peter with the human experience. Stan gave Peter the words while Steve provided the spidery look and most of the plot. From the beginning, they filled Spider-Man's life with frustrations but also with fun. Now let's take a look at Spider-Man, Peter Parker, with his "really tough life," through the dark clouds that follow him and the fun that fills his adventures. His struggles bring Spidey to life for us, maybe even make him our friend, and make his triumphs amaze.

Writer/editor Travis Langley (right) shares a laugh with Stan Lee in Philadelphia. Photo by Alex Langley.

1

Why Does He Keep Doing What a Spider Can?

Alex Langley

"Imagine learning what motivates such a man! Is it altruism or deep-rooted schizophrenia?"

—**Professor Miles Warren (not yet the Jackal)**[1]

"If I were dropped out of a plane into the ocean and told the nearest land was a thousand miles away, I'd still swim. And I'd despise the person who gave up."

—**apocryphally attributed to humanistic psychologist Abraham Maslow**[2]

Throughout his career, the wise-cracking, web-slinging, everyman hero Spider-Man frequently finds himself the subject of front-page news. There he's often depicted as, at best, a reckless threat to public safety and, at worst, an active menace.[3] Most of this news makes the front page of the *Daily Bugle*, a publication with such overt bias it could be argued as libel, so it should be easy enough to ignore.* It isn't. Regardless of the source or editorial slant, those words still hurt. The *negativity bias* refers to our tendency to better remember negative information and events compared to positive information

---

* Spider-Man tries to sue the *Daily Bugle* for libel in court. Unfortunately, his attorney expands the lawsuit to include all *Daily Bugle* staff—which includes Peter Parker. Naturally, Spidey drops the case (*She-Hulk* #4, 2004).

and events.[4] Few superheroes are as primed to be negatively biased against themselves as Spider-Man. His most fearsome foe is often his own self-image.

And this negative *Bugle* bias is hardly unique. Many of New York's own citizens loathe and fear Spider-Man,[5] and his interactions with the police would turn deadly for him if not for his spider-sense and agility.[6] The effects of Peter Parker's actions as Spider-Man extend, often disastrously, into his personal life. He can barely hold onto a job[7] or an apartment.[8] Without knowing he's Spider-Man, his own Aunt May notices the bruises, the torn clothes, and the disappearances. Worrying about him stresses her to the point of contributing to her frequent hospitalizations.[9] His friends and girlfriends tire of his excuses and ostracize him at times.[10] With his role as Spider-Man costing Peter Parker as much as it does, it begets the question: Why, true believer, does Peter Parker continue donning that costume? How does someone stay motivated when it feels like everyone is against them? Why in the world does Peter Parker continue on as Spider-Man?

Looking Out for the Neighborhood

Peter Parker's adventures as Spider-Man could be categorized as volunteer work—*very specialized* volunteer work, but volunteer work, nonetheless. Like real-world volunteers, Spidey's choice to help springs from an intersection of many factors, both external and internal. People's most common motives for volunteer work include wanting to help their community, gain understanding of themselves, enhance their self-esteem, or heed personal values that dictate the sheer importance of helping.[11] Peter Parker's most prominent motives seem to be his desire to help his community—from his Forest Hills neighborhood in Queens to all of New York City—and adherence to his personal values. Through both upbringing and heredity, Peter's family creates a strong sense of empathy, compassion, and responsibility in him, a combination of personality factors that are not only admirable but are critical elements in the choice to behave altruistically.[12]

But does he operate as Spider-Man primarily to aid others or to feed his own ego? At times, even Peter wonders that about himself, pondering at the end of one of his earliest adventures, "Am I more interested in the adventure of being Spider-Man than I am in helping people? Why do I do it?"[13] and later, "Can I be sure my only motive was the conquest of crime? Or was it the heady thrill of battle, the precious taste of triumph?"[14] It's a question of *altruism*, actions motivated toward improving the welfare of another, versus *egoism*, actions motivated toward improving one's own welfare. One reason Spider-Man resonates with audiences around the world is because both altruistic and egoistic tendencies exist within us all. Maybe there is a hero in us, but there's a self-serving jerk too. And yet we can count on the fact that despite some selfish thoughts, even going so far as to imagine using his powers illegally for personal gain,[15] Peter Parker will put on those tights time and time again and make the altruistic sacrifice.

Reasons *not* to help abound. People living in large cities are far less likely to offer help than those living elsewhere, with New York City seen as one of the most unhelpful cities in the entire world.[16] Given his nature as an emergency volunteer, Spider-Man helps everyone he can, regardless of gender, despite the numerous occasions in which (generally male) villains have used his desire to help others against him by posing as innocent victims.[17] He helps despite any and all risks.

Innocence plays a factor in altruism as well. We're more likely to help those whom we feel "deserve" our help, people whose suffering does not seem to result of their own irresponsible choices.[18] Although most people Spider-Man helps fall under the category of innocent victims, he's also likely to help imperiled supervillains and criminals regardless of whether they're mad scientists who experimented on themselves or unlucky guys who fell down in the wrong place (e.g., particle accelerator, vat of electric eels).[19] By choosing to help both everyday citizens and menacing villains, day after day at great risk to himself, Spider-Man takes actions that fly in the face of much of evolutionary psychology.[20] His ongoing heroics are an example of *courageous resistance*:[21] costly, ongoing altruism that requires incredible and sustained motivation.

Wealth and Fame

Cash, attention, and social media likes or views are *extrinsic motivators*, motivational factors oriented around external rewards. Peter Parker's earliest outings as Spider-Man involve trying to earn extra money for his family through wrestling and some fame for himself through TV appearances.[22] It all goes awry thanks to a robber who steals from the station and escapes due in part to teen Spider-Man's resolution to do nothing that does not directly benefit him. This robber, naturally, is the one who murders Peter's Uncle Ben, thus creating the tragic backstory and eternally guilty conscience that this book will address a number of times because Spider-Man thinks about them all the time. Not only does being Spider-Man offer few extrinsic rewards, it's expensive.[23] Peter's adventures often leave him so broke he lacks money for rent or replacement web-shooter cartridges. With few options for income, he resorts to taking photos of himself in action as Spider-Man and selling them to the very newspaper that hounds him. The pay, however, is generally a pittance, and Spider-Man's reputation suffers because of editor-in-chief J. Jonah Jameson's editorial grudge against him—leaving him more infamous than famous.

Ignored Rewards

Intrinsic motivation, the drive to perform acts for their own sake instead of external reward, is by far the stronger and more complex of the two primary motivational factors. Being Spider-Man may be a hard and costly endeavor, but it's not without some rewards. When we do nice things for others, we share in their good feelings through *empathic joy*.[24] When others are suffering and we help relieve that suffering, we share in their feelings of relief as well. During moments in which we feel bad about ourselves, *especially* when we feel guilty, acts of altruism can relieve those negative states and leave us feeling lighter, unburdened. Spider-Man often shares in the joys of those he's helping. He also has more than his share of guilt—as a superhero whose origin story centers around his personal selfishness leading to personal tragedy, guilt is an ever-present state of mind. His actions as Spider-Man provide fleeting moments of happiness but never a full reprieve from the guilt wedged into his psyche.

In addition to the sheer satisfaction of being a helper, being Spider-Man lets Peter Parker meet some of the greatest scientists on the planet, use cutting-edge technology, and travel to exotic locations all around the Earth, the universe, and the multiverse. These are experiences without tangible external value. They are rewarding in and of themselves.

Intrinsic factors similarly motivate Peter's fellow spider-heroes, while similarly costing them dearly. Miles Morales has a strong desire to help his community and adhere to his family-instilled personal values. Spider-Gwen (a.k.a. Ghost-Spider, Gwen Stacy of Earth-65) spends her days saving others to follow in the footsteps of her father, Captain George Stacy, and to help her wrestle with her guilt for letting her world's Peter Parker die. Cindy Moon (a.k.a. Silk), having lived the first decade of early adulthood alone in a bunker, relishes the superhero life as it gives her thrills and worldly experiences she missed out on. Ben Reilly, Peter Parker's often-deceased but repeatedly restored clone, shares the same genetics and childhood memories with Peter (sort of similar to the way an identical twin would). The lessons in Peter's memories, along with perpetually trying to make up for mistakes clone Reilly has made on his own (which get far too complicated to list here), direct his actions as the superhero Scarlet Spider.[26]

His Reward

When Doctor Strange pops into the astral plane, he usually doesn't have to worry about an audience. Members of teams such as the Avengers or X-Men operate with the support of their peers and often on secret missions unknown to the public. Spider-Man and his fellow spider-heroes, however, each tend to work alone (despite many team-ups) and in full public view. Not only does the need to keep people safe weigh on Spider-Man, he faces public reaction out on the streets in a way that most superheroes do not. When he accidentally webs up the wrong person, passersby will let him know, loudly: "You are so getting publicly shamed for this!"[25] In the age of smartphones, drones, and

AND A LEAN, SILENT FIGURE SLOWLY FADES INTO THE GATHERING DARKNESS, AWARE AT LAST THAT IN THIS WORLD, WITH GREAT POWER THERE MUST ALSO COME -- GREAT RESPONSIBILITY!

Peter learns the hard lesson about responsibility, including its imperative nature, which makes a big difference in terms of psychological impact and motivating power. It also shows the full quote, not the better-known, shorter version. *The Amazing Spider-Man* #4 (1963). Art by Steve Ditko.

video surveillance, a momentary misstep could live forever in infamy as #CancelSpiderMan* trends around the globe.

For most, this increased visibility would serve as a powerful demotivating factor. The presence of unhelpful, non-reactive bystanders in an emergency often creates a paralyzing mixture of social and survival cues. In such situations, *bystander apathy* can take hold and onlookers will withhold aid, not out of hostility, but out of apathy, confusion, and self-preservation. The more people who bear witness to an emergency, the less any one person feels responsible to help due to the general *diffusion of responsibility*. Peter Parker, it could be argued, feels a *suffusion of responsibility* in such situations. He feels responsible to act because he has the power to act.[27]

In fact, onlookers and innocent bystanders often motivate Spider-Man to do his best work. "Silence, attractive citizen!" he says as he swings into action, "I'm about to dazzle the crowd!"[28] *Social facilitation* occurs when the presence of an audience increases our performance beyond our normal

---

* The lack of a hyphen would drive him *crazy*.

limits. Spidey doesn't just thrive in the presence of others; he thrives *because* of them. Having the additional witness to his actions may increase his *arousal* (a combination of excitement and motivation) to the optimal levels along the *optimal arousal curve*. This inverted U-shaped curve correlates performance with arousal, illustrating the way in which too little will result in a lazy performance, and too much will result in a person "choking" or otherwise breaking down due to stress.[29] In the perfect conditions, however, we are just stressed enough to give our best.

The constant presence of an audience can also bring with it potential rewards. Spider-Man gets to see and feel the effects of his efforts more directly than other heroes often do. He gets immediate feedback, valuable for enhancing performance. Despite those who express ingratitude, many people he helps are truly grateful. Some honor him in different ways, such as naming their child after him* or offering free hot dogs for life.[30] Altruism research indicates that one factor that impacts the frequency and intensity with which a person will behave altruistically is whether or not those we're helping show gratitude.[31] Superheroes like Spider-Man aren't motivated solely by thank-yous and hot dogs, but it helps.

Why Then?

Spider-Man is not Oskar Schindler, who bribed, swindled, sweet-talked, and blackmailed anyone and everyone necessary to protect Jewish people from the Nazis. It is estimated that Schindler directly saved the lives of over 1,200 Jewish people, whose contributions and descendants are innumerable.[32] Spider-Man is not James Harrison, known to some as the Man with the Golden Arm, who found out during a routine blood donation that his blood carried a unique plasma composition that could protect infants from the immune disorder Rhesus disease. Upon this discovery, he spent the rest of his life making as many donations as he could—1,173 in total.[33]

---

* In such instances, he tells them his name is Ben (e.g., *Marvel Comics* #1000, 2019).

Oskar Schindler drained his fortune to save human lives and James Harrison drained a lot of his own blood, and yet each persisted. Neither saw his efforts as heroic. "I felt that the Jews were being destroyed," said Schindler. "I had to save them. I had no choice."[34] Similarly, Harrison said of his selfless donations, "It becomes quite humbling when they say, 'Oh, you've done this or you've done that or you're a hero.' It's something I can do. It's one of my talents, probably my only talent, that I can be a blood donor."[35]

Those heroes are real. They saved real lives and touched millions more. Spider-Man is not real, and yet a fictional example can inspire real people. The fact that he is not real can make it more comforting and easier to watch, thus giving readers, listeners, or viewers more time to learn from it. Like any other number of heroes fictional or real, Spider-Man pays for his efforts with his wallet, his blood, and how he spends his life. Like real heroes' efforts in our world, his within his stories are tireless, his contributions cumulative. Like them, he takes it upon himself to stop problems that are not of his doing because he is uniquely able to stop them. Spider-Man helps people because he enjoys helping people, and because if he does not, he feels no one will. He continues not for financial gain or prestige, but because it's the right thing to do. When he knows his effort has helped, that is his reward.

"Hope you were watching, Uncle Ben. 'Cause I did that for you. Kept everyone safe. Kept them from being scared. And I made it fun. It doesn't matter that most of 'em wouldn't have lifted a finger for Peter Parker. That's not why you do it. You do it 'cause it's the right thing to do."

—Peter Parker, your friendly neighborhood Spider-Man[36]

2

Why Do Heroes Stick? The Social and Psychological Functions of Hero Stories

Eric D. Wesselmann & Jordan P. LaBouff

"I believe there is a hero in all of us. That keeps us honest, gives us strength, makes us noble."
—**Aunt May (Rosemary Harris)**[1]

"Superheroes inspire us. They are engaged in a never-ending fight against crime and villainy. They fight the good fight even when they're tired, burned out, or have crises in their personal lives."
—**psychologist Robin S. Rosenberg**[2]

Spider-Man struggles with being a superhero, often sacrificing his personal desires to fulfill what he sees as his duty to use his powers in a socially responsible way. At times, he questions if his sacrifices make a difference, and he is tempted to quit. During one such low moment, he tells Aunt May and a child named Henry that Spider-Man has retired. Henry, a huge Spider-fan, leaves disappointed, and Aunt May argues that the boy "knows a hero when he sees one . . . Lord knows, kids like Henry need a hero. Courageous self-sacrificing people setting examples for all of us."[3] But what is it about heroes, and Spider-Man specifically, that inspires people such as Henry? What social and psychological needs do hero stories satisfy?

Psychologists focusing on *heroism science* often discuss the inspirational nature of heroes.[4] From this perspective, Spider-Man stories offer a wealth of heroic inspiration. Spider-Man writer J. M. DeMatteis has argued that "the belief in the ascendancy of the human heart, the essential nobility of the common man, has been at the core of all the web-spinner's finest tales."[5] Scott T. Allison, a psychologist interested in how heroism can be cultivated actively in society, wrote, "Every human being possesses one or more gifts to make the world a better place. Every human being is called to discover his or her gift."[6] Allison's argument resonates with former Spider-Man writer and group editor Tom DeFalco. "Spider-Man's message is simple. It's all about responsibility. If you want to be a good person, you have to be accountable for your actions," said DeFalco. "You also have a duty to use your talents to make this world a better place."[7]

Research suggests that we identify personally with our heroes, often bringing them into our self-concepts: how we view and define ourselves.[8] But what are the specific characteristics that lead us to label Spider-Man—and real-life individuals—as *heroes*? Why are these characters, and their stories of struggles and triumphs, so attractive to audiences worldwide?

Spinning a Heroic Tale

People often consume hero stories, whether those heroes are fictional like Spider-Man or real people in news stories. But these stories do more than just describe the actions of these heroes. They often reveal the motivations behind the actions. As Spider-Man author Paul Jenkins has noted, "There are elements that make a hero a hero, just as there are facets that make a villain a villain."[9] Psychologists describe such a set of elements as a *schema*, a collection of characteristics that exemplify a mental category that can help individuals classify the many diverse things (e.g., persons, places, objects) they experience daily into cognitively manageable, meaningful categories.[10] Such a category serves as a time-saving cognitive tool, allowing individuals to make evaluations quickly and effortlessly. Schemas about people help us determine what to expect as we interact with them, such as classifying whom we should befriend, trust, value, or emulate. In this case, the more traits a person exemplifies or behaviors they display that others consider heroic, the more likely they would be classified as a "hero" and lauded as an exemplary model.

Some cross-cultural research has examined people's lay perceptions of the characteristics that make someone a "hero." The researchers wanted to understand how people distinguish "heroes" from other similar culturally valued categories, such as "leaders" and "role models." Twelve descriptors emerged when examining the various ways people uniquely describe heroes. They considered heroes to be brave, courageous, determined, helpful, honest, inspiring, protective, and selfless people who show conviction, moral integrity, and self-sacrifice. Finally, they said that a hero "saves others."[11]

Spider-Man fits each of these descriptors. Because several of these descriptors are similar conceptually, we will combine some together. Whether Spider-Man is putting his life on the line fighting the ferocious supervillains Dr. Octopus, the Lizard, and Mysterio, or rescuing hundreds of New Yorkers from a runaway subway train, he can be described easily as *brave/courageous/saving others*.[12] Spider-Man's actions correspond well with the general cultural focus on bravery in heroism: putting oneself at serious physical risk for the benefit of others.[13] Many of Spider-Man's actions also can be described as *protecting/helpful* because he not only intervenes regularly in life-threatening situations with supervillains but also stops to help kids deal with bullies. When Spider-Man saves a kid from being beaten up for his lunch money, he thinks, "Some people might think stopping 'playground extortion' is pretty feeble! But I can't express how good it feels to make a little difference, to right small wrongs again."[14]

Further, Spider-Man often exhibits a sense of *conviction* or *determination* that helps him push past times when he feels like he has reached his limits to save other. One social psychologist argues that convictions rooted in one's sense of morality can provide individuals the courage necessary to pursue their moral goals even at great personal cost.[15] In a classic example, Spider-Man finds himself at one of his lowest moments when Aunt May is close to dying and only he can save her but he is trapped by wreckage. He

Spider-Man must lift literal weight off his back before he can save Aunt May in this frequently cited example of his persistence. *The Amazing Spider-Man* #33 (1965)

manages to find the willpower to continue on by thinking of his loved ones, especially Aunt May.[16] Similarly, even though he has tried to give up (or at least take a break from) his dual identity, he repeatedly feels drawn back because of his deeply held belief that his powers give him a responsibility to help other people no matter what, even if it endangers his relationships or health.[17] This sense of responsibility becomes the core of Spider-Man's worldview, which Aunt May and Uncle Ben raise him to view as a moral compass guiding his actions.[18] Spider-Man honestly believes in and strives to be consistent in practicing what he preaches. He is in what moral psychologists consider the laudable state of *moral integrity*.[19]

It is Spider-Man's moral compass and desire for integrity that ultimately drives his orientation toward *self-sacrifice*. As actor Tobey

Maguire said, "I don't think he particularly enjoys being Spider-Man."[20] In comics, Peter Parker has gone back and forth between loving and hating being Spider-Man.[21] He typically puts the well-being of others before himself, letting his loved ones down in his civilian life so he can fight for the greater good as his costumed alter ego.[22] He even resists telling his loved ones about his secret identity in order to protect them from harm or from getting enmeshed in his troubles, even if this means he must isolate himself from them.[23] Indeed, Spider-Man's selflessness illustrates the importance of being others-focused (rather than self-focused) in understanding the psychology of helping behavior. Making selfless choices despite occasional selfish impulses makes it even more of a sacrifice.

People often help others for complex reasons. Research suggests that when people are selfishly motivated to help others, they typically help someone only when it directly provides them some benefit. When people are others-focused (sometimes called empathically oriented, compassionate, or altruistic), they will help regardless of how it impacts them personally.[24] However, even psychologists who study empathy and prosocial behavior note that an overemphasis on others' needs can be harmful if it endangers one's own well-being. This trade-off is something Spider-Man continually struggles to find balance with.[25] Mary Jane tells Peter something similar when she calls him out on being "a poster boy for Obsessions R' Us" and reminds him that he needs to include his obligations to her and himself in his sense of responsibility.[26]

Finally, Spider-Man provides *inspiration* to those around him, from other superheroes like Firestar and Ms. Marvel to villains-turned-antiheroes such as Black Cat, Cardiac, and the Prowler.[27] Comics writer Brian Michael Bendis notes that when Spider-Man was one of the Avengers, his peers considered him "kind of the gold standard. He's the one that everyone else admires the most"[28] even though Spidey cannot easily see that in himself. In the Ultimates' universe, Captain America tells teenaged Spider-Man that when he grows up, "You're going to be the best out of all of us."[29] Moral psychologists argue that heroes provide a key social function by promoting morals and values, giving other members of the culture inspiration and a model to emulate.[30] Some data suggest that providing inspiration may be one of the most important traits that makes someone a hero.[31] Superhero stories can provide inspiration and a framework for how one thinks about their personal struggles.[32] Even simply being exposed to superhero images can increase both prosocial intentions and behaviors.[33] Heroic exemplars can inspire an increased sense of meaning in people's lives and the desire to reach one's ideal self.[34] Perhaps it is for these reasons that Spider-Man can inspire admiration even in in foes such as Doc Ock and one Green Goblin.[35]

Your Humble Neighborhood Spider-Man

Other heroism science researchers have identified *humility* as a quality central to heroism.[36] Humility is a widely valued quality and yet somewhat ambiguous and difficult to define.[37] Researchers who study humility describe it as the combination of at least three key qualities:

1. Humble people have an accurate view of their strengths and weaknesses. They don't overestimate (arrogance) or underestimate themselves (self-deprecation).

2. They are modest; they don't seek recognition or spend their attention or energy on themselves. Humble people are others-focused; they use their authentic strengths to, often quietly, step in to help those around them.[38]

3. Studies have demonstrated that humble people are more likely to be helpful to those in need—especially when their help is anonymous.[39] So, when a humble person is faced with a potentially heroic situation, they know what strengths they have, and put aside their own needs to help others.

Much of Spider-Man's heroism exemplifies humility. He recognizes his strengths and limitations, though he sometimes drifts into self-deprecation by underestimating his strengths and overestimating his limitations. Spider-Man also doesn't seek public recognition. During Marvel Comics' superhero *Civil War* comic book event, he only reveals his secret identity publicly when Iron Man convinces him that it's the best way for him to uphold the law requiring superhumans to register and work for the US government.[40] Again, Spider-Man focuses on others over his own well-being when making his choice. Like real-world heroes, Spider-Man seems to view his own accomplishments as less heroic than others view him.[41]

Heroes like Spider-Man model noble qualities like humility to which we all can aspire. But they can also show us the pitfalls of failing to be humble. There are plenty of stories where heroes become arrogant, where their pride or hubris comes before their fall. Data suggest that when people become overconfident, the quality of their work suffers and they tend to overextend themselves beyond their abilities, resulting in unnecessary risk and failure.[42] Further, they shift focus away from others' needs, making it easier to behave in a more hostile or aggressive way.[43] Some Spider-Man stories occasionally depict him as overconfident, reckless, or self-centered, such as when he causes massive property damage to a ship and interferes in a law investigation, prompting Iron Man to revoke his support for Spider-Man,[44] or when a self-satisfied Spider-Man compliments himself for catching Gwen Stacy as she falls from the George Washington Bridge, not knowing that in doing so he also may have accidentally killed her.[45] Spider-Man also becomes reckless when personal tragedies drive him to seek revenge against his enemies. Even though he recognizes he is being self-destructive by endangering innocent bystanders or ignoring his friends, Spider-Man still has trouble reining himself in.[46]

But Spider-Man sometimes offers another version of failing to be humble when he shifts his attention to overfocus on his own limitations— feeling deep shame over his inability to save everyone single-handedly. As he explains to Iron Man, "Look, when you can do the things that I can but you don't, and then the bad things happen, they happen because of you."[47] Researchers have shown that when we feel the self-focused emotion of shame, it can lead to *avoidance* and *inaction*—the opposite of heroism.[48] When Spider-Man's self-focus causes him to take responsibility for the consequence of actions clearly caused by villains, he fails to be humble and feels shame that prevents him from acting heroically. Harry Osborn (as Green Goblin) calls Spider-Man out on this, noting that his anxiety about potentially doing the wrong thing coupled with his guilt over past mistakes make it hard for him to act when necessary.[49]

By shouldering all the responsibility for a situation himself, he exhibits a form of egotism common to superheroes: the belief that they are the only ones who can solve a crisis. When Spider-Man falls prey to this egotism, he denies others the opportunity to be heroic because he takes on the responsibility alone. For example, Spider-Man prevents Black Cat from defeating the villain Tombstone supposedly to "protect" her and stops Tombstone himself. Black Cat is angry and tells Spider-Man that even if he has the best intentions, he still hurts her feelings and risks pushing her away.[50] Other times, Spider-Man ignores his own injuries and chooses to pursue supervillains alone when he would be better off having allies.[51] Ultimately, Spider-Man demonstrates the value of humility more often than not. He, like us, is most heroic when he authentically uses his strengths and supplements his weaknesses in service to the needs of others without dwelling on his own limitations or failures.

Helping Us Climb to New (Moral) Heights

Spider-Man film director Sam Raimi argues that the key strength of the character is his humble background and personal struggles, "the fact that he's a real person, he's one of us."[52] Former Marvel editor-in-chief Joe Quesada made a similar point: "I think the beauty of Spider-Man is that everyone—*everyone*—can relate to his character, everybody sees a little bit of themselves in Spider-Man."[53] Even though our friendly neighborhood Spider-Man has fantastic powers, he is as down-to-earth as heroes come: "The real me is Peter Parker, not some super powers, not a costume, but a real person."[54] Whether he is fighting cosmic-level crises, saving people from fires, or rescuing cats from trees, for him all life is worthy of protection and there "is no 'small stuff.'"[55] Thus, Spider-Man stories provide a great resource for encouraging what some psychologists have described as *banality of heroism*, the concept that everyone can be heroes in their own way by modeling heroic traits in their daily lives, using their personal gifts to make the world a better place.[56] Indeed, there have been several real-world examples of everyday people inspired by Spider-Man to increase the well-being of others, such as by feeding the homeless and visiting children's hospitals.[57] Perhaps

Spider-Man writer J. M. DeMatteis said it best, that Peter Parker "was, is, and always will be a kind, decent, compassionate, caring human being."[58] We don't need to be bitten by a radioactive spider to emulate these traits.

Eric D. Wesselmann, PhD, a professor of psychology at Illinois State University, regularly uses superhero stories to teach the psychology of moral decision-making and other psychological topics. He co-curates film programming and writes a blog for his local independent theater (The Normal Theater; Film CULTure). His published works include contributions to most of the volumes in the Popular Culture Psychology series. He first started reading Spidey in junior high when the "Maximum Carnage" arc was published and rereads it every few years and has nostalgic memories of the video game adaptation.

Jordan P. LaBouff, PhD, professor of psychology at the University of Maine, studies humility and how people's beliefs translate into behavior—and so his classes often analyze real-world and comic book heroes. He cooperates with art houses and theaters to study the effects of experiencing art on local communities. He has always loved Spider-Man's reminders to do what we can for others around us and that no need is too small.

3

Reweaving:
How Those Great Powers
Alter a Young Hero's Sense
of Self and World

Travis Langley

"Power doesn't always corrupt. Power can cleanse.
What I believe is always true about power is that power always reveals."
—**Pulitzer-winning author Robert Caro**[1]

> "Your story will change lives, Peter. That's your greatest power."
> —**Aunt May**[2]

When Peter Parker leaps out of a car's path, Cindy Moon accidentally webs her entire bedroom, or Miles Morales vanishes from sight, suddenly camouflaged,[3] those moments mark childhood's end more than the spider bites that cause them do. Each transformation offers a dramatic puberty metaphor,[4] which may be why so many prominent spider-heroes gain those powers during high school.[5] Peter, Cindy, Miles, and the version of Gwen Stacy nicknamed "Spider-Gwen"[6] are undergoing the already turbulent changes of adolescence when spider bites alter them faster and more wildly than puberty ever could. The onset of superpowers makes for the ultimate growth spurt.

At a time in life when identity crisis may approach its peak,[7] un-anticipated changes impact how teens see themselves and others, in-cluding how they evaluate themselves relative to family, friends, rivals, strangers, and anyone else they notice. Cognitive processes, even moral reasoning, grow more complex. Physical and mental changes remap the surrounding environment so that they see the world from new perspectives—dramatically so when the new point of view includes the tug of a webline, the feel of wind against the face, and the sight of the city when swinging in an arc between skyscrapers sixty stories up in the air.

Power as Developmental Milestone

We grow up. We change. We expect to become more capable and to gain new skills as we develop. Puberty rewrites the rules in ways that may delight, distress, or disappoint us. The smallest child may pray for a growth spurt that will let them stand tall above all peers, and some-times that happens; yet another person's changes—whether develop-mental, accidental, or pathological—make them feel betrayed by their own bodies.[8] *Change changes us.* Circular as that may sound, changes in our bodies and abilities produce changes in our self-concepts and patterns of behavior, in ways both good and bad.

Each young spider-hero's origin story becomes their personal *rite of passage*: their ceremonial transition between childhood and adult life, a time of *identity reconstruction* when each individual leaves behind the roles of early life to recreate themselves as adults.[9] Whether growing up or gaining superpowers, adolescent changes in abilities and physique alter the ways in which we relate to the world and see ourselves. The pseudonyms some adopt—Spider-*Man* for each of the boys and Spider-*Woman* for Gwen—do indicate that all of these youths want to be treated and seen as adults.

Though the spider bite sets this process in motion, that inciting in-cident is not the moment they know they're changing. It is not the first whisker, the first crack of pubescent voice, the first surprise by bodily fluids. However traumatic a spider bite may be, few people who have

Peter discovers his spider-powers in *Amazing Fantasy* #15 (1962). Art by Steve Ditko.

been bitten would list it among life's significant milestones.* In terms of self-discovery, the milestone that divides each young hero's life before from life after is the moment the powers manifest.

Peter Parker's first display of spider-powers lays the foundation for them all.[10] "Wrapped up in his thoughts" as he walks down the street, Peter nearly gets hit by a car. Reflexively he leaps out of its path and clings to a brick wall. The astonished teen finds he can scale the wall easily. Reaching the top, he grabs on to a steel pipe, which he crushes as though it were paper. He has gained "the proportionate speed, strength, and agility of a spider."[11]

---

* Being born, learning to walk, graduating high school, getting married, getting bitten by a spider . . .

No one has prepared him for this. Who could? Even teens who've been told what to expect as they develop get caught off guard by the reality, and not everyone enters puberty forewarned. Real teens may be reluctant to discuss changes in their bodies and abilities. Fear of rejection may make them wary of disclosing how different they feel. Even the popular kids—sometimes especially the popular kids—worry about getting alienated by peers. And so they may keep secrets. Some share with peers, perhaps using *pubilect* (teen-specific slang) to bond with one another while distancing adults,[12] but others feel they have no one they can talk to.

Our spider-heroes each have reason to feel more alien than ever before. As Peter marvels at his new powers and puts them to the test, he also wonders what in the world he should do with them. Little does he know that elsewhere in the neighborhood, a young woman bitten by the same spider will uncontrollably spray silky webbing from her fingertips all over her room. When her parents rush in, they find her sitting embarrassed and baffled on the floor. They comfort her, as any good parent should, but they cannot fully reassure their daughter because none of them understand this.[13] Many teens share this experience, such as LGBTQ+ youth who may neither understand their own feelings nor have parents who have any inkling on how to respond, and too many have reason to fear rejection by their own families.[14] The Gwen Stacy who becomes Spider-Woman (then Spider-Gwen, then Ghost-Spider) worries how her father will react. She feels all alone, even haunted.[15] After a few stumbles on his own, Miles at least can seek advice from his world's Spider-Man's loved ones. Aunt May encourages Miles both to embrace the mantle of Spider-Man and to be his own person without second-guessing: "Don't do what Peter Parker would do. Do what Miles Morales would do."[16]

The changes do not end with those milestones. Even without the adventures and misadventures their crime-fighting paths may take, the powers themselves will continue to make changes in them and their perspectives.

The "Spider" in Spider-Man

No one else had to know the powers came from a spider. A Golden Age superhero who gains super-speed from a transfusion of mongoose blood dubs himself the Whizzer, not Mister Mongoose. The spider-bites apply no wholly arachnid qualities to Peter, Gwen, and Miles. Not even crawling walls is exclusive to spiders. Lizards do it. The X-Men's Nightcrawler does it.[17] The Prowler and others use special equipment to do it.[18] Silk's organic webs are more clearly spidery, but she goes into hiding for ten years and does not yet become a superhero. No, Peter, Gwen, and Miles embrace and declare their spidery origins by choice.

Through *introjection*, they identify so strongly with the spider symbol that they incorporate it into superhero identities.[19] As a *symbol* (anything that represents something else), the spider shape or the webbing may embolden each of them through association with a creature they find strong, fearsome, or humble. It certainly evokes fear in many criminals. Unfortunately, it does that in many citizens as well. *Arachnophobia*, the fear of spiders and usually other arachnids, ranks among the better-known specific phobias, possibly *the* best-known one.[20] Even people whose reactions to spiders are not clinically *phobic*—not severe or intrusive enough to interfere with functioning—often find them unnerving. Identifying with a symbol so divisive may reflect the characters' mixed feelings about themselves.

Crawling, Jumping, Spinning Through Space

As soon as Peter climbs that first wall, his world grows taller. Jumping between buildings extends his *cognitive map*, his mental representation of his physical environment. Regardless of our knowledge that buildings are tall, we mainly relate to their space in two dimensions, with each floor a flat geometric plane we walk along. Elevators and stairs, though moving us through the third dimension, move us to the building's level surfaces where most of us spend our time. Through repeated rehearsal, firefighters begin to think differently about surfaces they climb and to feel differently about the space, all the while staying alert for flames or objects that can come at them from any direction.[21] Tree-trimmers, communication tower technicians, skyscraper construction workers, and others working high-altitude jobs develop new perspectives and new ways of feeling for a world that reaches through all three dimensions while pinned one way by gravity. Together, climbing and jumping reshape the environment and increase awareness of object heights without even ascending buildings. Basketball players progress from simply thinking about the goal's height to developing a feel for it as well. Gymnasts and many other athletes move through three-dimensional space as befits their respective sports, while Spider-Man backflips through that kind of space over his foes.

Web-slinging takes Spider-Man to new heights, new angles, new directions, and so his cognitive map grows. Fans may argue that web-slinging is no superpower because Peter Parker uses web-shooters and special web-fluid. For some of the spider-heroes, notably Cindy Moon or symbiote-powered characters such as Venom (and eventually Spider-Gwen), shooting webs is a superpower. For Peter Parker, outside of the film version played by Tobey Maguire,[22] it usually is not. Keep in mind that Peter invents the technology himself.[23] His first power is his intelligence. Rapidly inventing his tools requires great *analytical intelligence* (ability to think convergently and solve problems through logic)[24] and *creative intelligence* (ability to think divergently and generate imaginative solutions). Even in versions where he bases the web-fluid on a formula his father came up with, Peter completes the inventions himself.[25] Enhanced physical abilities enable him to use them effectively.

Regardless, Spider-Man's superhuman use of the web-shooter to swing his way through the city extends his personal domain through all the space between and around the buildings, through all the air overhead. Web-slinging changes how he interacts with the city and its people. He develops an intricate knowledge of New York City to traverse it and an intimate connection because swinging between buildings keeps him tethered to them. His *practical intelligence* (ability to learn through unprompted observation) constantly adjusts his 3-D cognitive map. This method of transportation and climbing surfaces others cannot reach keep him at a distance from everyday people and most of his fellow superheroes. Spider-Man can be both connected to the city by his webline and yet far from people he saves, sometimes webbing people to safety without touching ground himself. No other superhero spends so much time at unusual angles or simply upside down, not even the bat-themed hero whose namesake *sleeps* upside down.

That 3-D cognitive map is more accurately a 4-D cognitive map to account for time because Spider-Man stays in motion. When moving through the air, he must maintain continuous control, feeling the tension through the webline and adjusting his body all along the way. Though the average person may not go swinging through the city, motion requires *temporal awareness*, a conscious or unconscious sense of time and timing. Through much of the twentieth century, most perception research took place in laboratory settings with stationary observers directed to view motionless stimuli. In the 1970s and into the 1980s (essentially the Bronze Age of Comics), a group of psychologists made the point that this traditional method lacked *ecological validity*: It was not true to real life.[26]

Webbing also extends Spider-Man's sense of physical self. Even when it's artificial web-fluid mixed in the lab, webs become an extension of his body no less than a hockey player feels the hockey stick—and, through it, the puck and ice—or a swordfighter feels every waver of the blade. Webs let Spidey reach far beyond the limits of his hands and arms to catch people who are falling or to stop criminals in their tracks.[27]

Spider-Man's cumulative time spent maneuvering physically risky aerial feats may have a negative effect on his well-being. Circus performers, particularly aerial acrobats who perform under similar conditions to Spider-Man, tend to show poorer mental health than most in the general population.[28] Correlation does not prove causation, of course. Perhaps people with a propensity toward lower mental health are drawn to the risks of acrobatic circus life, but perhaps not. Perhaps a third factor such as sensation-seeking brings these together. The parallel does raise questions about the possible effects that near-daily high-wire danger and occasional tragedy among performers might have on a person's sense of wellness.

The more immersive Spider-Man videogames may offer players some clues as to how these experiences feel to Peter, Miles, and pals. Combined with the player's ongoing physical activity in adjusting their character's movement, the better *haptic technology* simulates some limited motion and touch sensations through pressure, vibration, and motion of controllers, gloves, or other devices.[29] Different games may also work on the player's *proprioception* or *kinesthesia* (sense of body position and movement relative to self), their *vestibular sense* (sense of balance and spatial orientation relative to environment), and the *sensory interaction* between vision and balance that makes a viewer feel the lurch of a roller coaster when only watching a film. Not unlike the way a player's "feel" for the game will improve, make anticipatory responses to intercept items, or otherwise get their timing right,[30] and even show alterations in the brain,[31] Spider-Man's senses and resultant neurons change—on a larger scale—through the application and extension of his activities.

Another superpower also plays a critical role in enabling Spider-Man and friends to swing safety through the city: the preternatural spider-sense.

Danger!

Even though Spider-Man's origin makes no mention of the spider-sense, it comes up in early issues of his own comic book series.[32] In later years, the power is referred to as extrasensory, more specifically prescient. Still, it seems implicit in the origin. In the scene when Peter first discovers his powers and jumps clear of the speeding car, how does he know to jump? The text says he "unthinkingly leaps."[33] Later depictions, such as the 1977 film starring Nicholas Hammond and 2000's origin in the *Ultimate Spider-Man* comic, clearly present the spider-sense warning him of the car's approach.[34]

A National Wildlife Federation blog addressed the question of whether spiders have a danger-detection ability akin to Spider-Man's:

> *Spider-Man is able to sense danger lurking near, the warning signal coming as a pain in his head that varies with the intensity of the threat. Spiders can detect danger coming their way with an early-warning system called eyes.*[35]

Their vision isn't even that good. Spiders do not have a true "spider-sense" to speak of. The closest they come may be in picking up subtle environmental changes through *trichobothria*, the tiny, sensitive hairs on their bodies. Vibrations picked up through webbing may extend that, but webbing has never been requisite for Spider-Man's danger sense (except possibly in Sam Raimi's version).

Scientific explanation of how it functions notwithstanding, psychologically the spider-sense taps into sensitive Peter's tendency to obsess over the possibility of something bad happening. For years, the power will remain exclusive to Peter Parker. Young Peter worries intensely and most of the time. In the wake of Uncle Ben's murder, he rarely allows himself to relax for fear that such tragedy may strike again. His spider-sense acts as an extension of what may have been a potential toward *hypervigilance*, excessive alertness to possible danger. The spider-sense may lessen Peter's worries about what *might* happen because he now knows for certain whether danger is coming or not (usually), thus removing the ambiguous dread felt by others suffering from anxiety and hypervigilance. His worries tend to be specific.

Cindy Moon's decade of isolation keeps her from adapting to her Silk-sense (as she prefers to call it, rather than spider-sense or Spidey-sense). New York City, filled with risk in all directions, hits her like pins on raw nerves. Unaccustomed to the buzz, Silk calls Spidey to ask, "How do you deal with all the static?" He knows what she is asking but can only recommend that she find balance by attending to all the city's other sensations as well, and he reassures her, "You're gonna be okay, Cin. You just need time."[36] Her social anxiety likely magnifies the ongoing prickle.

What does the spider-sense have to do with their spatial awareness and maneuvering? Spidey realizes its value in this regard when the power gets temporarily disabled. Swinging his way to a crime scene, he shoots a webline onto crumbling brick and falls. It hits him: "All this time, my spider-sense must've prevented me from making those kinda shots—from web-slinging like that." He has "never realized all the ways the power affected so many of the things I do."[37] Perhaps part of the reason Spider-Man works more often without a partner is because the tingle in his head makes the most reliable partner he could ask for.

The "Man" in Spider-Man

Except for the wall-climbing part, the powers visible to others consist only of basic human abilities magnified—no more distinctly spidery than the kind of enhanced strength shown by Captain America or Jessica Jones. Only by calling his agility, speed, and strength "proportionate to that of a spider" does Peter associate those powers with arachnids. He makes that assertion before any quantitative tests, though, and science seems to contradict his interpretation.[38] These powers make Spidey and company superhumans but not spider-humans, and do not characterize their superhero identities. In many ways, the powers affect their everyday lives more than the obviously spiderific powers. Peter does not have to dodge speeding cars and aggressive bullies every hour of the day. Even without becoming a superhero, suddenly growing stronger, faster, and more dexterous than peers can make the adolescent feel more adult (again, Spider-*Man*, Spider-*Woman*).

One important, if less obvious or famous, superpower may also help the young heroes live in ways that are more reckless and careless, that create the feeling of having the freedom and independence youngsters look forward to in adult life. "One of the first things to remember about Spider-Man is his extreme durability."[39] Super-stamina not only helps him endure and persist in the moment but also speeds subsequent recovery through remarkable healing. Merely knowing about his own durability can build personal tenacity and boost his persistence to keep going despite stacked odds. Unlike Wolverine and Deadpool, whose bodies may regrow severed limbs,[40] stories set in future timelines and other situations show that if Spidey's limbs get amputated, they do not grow back.[41] Still, he can recover from almost any injury, and he knows that. The greatest impediment to his healing comes from his own behavior: He won't let himself get the rest he needs for it to work. When a bullet wound heals almost completely overnight, he muses, "Guess all I needed was a good night's sleep so I could recuperate."[42] And yet he keeps getting in his own way. After breaking his arm,[43] Peter must wear a cast for weeks until he finally collapses onto his bed and sleeps twenty-four hours. Waking with it finally healed, he shatters the cast. "All I needed was one good night's sleep and I'm better than ever! It's hard to believe I've been on the go every minute since I broke my arm!"[44] His stress-related ulcer lasts longer than it should[45] and resurfaces later because of his lifestyle choices.[46]

For Peter Parker, feeling more like a mighty man may also get into masculinity issues. After all, how does he first decide to put his new powers to use? He becomes a wrestler. The boy who has not managed to fend off bullies enters the testosterone-splashed ring where he physically overpowers his opponents, one grown man after another.[47] In the eyes of many, wrestling with all its aggression and smack talk promotes *hegemonic masculinity*, the view that boys should be tough and men should dominate in society.[48] Remember, the wrestling first takes place before the stories mention the spider-sense. He wins through agility and brute strength when he could use other powers to make money other ways. According to one story, the spider-sense could help Peter win a fortune gambling, such as when he beats the Kingpin at poker and donates the money to charity,[49] but he refrains out of social responsibility.* It would feel like theft. Although he couldn't enter legal poker games at age fifteen, someone with his powers could make money in other ways without going straight to aggressive man-on-man competition. He wanted to fight.

The Adventure Begins

The adolescent spider-hero embarks on a life filled with fun adventure and great tragedy, where each gets the opportunity to make a difference in people's lives by helping where they can. When Lyndon B. Johnson biographer Robert Caro said that power always reveals, he added, "When you have enough power to do what you always wanted to do, then you see what the guy always wanted to do." Of the four characters this chapter compares (Peter, Cindy, Gwen, and Miles), none of them rush to become heroes. Peter wants to make money to help his uncle and aunt, Gwen wants to have fun, and Cindy and Miles want to keep it private. Power alone does not bring out their superheroism. Each needs a catalyst, some inspiration or tragedy, to bring out their heroic sides, but they do already have those sides latent within themselves.

---

* And is poker really dangerous enough to set the spider-sense abuzz when playing opponents who aren't Kingpin?

Other powers emerge at times, and several of them have powers unique to themselves. For both Cindy and Miles, their first manifestation of power (her unleashing silky webs; him turning translucent when distressed because his father and uncle are arguing while failing to listen to what Miles has to say)[50] distinguish them from everybody else. Although, Miles's manifestation is somewhat representative of them all: Every spider-hero hides. Each can lurk in shadows and unseen corners, in all directions and out-of-the-way places where observers tend not to look. Several grow up feeling overlooked before gaining powers, only to conceal their true nature and lifestyle from others once the powers arrive.

In each identity, Peter and the others hide parts of who they are. They try to partition the superhero self from the civilian self even though those superheroes keep showing up in the lives of everyone around them. Concealing important parts of themselves in one area allows them to reveal more in the other, as they strive to remain true to seemingly contradictory truths about themselves—which is not so far removed from how people, particularly teens, already feel about themselves. Superhuman powers enable them to achieve extraordinary things while their human natures yearn for some semblance of ordinary lives.

"I didn't choose to get bit or gain these great powers. All I ever planned on was being plain old Peter Parker. I never asked to be Spider-Man. It just happened. So all I can do is try to make the right choices, no matter how many weird places they take me."

—Spider-Man[51]

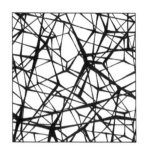

Before the Bite: Psychosocial Stages of Parker Development

"My name is Peter Parker, and I've been Spider-Man since I was 15 years old."
—Peter Parker[1]

Psychologist Erik Erikson's model of eight *psychosocial stages* emphasizes social influence as the primary force that shapes personality.[2] Healthier outcomes in the first five early periods give each person qualities that help them relate to others and self throughout life.[3]

Basic Trust vs. Mistrust (about 0 to 18 months). In comics, Peter Parker is an infant when parents Richard and Mary Parker die. He will grow up with no memory of them[4] even though he knows them during his first year. Their involvement as loving caregivers gives him hope, which Uncle Ben and Ben's wife, May, nurture, but the abrupt disappearance from his life likely leads to many inconsolable tears and rattles his emergent ability to trust.

Autonomy vs. Shame and Doubt (age 18 months to 3 years). Uncle Ben and Aunt May encourage Peter to be *autonomous*, to act independently rather than to feel *shame* for trying to do things himself. Their occasional overprotectiveness and his lack of interaction with peers may foster some of his self-doubt, but for the most part, Spidey is one autonomous superhero.[5]

Initiative vs. Guilt (about age 3 to 5 years). The guy who invents webshooters, dons a spider-themed costume to make money as a wrestler, and then swings about to fight crime by himself has developed great *initiative*, initiating new activities independently. He is also famous for his burdensome sense of *guilt*. Although his guilt focuses on things that happen later, the ability to feel guilt tends to originate early. Aunt May can be fearful and shows a strong sense of guilt herself, which he may pick up on, and sometimes her words can be harsh.[6]

Another possibility lies in Erikson's original view of how these stages work: He believed a chaotic or unsuccessful outcome in one stage will make later crises more difficult. The disruption in Peter's early ability to trust may still influence development in these other areas, and at this point he is old enough to know other kids have parents. Guardians Ben and May, hoping for the parents' return, never adopt Peter. Even so, adult Peter thinks back, "Maybe my real parents were dead, but never once did I feel lonely or that I was missing anything."[7] He doesn't know loneliness until he goes to school.

Industry vs. Inferiority (roughly age 5 or 6 until puberty). For many children who lose their parents, poor grades and behavioral issues are common,[8] but not for Peter. Encouraged by uncle, aunt, and teachers he impresses, Peter develops a strong sense of *industry*, a feeling of capability and competence. He knows he has a range of knowledge and skills.

Identity Achievement vs. Role Confusion (puberty until early adulthood). In the comics, the spider bites Peter Parker at age fifteen.[9] The boy has barely started figuring out who he is when his world flips upside down. Despite certain stable traits and sense of self (*identity achievement*), his life will fill with chaos and much *role confusion*, leaving him adrift and unsure how he fits into anything. During this struggle for personal identity, Peter gains superpowers and loses a father.[10]

Unlike Sigmund Freud who only outlined stages for growing up (and based them on sexual maturation),[11] Erikson added three more stages for adult personality development because he saw patterns of change throughout the lifetime.[12] Peter Parker, however, has not yet reached those adult stages when Spider-Man first swings into action.

—T. L. & T. A.

4

Along Came a Spider-Mentor

Sy Islam & Gordon Schmidt

"I'm just trying to help, that's all. I've been on a parallel road to yours for a long time and I have the advantage of being able to see down the road a bit to what's coming. I'm trying to straighten out some of the curves coming your way."
—Ezekiel[1]

"A mentor is someone who allows you to know that no matter how dark the night, in the morning, joy will come. A mentor is someone who allows you to see the higher part of yourself when sometimes it becomes hidden to your own view."
—Oprah Winfrey[2]

Peter Parker begins his time as Spider-Man as a young man struggling with his new powers and beginning to undertake more adult responsibilities in life. Like many other fictional heroes, Peter is an orphan, but unlike others, he faces many unique difficulties in managing his life. As such, he is looking for help and guidance, whether he realizes that consciously or not. Unlike similar teenaged heroes such as Ms. Marvel, Spider-Man does not have a mentor to whom he can consistently turn. Mentors can provide a major way to help the young and/or inexperienced develop themselves. *Mentorship* is a developmental relationship in which a *mentor* provides advice and developmental opportunities to a protégé (or mentee).[3] For a young man becoming a superhero, as with so many opportunities in life, such support could prove beneficial to his success as a crime-fighter and his ability to balance the hero and civilian life.

Spider-Man's origin focuses on the loss of a major mentor: Uncle Ben.[4] His loss and example inspire Peter toward a philosophy that "with great power, there must also come great responsibility." This mantra will steer Peter as a superhero. It helps him stay on the right path and maintain his mission as Spider-Man.[5]

After losing this mentor, Peter looks for inspiration from others. In one of his earliest adventures, Spider-Man faces his first major career defeat by Doctor Octopus and wonders if he should quit.[6] Spider-Man gains confidence to continue from a speech the Human Torch gives at Peter's high school, effectively becoming a peer mentor whose words inspire Spidey to keep trying. Characters such as Robbie Robertson at the *Daily Bugle* and Captain George Stacy with the NYPD offer people for Peter to look up to, but he always feels a need to stay guarded because their intelligence could lead them to figure out his secret identity. Thus, he has potential mentors but cannot engage with them fully for fear of discovery.[7]

True mentorship for Spidey begins when he identifies a mentor more like himself in Ezekiel. Peter identifies Ezekiel by noting that he has similar spider-powers: "You're the only other person in the world who knows what it's like to be me, to do what I can do. There are a lot of questions I want—need—to ask you," he says to Ezekiel (before Cindy Moon and Miles Morales enter his life).[8] Though Ezekiel is later revealed to be villainous, he can mentor Peter to recognize the mystical component of his spider-powers.

Spider-Man acts as both mentee and mentor to different people and at different times. The psychology of mentorship offers some insight into the reasons mentors are necessary and why people become mentors.

A Web of Mentors

People crave relationships, and Spider-Man is no different. From the first panel in his first story, Peter Parker is a wallflower set apart from others his own age.[9] Peter desires to belong to a peer group and build relationships but feels isolated. This isolation initially worsens after he becomes Spider-Man because the responsibilities interfere with building and maintaining relationships. He generally fights crime alone and does his schoolwork alone. It takes Peter a long time into his college career to build a strong network of friends. His life as Spider-Man greatly reduces the amount of time he spends with them, however.

People often desire a mentor to share ideas or to provide support through difficult times. Mentorship is commonly considered an important part of career development as it provides opportunities to develop skills and a social network.[10] Mentoring also allows mentors to improve their job performance and revitalize their careers.[11] For a hero like Spider-Man, taking on a mentorship role is especially important because of how he developed his superhero persona. As an individual hero working without a partner or team in most cases, he doesn't have the luxury of getting advice from others, and as someone who maintains a secret identity from nearly everyone, he struggles to find individuals to whom he can confide about struggles in his personal, professional, and superheroic life.

Building a Web

Peter experiences challenges managing his day-to-day life. This is a key factor in his desire for a mentor. From financial challenges to supervillains, he is under the kind of consistent stress that leads many people to seek guidance.[12]

Attachment theory describes how people build relationships whether romantic or friendly, starting with how securely a person during infancy connects with a primary caregiver and how that caregiver teaches the young one to relate to others.[13] Attachment theory posits that when people face threatening situations, they will often revert and look for comfort from an attachment figure or caregiver—the *safe haven* function of attachment.[14] Once the individual has found the caregiver, the caregiver reciprocates with the necessary support to help the individual advance. This dyadic approach helps us understand the give and take between mentor and mentee.

Peter finds some of this support in the people he has in his life. In the hostile environment of the *Daily Bugle*, Peter finds support in the form of editor-in-chief Robbie Robertson. Where J. Jonah Jameson is out to smear Spider-Man, Robertson models journalistic ethics by supporting the truth about Spider-Man. Robertson guides Peter in his journalistic career while JJJ does not.

Aunt May provides Peter's most prominent emotional support and source of encouragement.[15] She greatly encourages his schoolwork and newspaper job. While she offers emotional support and gives Spider-Man purpose in many of his adventures, she is not able to help him with his superhero work. Conversely, while Aunt May supports Peter, she often unknowingly makes his life more difficult by expressing negative feelings for Spider-Man, calling him a "menace" or "dreadful."[16] Peter does not feel she will accept his superhero life and worries constantly about what would happen should she find out.

Despite this, Peter looks to Aunt May as a mentor. She may not have the same superpowers or interests, but Peter sees the importance of the content of her words. Rather than an occupational mentor, she is a mentor for the kind of person Peter wants to be. Aunt May often gives Peter the advice he needs to continue in his battle against supervillains. Though Aunt May isn't fighting the Green Goblin, she has faced many of the same stressors Peter has. It's through this shared hardship that Aunt May can tell Peter to enjoy the "moments of joy" between "moments of hardship."[17] Aunt May has always been a strong mentor guiding him with the advice to "not be a quitter" that leads Peter to return as Spider-Man.[18] Peter may not always recognize Aunt May as a mentor but he has learned important lessons from her that have impacted him as a superhero.

This lack of an overt, superheroic mentor early on in his superhero career may have limited Peter's effectiveness as a superhero. When Otto "Doctor Octopus" Octavius takes over Peter Parker's body and operates, temporarily, as both Peter Parker and Spider-Man, he notes, "I have spent a month inside Peter Parker's head. And I have found him wanting. He was a man of limited vision. No plans. No schemes. Just blindly going from one thing to the next."[19] Octavius vows to be a "superior" Spider-Man and begins to make some improvements on Peter's style of superheroics by using monitoring bots and other technology.

Would Peter have been more effective if he had received mentoring earlier on in his career? According to Octavius, the answer is yes. In one of Peter's first actions as Spider-Man, he attempts to join the Fantastic Four because he believes they could pay him to do his superhero work. Peter thinks they will "jump at the chance to have a teenager with superpowers working with them." When the Fantastic Four reject his proposal, Peter says, "You're like all the rest, ready to believe the worst of anyone."[20] Peter understands that he needs some support whether social or otherwise, and his first attempt at gaining a mentor gets thwarted by his misunderstanding of the Fantastic Four.

Peter's actions underline another key element in mentoring explained through *self-expansion theory*,[21] which suggests people attempt to increase their effectiveness by developing perspectives, resources, and identities to achieve their goals.[22] This process of expansion requires a delicate balance. Sometimes if an individual feels there is too much happening and there are too many resources being utilized during mentorship relationships, if their mentor is asking too much of them, they feel a stressful state of *overexpansion*. If the individual feels they are not getting enough development through relationships, then they feel an unfulfilled state of *underexpansion*. Unfulfilled underexpansion can lead to reduced effort at work and dissatisfaction. Overexpansion can lead to feelings of being overwhelmed or losing a sense of oneself.[23]

As Peter struggles to make his way through his life as Spider-Man, he searches for potential partners or mentors. Upon meeting J. Jonah Jameson, he tries to expand his perspective and access the resources J. Jonah Jameson has after rescuing JJJ's son, John Jameson.[24] Although Spider-Man is successful in saving John Jameson's life during a shuttle malfunction, Peter learns later that his good deed is not paid back in kind. JJJ's lack of empathy and support show that he's not a good mentor for Spidey. Peter's search for a mentor must continue.

Searching the Spider-Verse for a Mentor

As Peter Parker starts to operate as a superhero, he finds that there are few who can relate to this experience. Spider-Man spends most of his career as an individual hero with very little team experience until his later, though erratic, stints with teams such as the Fantastic Four and Avengers. While Peter Parker isn't often part of a formal team, he does develop strong relationships with several heroes who serve as mentor figures, usually peer mentors. Across Spider-Man media (comics, TV, movies), we see Peter Parker both serving as a mentee and a mentor. But the question remains: How does a superhero find a mentor?

A potential answer to this question can be found in a model to pair mentors and mentees based on *goodness of fit*, i.e., how well a mentor and a mentee connect with and complement one another.[25] The model views mentoring relationships as dyads or pairs who are engaged in a social exchange. The relationship is built around an alignment between the mentor's and mentee's preferences, incentives, and valuations. Mentors and mentees who mutually benefit each other maintain the relationship. Once the relationship stops being fruitful, the relationship ends. In Peter Parker's early career, he reaches out to the Fantastic Four to try and find a mentor or a guide who is a good fit (and, admittedly, to see if they would pay him a salary).

Between any pair of mentor and mentee, there exist endowments, preferences, and mentoring content. *Endowments* are the social capital, knowledge, and experience brought to the relationship by the mentor and mentee. *Preferences* represent the value of communicating and receiving different kinds of knowledge. *Mentoring content* represents the information exchanged, whether it's a referral to another individual, or information about office politics, or a key piece of knowledge needed to move forward in one's career.[26] Peter initially disregards some potential mentors like Uncle Ben because he may not recognize the value of the content they provide. A mentor-mentee relationship is most effective when a mentor has knowledge that the mentee desires that which furthers the mentee's career. The mentor receives the benefit of improving the organization, developing a new colleague, and showing greater leadership within the organization. In the case of Ezekiel, the mentor learns a lot about himself from Peter and realizes the mistakes he's made in his own life and how he's used his powers. This sort of self-reflective epiphany exemplifies the *working alliance*, a collaborative and mutually beneficial bond connecting mentor and mentee.

An important factor impacting the relationship between the mentor and mentee is perceived similarity. Similarity can lie at the heart of an effective working alliance,[27] important because it shapes perceptions of compatibility. In the Ultimate universe, after gaining his powers, Peter starts to change—growing more arrogant, giving up his old interests, and acting like a different person. Uncle Ben provides him feedback and advice, which Peter quickly rejects because he sees Uncle Ben as someone who can't understand his situation any longer (and Uncle Ben lacks critical information about Peter's new powers and situation).[28] And, in the same way it plays out in the earliest version of Spider-Man's origin, Uncle Ben's death spurs Peter to learn an important lesson. Had Peter recognized the value of Uncle Ben as a mentor before his death and evaluated what Uncle Ben had to offer differently, he may have received more from the relationship. Because of the dissimilarity, Peter rejects Uncle Ben's advice until it's too late.

Peter Parker and Otto Octavius have sometimes been depicted as mentor and mentee.[29] They connect over a shared love of science, with the older scientist serving as a helpful mentor to Peter both in his academic work and his love life. Octavius's advice serves as a warning to be more honest with oneself about what and whom you love.[30] Peter listens to Otto because he sees the value of what Octavius says through the similarity that they share. When nanotechnology negatively manipulates Otto's brain, the arrival of the new supervillain worries Spidey, but the loss of this mentor also saddens him.

Iron Man and Dr. Strange each mentor Spider-Man from time to time, particularly in the Marvel Cinematic Universe. Peter and Tony share important similarities as scientists.[31] Peter looks up to Tony as a tech mogul and desires a mentoring relationship. Over the course of several films, Tony comes to care for Peter and provides him with material support (i.e., a new costume) and advice to get through the difficulties of the superhero experience.[32] In the pages of Marvel comics, Tony turns to Peter for support during times of conflict with other heroes such as during Civil War when Peter works closely as Tony's assistant.[33]

Dr. Strange also mentors Peter on occasion, particularly on occasions where the world of science gets left behind. When Spider-Man faces different foes and relives challenges from his past, Strange provides Peter with words of encouragement and the clue he needs to stop the villains tormenting him.[34] Spider-Man also asks Strange for advice on handling anonymity and for material support in the form of a forgetting spell (when said advice does not yield positive results) in comics and later in film.[35] Dr. Strange is there for Peter when needed, as any good mentor should be.

Spider-Man and His Amazing Mentees

Over his career as a superhero, Peter Parker often inadvertently winds up acting as a mentor himself. Mentorship relations are often established between a more experienced individual and someone with less experience, but mentors can also be peers.[36]

Miles Morales draws upon knowledge of his world's deceased Peter Parker for indirect mentorship that is *parasocial* (social-like but without two-way awareness of each other). *Ultimate Comics Spider-Man* #12. Art by David Marquez.

Once they finally cross universes and meet, Peter becomes a strong mentor for Miles Morales, who is still new to being a Spider-Man.[37] Miles sees Peter as someone who is similar and who has important information to share. They develop a strong working alliance because of their shared powers and experiences. The two Spider-Men discuss their families, their concerns, and fears about certain threats. The relationship between mentor and mentee allows Miles to benefit from Peter's experiences while Peter can feel good that he's guiding a future Spider-Man. They can share the burden of having great power and responsibility.

Even Peter's non-superhero life requires him to be a mentor sometimes. One of his greatest challenges is taking on the role of teacher. As a teacher, he is often seen mentoring students. Research has shown that students benefit from mentoring relationships with teachers exhibiting increased competence and positive relationships with their mentors.[38] As a diligent student who took time off, Peter is able to call out when students try to use him as an easy cover. One of his students, Jordan, desires to be a marine biologist and sees Peter's absenteeism as a teacher as a quick ticket to getting easy support for his application to the University of Miami. Peter sees someone like himself who has a "passion for science" and takes Jordan under his wing but promises to be "tough on him.[39]

We see Peter's capacity for mentoring troubled students as a teacher in Charles Xavier's School for Gifted Youngsters. Peter is tasked with teaching the students most likely to become supervillains. His affable nature and penchant to push back make him an ideal fit for these misfit characters.[40] A peer mentor may also provide useful support. A *peer mentor* is at the same level within an organization as the mentee. Peer mentors can offer support by reflecting an individual's current experiences back to them from another functional area in the organization.[41] A prominent peer mentor for Peter is Matt Murdock, Daredevil. After the death of Peter and Matt's friend, Captain Jean DeWolff, the two superheroes find themselves in conflict over how to handle her murderer, the villain Sin-Eater.[42] Peter can respect Matt as a lawyer and fellow superhero, but during their conflict in this story, he ignores the man until Matt is able to get Peter to listen by calling him by his real name. The two later discuss their different approaches to the case and reveal their secret identities to each other. Peter is angry that he has lost so many people to villains like Sin-Eater, but because he values the content of what Matt is saying, he listens and eventually agrees that killing a villain or even allowing Sin-Eater to be killed is not the right path for Spider-Man. Despite the conflict that Daredevil and Spider-Man have, they always have a strong *working alliance*: a relationship built on mutual trust and respect. Even when Matt has faked his own death, Peter finds him and reveals that he feels that Matt is the closest thing he has to a kindred spirit.[43] That shows the depth of their relationship and their ability to mentor each other.

Spider-Mentors and Spider-Mentees

As a lonely teen and a superhero who usually fights on his own, Peter Parker always needs mentors, whether he realizes it or not. He has struggled to find mentors who fit his unique needs and to recognize the potential mentors already in his life. Finding the right mentor can be difficult for anyone and developing that relationship takes time. However, when that mentorship is successful, it can have a positive impact on a person. Peter's life and work as a superhero benefit from his mentors both superheroic and otherwise. As he has gained experience, he has become a mentor. In an era where there are more Spider-Men, Spider-Women, and spider-people than ever before, Peter Parker will need to continue to strive to be an amazing and spectacular mentor.

Sy Islam, PhD, is vice president of consulting with Talent Metrics and an associate professor of psychology at Farmingdale State College. Through Talent Metrics, he has consulted with Fortune 100 companies such as IBM and teams like the Florida Panthers. He co-authored *Leaders Assemble: Leadership in the MCU* about teaching leadership using the Marvel movies. He is working on a book about leadership in *Avatar: The Last Airbender.*

Gordon Schmidt, PhD, is a professor of management and the director of the David and Sharon Turrentine School of Management at the University of Louisiana Monroe. He researches leadership and the future of work. He consults with organizations on these topics. He co-wrote *Leaders Assemble: Leadership in the MCU,* teaching leadership through Marvel superhero films, and edited a book on social media use in employee selection. He is writing a book teaching leadership through *Avatar: The Last Airbender.*

5

From a Leap to a Spark: Miles Morales and the Coming-of-Age Experience for Latinx and Black Heroes

Richard-Michael Calzada

"I see this spark in you. It's amazing. It's why I push you. But it's yours. Whatever you choose to do with it, you'll be great."

—Jefferson Davis Morales to son Miles[1]

"Psychotherapy for black people needs to be a safe space where they can talk about racial trauma, with an assurance their experiences will be heard and without fear it will be used as a weapon to subdue."

—Black Men on the Couch founder, psychotherapist Rotimi Akinsete[2]

Born out of the Ultimate Universe, Miles Morales is the first Black and Latinx Spider-Man. Miles being biracial isn't new for Marvel. He isn't even their first biracial Spider-Man. Miguel O'Hara (Spider-Man 2099), a geneticist of Irish and Latinx descent, holds that distinction.[3] However, Miles's journey offers an in-depth look into young adulthood for a person of color that is both timely and grounded in multiculturalism. Miles dives into superheroism while struggling to define himself. From discrimination to grief to intense social and academic expectations,

Miles faces a mix of personal obstacles. Joined by mentors and super-villains alike, he explores more about what race and family mean to him. His upbringing and social support system offer a look into what many young men of color need to thrive and realize their full potential.

When Ethnicity and Culture Clash

As a boy of Puerto Rican and African American descent, Miles often feels at odds with cultural norms seen in both the Black and Latinx communities. In the comics, he remarks about not wanting to be known as the Black Spider-Man, but rather Spider-Man.[4] He wonders aloud to his friend Ganke why the media make his skin color such a salient part of his newfound superhero identity. Miles wants to be recognized for more than his race, and he is disappointed when others are unable to do so.

His parents are Rio and Jefferson "Jeff" Davis Morales, a Puerto Rican nurse and an African American police officer, respectively. Miles sometimes finds himself at a loss as to which cultural norms and traditions he wants to follow and which he wants to set aside. The concept of *familismo* is clearly present when his mom brings Miles's grandma Gloria over to chastise him for his slipping grades. Though it starts as Rio's idea, she quickly realizes the situation is getting out of hand when Gloria takes Miles's phone away, thereby hindering his ability to do his duty as Spider-Man.[5] While family remains a high priority in many Latinx and Black communities,[6] it also often entails clashes between generations and along differing personal values. Clearly, respect and *simpatia* are easier for some families to abide by than others.

Though part of a strong family unit, Miles also encounters, and at times internalizes, more Western individualistic traits such as asser-tiveness, self-reliance, and seeking out personal happiness.[7] Even so, his parents often try to make critical life choices on his behalf. His mom and dad lead him to Brooklyn Visions Academy to enter a char-ter school lottery in which only forty of over seven hundred students are selected. While Norman Osborn and his scientists work to create the perfect genetically enhanced spider, Miles gets chosen as the final student to enter the academy. His lottery number *42* foreshadows the inevitable transformation Miles will undergo once he crosses paths with the enhanced spider.[8]

Family clashes can extend across households. When Miles feels confused and struggles to understand his feelings, he often turns to his uncle Aaron for guidance. His dad and uncle often butt heads. Readers may find this as no surprise, given that both Jefferson and Aaron lead their own double lives: Miles's father as an agent of S.H.I.E.L.D. and Uncle Aaron as the Prowler or Iron Spider.[9] This conflict is juxtaposed with traditional Latinx and Black norms, namely that family is paramount and often takes precedence over other significant relationships.[10]

Social Ties and the Comfort of Friendship

Miles doesn't always handle the perils of young adulthood with ease. These struggles—dating girls, turning in his homework on time, and coming to grips with his changing body—become more manageable with the support and encouragement of his friends. Although he quickly gets to know such heroes as Captain America, Ghost-Spider (Spider-Gwen), and Dagger, Miles remains closest to his best friend, Ganke.* Both Ganke and their roommate, Judge, quickly adapt and learn how to conceal Miles's alter identity from prying eyes. As a result, Miles can dedicate more time to his studies while also dating his world's Kate Bishop.[11] In a moment of levity, Ganke even refers to himself as Miles's guru, which reinforces how their friendship is built on both humor and typical teenage awkwardness.[12]

Miles continues to explore his identity from an ethnic and racial standpoint. In class, Miles is unable to answer a basic question about the novel *To Kill a Mockingbird*,[13] to which his English teacher responds by reminding Miles that countless other kids in the world aren't as

---

* FYI: Ganke Lee's characteristics and personality in the comic books manifest as the character Ned Leeds in live-action films, starting with *Spider-Man: Homecoming* (2017 motion picture).—Editors.

fortunate to be able to learn in a classroom setting.[14] This comment captures the duality that young men of color often face, as they tend to receive more critical motivation and guilt-tripping about the opportunities presented to them, especially compared to their White counterparts.[15]

Growing Up in Different Systems

Social ecological theory offers a clear picture of psychological development during adolescence as outlined at five levels: the microsystem, mesosystem, exosystem, macrosystem, and chronosystem.[16] Miles doesn't exist in isolation, but rather in a complex system involving family values, cultural norms, laws, and superhero ideologies. He experiences uncertainty on a *microsystemic level* (within himself, his family, and his peer groups) and a *mesosystemic level* (the level of interaction between key subgroups, such as between his family or school staff and less traditional groups such as S.H.I.E.L.D.).

Young Latinx males often undergo institutional violence and mistreatment from authority figures, such as teachers, school resource officers, and rival members of different peer groups, including gangs.[17] Thus, Miles stays aware of how others perceive him. As the son of a police officer and a nurse, he shows standards of model teen behavior higher than those of the average student. His vigilance is a way of not only keeping himself accountable but also surviving a harsh world. (Note: *Vigilance* would prove appropriate for the life he leads even if sometimes misplaced, rather than *hypervigilance*, which would be excessive.)[18] Even before becoming a Spider-Man, this gives him a different kind of Spidey-sense than the one Peter Parker had to hone as a means of self-preservation.

Miles often skirts the line between being a model student and troublesome for his teachers. For any parent, the challenge of seeing a teen struggle with grades and social interaction is no minor experience. However, research suggests that Latinx parents especially focus on preparing their children for the harsh realities many people of color face. Socially and economically, Latinos, Hispanics, and Blacks are more

likely to be viewed as less driven and expected to engage in socially un-
acceptable behaviors, such as joining a gang, than their White counterparts.[19] These assumptions are largely unfounded. When compared to
other youths, around 89 percent of Latino youth reported having high
career aspirations for themselves. Their barriers to self-actualization are
also evident, as the same sample population of teens surveyed had a
higher school dropout rate than their counterparts. Many Latinx and
Black adolescents are unable to fulfill their higher education goals due
to financial burdens and the desire to provide for their families, a decision that often comes at a great cost to their personal aspirations.[20]

His giving nature and playful demeanor often conflict with Miles's
more serious responsibilities. However, he relies on humor to cope with life's
hardships. When used appropriately, humor serves as one of the healthiest
defense mechanisms, protecting us against anxiety and helping us manage
our way through life.[21] Miles jokes around with everyone—including villains such as the Rhino, who doesn't mind giving the young man a beat-
down.[22] Thanks to both his quips and his sense of compassion (and his sense
of humor being less antagonizing than Peter Parker's), Miles manages to
team up with the Rhino to get to the bottom of another threat to the city,
this one led by the crime boss Tombstone.[23] The use of humor, while at
times a form of deflecting, can also serve young minority individuals well as
it allows them to make unexpected alliances and stand a greater chance of
getting through prolonged hardship.[24]

Stepping into Self-Actualization

From his earliest appearance, Miles proves himself compassionate,
hardworking, and dedicated to his friends and relatives. Others are often blind to this teen's nobler qualities. After he becomes a new Spider-
Man, many citizens initially see him as a brash kid disrespecting the
image of New York's fallen hero, Peter Parker, who has died in their
world.[25] Judgments like these are all too common for both African
American and Latinx teens, many of whom suffer a serious blow to
their self-esteem as a result of receiving criticism as if they have in-
truded on someone else's domain.[26]

Young Miles remains connected with the living, ever-evolving, and sometimes threatening reality (or in some cases, the numerous realities) of NYC and beyond. His biggest priorities are making good grades, finding and keeping quality friends, ensuring the safety of his loved ones, and making his family proud. During a sit-down talk, Uncle Aaron encapsulates Miles's desire for acceptance and support in the face of adversity. "Boys shouldn't have to fight the way we had to," Aaron tells him. "You learn. You study. And you make the world the way you want it to be, not the way it is. You make it. Don't let people make it for you."[27]

Machismo: Living with a Hardened Exterior

Mental health presents an often-minimized gray area, particularly for those in Latinx and Black families. In a qualitative study, Latino males ages 12 to 19 were surveyed regarding educational goals in light of community violence prevalent in their communities. Those young men reported witnessing and often being directly victimized by acts of violence, typically at the hands of peers, school resource officers, and police. The majority of interviewees also referenced being victims of gun violence and, for some, losing a friend or loved one to sudden acts of aggression. Despite the psychological damage and dangerous environment they were in, most interviewees reported aspirations to attend some form of post-secondary education. They demonstrated persistence in completing their high school goals, even as expulsions, suspensions, drug use, and negative peer interactions threatened their efforts.[28]

Another study found clear disparities in ethnicity and self-reported depression in a sample population composed of immigrants from Cuba, Puerto Rico, the Dominican Republic, Mexico, and other Central and South American nations. Of the five groups surveyed, Puerto Ricans reported the highest rates of depression. Those with higher educational attainment were less likely to report depressive symptoms than their counterparts.[29]

Machismo, a common cultural value within Latinx communities, refers to an expectation that a male's character will be determined by his ability to be strong, respectful, and directive, especially when it comes to fatherhood and leadership. It is a value that plays a critical role in how Miles thinks, acts, and behaves. This approach is often seen as taking charge, sometimes to the point of physical aggression.[30] While *machismo* has been associated with relationship difficulties and, in some cases, violence, it can also be expressed in a more positive light. For example, when a father uses authoritative (*not* authoritarian) discipline to help raise his children and leads by example as a positive role model, he demonstrates healthy masculinity. In a similar vein, Miles learns how to be tough yet courteous from both his mom and dad.

For Miles, another aspect of success means connecting with others. His superpowers extend beyond web-slinging and wielding superhuman strength. Miles is multilingual, communicating in English, Spanish, and ASL[31] with ease. His sense of fluency with his community is impressive, as seen when he walks down his neighborhood street and greets most everyone he sees by name and in their native language.[32] Miles knows the trials and tribulations of his friends and family, which strengthens his sense of empathy and compassion. Language becomes his way of identifying with and supporting others, especially during times of social unrest.

Grief at a Young Age

Miles has barely reached his teens when he starts saving the city in the wake of Peter Parker's death, a task no one can prepare him for. Mourning the death of a hero Miles looked up to is the first of many unexpected losses he must face on the road through young adulthood. His grief is also influenced by his values and cultural norms, many of which begin within his family. For example, he must witness not only his dad's brief disappearance after Miles reveals his Spider-Man identity to him[33] but also his uncle Aaron's death by gun violence.[34]

Being a superhero comes with the weight of death, loss, and uncertainty. The risk of exposure to sudden brutality in everyday life is compounded not only by Miles's environment, but also by how others perceive him. For many Latinx individuals, growing up in *el barrio* can be just as risky as being raised in the ghetto.[35] It comes as no surprise, then, that Miles isn't always able to joke or tough his way out of intense grieving. When Miles finds a mysteriously resurrected Peter Parker in his old apartment, alive and well, Miles remains in a stunned silence for several seconds. In their subsequent shouting match, Peter snaps at Miles about him not having been forced to take up the mantle of Spider-Man.[36] Their initial (though soon resolved) confrontation encapsulates some notable elements of bereavement, including overt anger, disbelief, and the use of personal attacks to get one's point across.

Research in psychology also highlights distinctive traits of loss and bereavement among Latinx and Black communities. For example, those African Americans who were part of a close-knit group of friends and family members reported higher levels of distress in the wake of a close family member's death than their respective White counterparts. Kinship also played a significant role in how African Americans experienced bereavement. The individuals surveyed reported significant contact with their deceased loved ones through spiritual practices and recollective experiences. However, those who mourned the deceased also engaged in little to no disclosure to others about their grief process.[37]

Racism and the Many Shades of Discrimination

Racism is perhaps the most dangerous form of oppression young men of color face. Miles struggles with identifying with versus separating from his racial identity. Telling Ganke he wishes to be known as Spider-Man rather than the Black Spider-Man expresses internal conflict typical for someone his age. He's experiencing a moment of ethnic identity development known as *moratorium*, a conflict between the desire to immerse himself in his ethnic identity or to distance himself from it.[38]

Systemic barriers are entrenched in our society. Black, Native American, and Hispanic children are six to nine times more likely than White children to reside in areas stricken by poverty.[39] The US incarceration rate is almost eight times higher now than its historic average.

Among African American men who earned their high school diploma, close to one in ten were incarcerated in 2008. Low educational attainment has been strongly correlated with Black and, to a lesser degree, Latinx men being sent to jail or prison.[40] For Miles, education is a do-or-die effort, as is his role as a superhero, and as a Black/Latinx young man, he must consider the impact his culture has on his aspirations more so than his White counterparts.

Clinical Interventions

The interconnection between heritage, language, and culture reinforces an important point: If any mental health interventions are to be effective with teens of color, they must take into consideration and honor the values and culturally tied practices that comprise the individual's worldview.[41] As children develop their ability to rationalize, anticipate consequences of their actions, and articulate their needs, they typically become more refined. Identity grows more nuanced and firmly rooted in one's sense of self. Gender, sexual orientation, and masculinity often loom at the forefront of many young men's thinking. Researchers have found that the stereotype of Latinx men being overly domineering, sexist, and driven by romance shows a reductionistic mindset for what is a wide spectrum of behaviors seen across various Latinx groups.[42] What's more, the tendency for racial majorities to peg many Latinx men as domineering demonstrates more long-standing racist practices, as the generalizations to view men as insatiable lovers and power-hungry abusers is not unique to any one particular race or ethnicity. The term also stems from a broader system, namely patriarchy, which has been shown to cause damage to families regardless of ethnicity or demographics.[43] For Miles, sticking to respect and truthfulness is more important than being seen as the toughest or most attractive young man on the block.

Research suggests that mentoring provides a critical component of competent clinical interventions for young men of Black and Hispanic descent. In *critical mentoring*, a mentor has the ability to stay continually aware of cultural, social, political, and economic oppression that afflicts young men and women of color.[44] Well-trained mentors are able to recognize their own biases and values, share the most important values with their mentees, and offer their young charges protection in the form of genuine, compassionate, and culturally sensitive guidance. One program that captures the spirit of mentorship is the My Brother's Keeper Alliance (MBKA). Launched by President Barack Obama in 2014, MBKA was developed to address enduring inequality and empower all young men of color to thrive. By closing the educational and labor force gaps permeating our society, MBKA allows for disenfranchised minoritized boys and men to realize their full potential and achieve a lifetime of well-being.[45] Safe and supportive communities can and often have arisen from such initiatives.

A closely related term, *critical consciousness*, is the ability of the mentor to recognize and respond to the unique cultural and environmental needs each young person has, then engage the mentee in a discussion of how best to meet their needs in a historically hostile society.[46] A healthy mentoring relationship in which adults and teens can have meaningful conversations regarding race, gender, academic performance, and personal identity can positively shape youthful perspectives. Miles has several mentors. From his own dad to his uncle Aaron to Ghost-Spider to the original Spider-Man to Mary Jane Watson, each teaches him invaluable lessons about forgiveness, mercy, and staying true to oneself. When torn between lying and telling his girlfriend Kate Bishop about his secret identity, Miles speaks with Mary Jane Watson and gets her perspective on what did and didn't work in her relationship with the late Peter Parker. MJ listens empathetically to Miles, validates his struggles, and encourages him to be sure that his and Kate's love is the real deal because dropping such a big revelation on her will test their relationship like nothing else.[47] His mentors are also human and flawed. They suffer their own losses and shortcomings, which is true to real-life mentorship. He sees firsthand the ways in which Peter Parker and Ghost-Spider fail to manage the balance between their personal lives and superhero lives. By learning from other heroes' regrets and battles with depression and anxiety, Miles learns how to better take care of himself and not repeat the same mistakes.[48]

Taking off the Mask in the Counseling Room

Rising above systemic barriers and oppression, Miles Morales serves as a beacon of hope for people of color, particularly young Latinx and Black males. As he faces grief, racism, and supervillains, one common concern emerges: the need for Miles to take care of his mental health.

Research indicates that for people of color to be best served in the counseling room, less conventional therapeutic approaches must be utilized. Counseling and psychotherapy are deeply rooted in White heteronormative ideas, experiences, and theories, which seldom translate to an accurate or helpful understanding of the unique struggles and successes Black and Latinx individuals experience.[49] From the start, practitioners must enter each session with an open mind and a genuine curiosity. A *trauma-informed approach* often helps, as it allows the client to feel safe and heard while talking about particularly upsetting events they have endured, such as armed robbery and police brutality.[50]

It is important to provide counseling that is grounded in a person's unique identity, needs, and culture. *Multicultural counseling and therapy* (MCT) is founded upon the importance of meeting a client or patient where they are, rather than where the clinician believes they should be. Key client resources, including the immediate support of friends and family, are recognized and affirmed. Indeed, for many Black individuals, there is a strong correlation between the ability to weather depression and the presence of family support.[51] By adopting a curious and kind approach, therapists can help enable clients like Miles to share their story without them feeling the need to withhold or withdraw.

All superheroes have struggles. Like most teenagers, Miles has a chaotic life with many moments of success, defeat, and self-doubt. Compassion and humility are powerful attributes in recognizing and responding to the racial reality that is, for so many Black and Latinx teens, all too harsh. Discomfort on the part of the mental health provider is just as natural; privilege and unawareness often serve as cushions to unpleasant feelings and paradigm shifts for clinicians, particularly those who are White.[52] To be present, it is important to be open to each client's lived experience and continually challenge personal biases and prejudices, both inside and outside the therapy room. Miles shows how, even in the face of fear, anyone can take a leap of faith—and survive. The power to heal starts with listening to another person's story, empathizing with them, and exploring the inherent hope and strengths tying all communities together. Only then can their true superhero identity emerge.

 **Richard-Michael Calzada, MS, LPC,** is a Texas native who has been navigating his own Latinx identity since birth. He is a Licensed Professional Counselor and specializes in providing multicultural services to people of color, the LGBTQ+ community, and those struggling with depression, anxiety, and grief. Richard-Michael has worked in the mental healthcare field for a decade. In his spare time, he enjoys writing fiction, playing with his cats, gaming, and spending time with his partner.

 **Vanessa Hintz, PsyD,** a licensed clinical psychologist in Wisconsin, earned her doctorate in psychology from the Chicago School of Professional Psychology. Dr. Hintz has served on panel discussions of the manifestations of psychological concepts in American popular culture. An active proponent of diversity, equity, and inclusion, she works collaboratively with individuals to understand how each person makes meaning of the world within their various cultural contexts. Vanessa Hintz provided mentorship and other chapter assistance on this chapter.

6

Finding Your Inner Superhero: Adolescent Moral Identity Development

Apryl Alexander

"I've never been more confused about my responsibility."
—Miles Morales[1]

"When I discover who I am, I'll be free."
—author Ralph Ellison[2]

The pathway to adulthood challenges even super-heroes. Imagine navigating the awkwardness of high school, then you get bitten by a radioactive spider! When reflecting on adolescence, many of us think about the physical and emotional changes associated with puberty. Adults discussing teen life often dwell on their risk-taking, sensation-seeking, and flawed decision-making.[3] However, cognitive and behavioral development also evolve dramatically during this time. Developmental psychologists have found that cognitive development continues through about age twenty-five, particularly in the growth of the prefrontal cortex of the brain responsible for reasoning, information processing, and decision-making.[4] During this time, teenagers are also attempting to find their sense of self, personal identity, and purpose in their family and social groups.

Many early Spider-Man comics and later revisions center around navigating identity during this period of adolescent development into early adulthood (often called *late adolescence* or *emerging adulthood* by child development researchers).[5] Superheroes make many difficult decisions, including navigating their own moral compass. Teenagers and superheroes both have to weigh the risks and benefits of what they will do when presented with novel situations. Attitudes and morals aid in guiding youth through their challenges. Peter Parker and Miles Morales, both teenagers as they assume the Spider-Man identity, face trials of morality in their personal lives as well as their hero lives.

Moral Development

Fifteen-year-old Peter Parker of the Forest Hills neighborhood in Queens, New York,[6] must navigate all the usual tasks of being a teenager, such as going to school, navigating friendships and romantic interests, dealing with bullies,[7] and even maintaining a summer job.[8] During his early adolescent stage of development, new situations frequently challenge him as a teenager and superhero alike.

American psychologist Lawrence Kohlberg posited three levels of moral development: preconventional, conventional, and postconventional.[9] The *preconventional level* (in early childhood, before learning moral conventions) involves avoiding punishment and attaining pleasure. The person may not understand or care about the fact that other people want things too. The *conventional level* (typically developing throughout elementary school years and adolescence) develops as the individual becomes motivated and concerned about mutual problems. The person wants acceptance and seeks social approval from others, particularly others they see as superior. Finally, during the *postconventional level* (more mature moral thinking, which not everyone develops) the person develops autonomous moral judgment governed around a universal set of principles such as fairness and justice. In the early comics, Peter appears to get thrown into the conventional level of moral development. Uncle Ben and Aunt May serve as adult figures who are caring and compassionate and act as Peter's guide to who he wants to become in life.

However, Peter finds himself further pushed to think about his concern for others in this conventional level as he faces further adversity. As unexpected hardships occur, moral injury can develop. *Moral injury*, the experience of trauma characterized by guilt, shame, and/or an existential conflict,[10] originated as a term for military members and veterans but has also been applied to healthcare workers in thinking about actions/inactions that violate their moral code. Uncle Ben's preventable murder serves as Peter's incident of moral injury.[11] Those who experience moral injury feel as though their moral values have been violated by the actions of themselves or others, and they face *guilt*, regret experienced through an evaluation of oneself and one's own behavior in relation to ethics, norms, and values.[12] The loss also places his family in even worse financial turmoil,[13] which is a lot for a teenager to cope with. Ultimately, Peter comes to terms with his moral injury through examining his purpose and following the mantra that Uncle Ben has left with him.

For Peter and his identity as Spider-Man, much of his coping takes place in the form of risk-taking behaviors—another marker of adolescence. While most adults focus on negative risk-taking among adolescents, teenagers also demonstrate a capacity for *prosocial risk-taking*—doing risky things for prosocial purposes. Prosocial risk-taking includes speaking out against popular opinions, beliefs, or authority, along with assisting family and peers.[14] Perhaps because it figures into a broader pattern of generally taking risks, *negative risk-taking* (taking unhealthy, dangerous risks such as texting while driving) is positively correlated with *positive risk-taking* behaviors (e.g., standing up for your beliefs, developing friendships).[15] Developmental and environmental changes may contribute to risk tolerance and prosocial tendencies that occur during the transitions from early to mid-adolescence.[16]

Finding Your Hero Identity

Peter Parker and most of the Spider-Men (like younger Miles Morales, future Miguel O'Hara, clone Ben Reilly) find themselves

Aunt May points out a problem with *identity foreclosure,* making a lifetime commitment to a value or role (in this case, protector) when too young to know the options. *The Amazing Spider-Man* #532 (2006). Art by Ron Garney & Bill Reinhold.

having to balance their personal and professional (superhero) identities. For most of them, they do not initially see the two as integrated. However, their personal morals contribute to who each is as a hero. During adolescence, teenagers experience *ego identity development,* finding one's stable and formulated identity through the exploration of abilities and interests.[17] *Ego identity* extends through at least four distinct ego identity statuses: identity diffusion, identity foreclosure, moratorium, and identity achievement.[18] *Identity diffusion* covers individuals who have not committed to a particular identity but are not exploring who they are either. Individuals in a *foreclosed* status of development have committed to a particular identity based on expectations imposed by others (i.e., family, friends, culture) without any personal exploration. During *moratorium,* individuals engage in exploring who they are without yet committing to a particular identity. Finally, *identity achievement* occurs when a person commits to a particular identity after having explicitly explored what that identity means.

Adolescent Peter may be in moratorium all along. After becoming Spider-Man, he continues exploring who he is both as a person and as a superhero. At times, Peter assumes these to be distinct rather than integrated identities. Comics character psychiatrist Ludwig Rinehart explores the ego identity status of Spider-Man, noting, "You see, he is in a fantasy world now! But, of course, he is a human being! It is only a matter of time before his id and his ego get so confused that he forgets who he really is and then he will suffer a severe breakdown!"[19] Even though Dr. Rinehart turns out to be Mysterio in disguise, he correctly remarks on the challenges Peter faces in the moratorium identity phase. Peter's confusion is also exacerbated by his inability (or refusal) to share his superhero identity with loved ones, particularly his caregiver Aunt May. Adolescents often look to caregivers as models in navigating decision-making, particularly concerning moral challenges, and Peter's choice to isolate himself as Spider-Man also isolates him from typical sources of guidance.

Eventually, older adolescents and younger adults become better able to make moral decisions for themselves instead of following rule-bound social norms and expectations.[20] *Future orientation*, the capacity to project events into the future and think about the long-term consequences of one's behaviors, increases through late adolescence.[21] As we see Peter transition into college,[22] he appears more committed to examining how he can juggle all of his roles and obligations (i.e., to superheroism, to college, to job, to friends, to girlfriend, to a frequently ill Aunt May). His identities ultimately become more congruent, and he reaches identity achievement.

Community Hero

In another NYC borough, Brooklyn, we have Miles Morales. His heritage as an Afro-Latino teenager, although not always central to the story, is important to note. His culture often lingers in the background of the stories: We witness him speaking Spanish with his Latina mother at home, he wears hoodies while shopping local bodegas, and he shows a strong interest in hip-hop.

In fandom, some debate surrounds the notion of racebending characters (i.e., taking established characters and changing their race).[23] When the mask Miles wears gets damaged and partially exposes his face, a reporter notes his apparent race, which is not how Miles wants to be defined.[24] In essence, he wants to be known for his actions and commitments to community rather than his racial/ethnic identity. In his conceptualization of moral development, Kohlberg believed that all people across all cultures exhibited the universal concepts of morality.[25] Miles just wants to be Spider-Man. However, some individuals might interpret this approach to storytelling as incorporating racial colorblindness. For instance, scholar W.E.B. Du Bois discussed the notion of *double consciousness*,[26] where Black people often balance integrating their sense of self and Black identity with the need to placate to whiteness and the White gaze. Having a positive racial identity is a protective factor against the physical and mental health impacts of discrimination.[27]

It is important to not ignore racial and ethnic heritage for Miles in describing his hero identity, particularly when it is relevant in his own family and in the diverse community of Brooklyn. As the experiences of Spider-Men are not monolithic, neither are the experiences of Black boys and men. *Oppression* occurs when one group of individuals abuses their power (interpersonal, structural, institutional) to benefit themselves at the expense of another group. Oppressive social and political systems are contextual factors that influence a youth's potential for positive development.[28] Even within comics, harmful stereotypes and tropes can be perpetuated. Marvel writer Yehudi Mercado apologized when critiqued about stereotypes in his writing of Morales in an alternate universe where he becomes Thor.[29] Therefore, when possible, it is important to note his culture and the importance of his presence as an Afro-Latino adolescent.

Family plays a major protective factor in his life. Miles's mother and father are important figures throughout the comics, often offering him support and guidance through his troubles in school. Eventually both parents discover his identity as Spider-Man and still provide him with the support to grow and develop his identity, both as a teenager and as a superhero. This type of *authoritative parenting*, which emphasizes warmth and support, is beneficial in promoting moral development in adolescents.[30] In many cultural and ethnic groups, extended family members have a significant role in a child or adolescent's upbringing. Uncle Aaron tries to fill that role. Miles admires his uncle despite his parents' open guardedness toward Aaron, given his criminal history.[31] Uncle Aaron tries to give up his criminal behavior as the Prowler, but frequently relapses. More than once, Miles witnesses his uncle actively committing a crime.[32] As Miles is developing as a teen and superhero, he learns to navigate his complex relationship with his uncle, torn between his desire to save him and to protect his community, and reflect on how he feels that his uncle's behavior clashes so strongly with his own ethical code.

As with Peter, Miles's peer group plays a significant role in his life. Ganke Lee, his roommate at Brooklyn Visions Academy, is the first person to learn about his identity as Spider-Man.[33] Ganke not only keeps his friend's identity secret, but he also aids in providing supplies and technology to Miles, and supporting him through the emotional challenges of being Spider-Man. Miles recognizes the importance of his role as Spider-Man in serving as a role model for youth in his neighborhood, as well as his sister Billie.[34] His family, peers, and community also foster his sense of duty to his community and activism. For adolescents, activism and an orientation toward activism is a part of *civic development*,[35] the emergence of civic beliefs, attitudes, and behaviors over time.[36] When trying to save a group of foster children who were trafficked by Tombstone, Miles notes that "the people around us are our great responsibility."[37]

Balancing on a Web Line

Both Miles and Peter have to juggle keeping their communities safe, serving as a role model, and navigating daily living. The responsibility of being a superhero often leads to their *adultification*, placing adult expectations on teens and children. While adultification can be seen as positive[38] in that it teaches youth responsibilities, it can also rob adolescents of their youth. For instance, Peter feels immense pressure to provide for him and Aunt May after Uncle Ben's death.[39] Moreover, Black youth are more likely to face adultification through racism. Adultification may be "rooted in the legacy of racial discrimination in [the United States], which historically included responding to Black youths' childlike behavior more punitively."[40]

In real life, adults must be cautious of tasking youth with great responsibility as they are developing into their own identities. Although adultification can provide youth with great life skills such as self-confidence, empathy, and problem solving,[41] it is important not to deprive them of their youthful engagement. Further, adultification can lead to unsafe situations such as interacting with dangerous people. Adolescents learn through naturalistic exploration and positive risk-taking behaviors under the safe supervision of adults. Reaching identity achievement happens when adolescents and emerging adults learn about who they are and who they want to become. Spider-Men reach that stage when they realize their prosocial values not only benefit the ones they love and their communities but are part of their authentic selves. This is what we hope for in all youth—for each to develop into their own superhero.

Apryl Alexander, PsyD, is the Metrolina Medical Foundation Distinguished Scholar in Health and Public Policy in the Department of Public Health Sciences at the University of North Carolina at Charlotte. Her research broadly focuses on violence and victimization, human sexuality, and trauma- and culturally informed practice.

7

Into the Spidentity: The Multiverse of Personality and Identity

Alex Langley

"I learned to recognize the thorough and primitive duality of man. I saw that, of the two natures that contended in the field of my consciousness, even if I could rightly be said to be either, it was only because I was radically both."

—Mr. Hyde, alter ego of Dr. Jekyll[1]

"The best way to find yourself is to lose yourself in the service of others."

—activist and civil rights leader Mahatma Gandhi[2]

We all exist in a multiverse of sorts. We spend much of our time thinking about what we've done, what we're doing, what we should do, as well as what we could have done, could be doing, and might do. Within each of these universes exists an alternate self—the person we might have been or could still be if a single decision would go differently. Some choices we deliberate over before they're made or ruminate over after they're done. Others happen in the blink of an eye.

Peter Parker's decision to adopt the alter ego of "Spider-Man" happens with almost whimsical casualness. "I'll need a name," he says, donning his homemade costume. "Well, guess Spider-Man is as good as any!"[3] As teenagers, we begin making decisions that affect us for the rest of our lives. Few teens, however, make decisions that carry as much impact as Peter Parker's decision to become Spider-Man. His choice irrevocably changes not only the direction of his own life but also the lives of his loved ones and countless strangers he directly and indirectly helps. In donning his costume, he makes a choice that creates a new branch to the multiverse of his identity, and in the process begins exploring his sense of self in ways he never had before.

Who is Peter Parker? Who is Spider-Man? And how are these not the same question? As one person, he has one personality but with dual identities. *Personality* refers to a person's characteristic pattern of behavior, both overt (actions visible to others) and covert (invisible thoughts, feelings, and other mental processes), distinct from other people.[4] It is who you are psychologically no matter how differently you express that in various circumstances, whereas *identity* (1) is an idea of who you are and (2) considers all traits whether psychological, physical, or interpersonal.[5] Personality encompasses one's sense of identity and interrelated concepts such as self-concept, self-esteem, and self-control. One personality can have several identities: Who we are with grandma is not who we are with friends; celebrities are not the same in interviews as they are at home; and who you are online is not necessarily who you are in the real world.

Dual identity is not unique to superhero characters, but the distinction between superhero persona and secret identity can help illustrate, perhaps in an exaggerated way, complexities of real personality development. Few superheroes can demonstrate that better than the man who's also a spider. His depictions demonstrate identity issues and principles throughout personality psychology. After *personality psychology* emerged as a distinct area in psychology, not simply as a topic within Freudian psychoanalysis, some of the most popular perspectives to emerge have been the lifestyle, trait, and humanistic existential approaches (all of which would have plenty to say about Peter Parker and his supporting cast). Because personality makes him stand out among superhero characters, personality plays an important part in defining his enemies and friends as well.

Black Suit, No Tie

The choice to become Spider-Man enables Peter to explore his personality through the new identity he's created. No longer is he simply Peter Parker, teenage bookworm. Now he's also Spider-Man, wall-crawling superhero. Spider-Man can act with a directness that Peter Parker generally can't afford, swinging into action with fewer concerns for what others will think of his behavior. Peter second-guesses himself constantly. As readers privy to both his inner thoughts and his outer behaviors, we see the contrast between what he wishes he could do and what he must do in order to stabilize his life. Spider-Man generally gets to act more directly and speak more honestly than Peter Parker does because the social situation allows for such behavior (though as Spidey he still spins his share of quick lies and cover stories even while in costume).

Being Spider-Man allows Peter to take preexisting aspects of himself and adjust them to the situation. Such behavior matches the *social-cognitive learning theory of personality*: While personality may be stable and consistent over time, it varies in different situations (and those variations are similarly stable and consistent over time).[6] Peter tends to be "Peter," and Spider-Man tends to be "Spider-Man." For one to behave like the other would strike people as odd and out of place. Peter and Spider-Man are similar, but different enough in the way they present different aspects of personality known as *traits*, habitual patterns of thought, behavior, and emotion.[7]

Swinging Across the OCEAN

Often, like the strands of a web, traits stick together. The person who is highly outgoing also tends to be a bold, talkative, enthusiastic person who seeks excitation and needs other people so much that solitude is boring—a set of traits collectively known as *extraversion*, the opposite of which would be *introversion*. Someone who is generally introverted can show many of these traits without possessing them all.

Extraversion/introversion was the earliest such webbed-together cluster of traits, known as a *personality factor*, widely recognized in personality psychology. The best-studied personality factors are known as the "Big Five" or *OCEAN model* for openness, conscientiousness, extraversion, agreeableness, and neuroticism.[8]

Peter Parker may be a shy bibliophile in high school, but in his adventures as Spider-Man he comes to discover that he loves new experiences and frequently engages in activities that are novel and thought-provoking. As Spider-Man he has a high degree of *openness* (a.k.a. *openness to experience*), the factor that covers curiosity, intellectual flexibility, and desire for variety of experience. As Peter Parker he often hides his true joy over experiencing new things in many areas, save for his lifelong love of science.

Conscientiousness refers to a person's need to be diligent, punctual, productive, and cautious. Peter graduates high school with a full scholarship and eventually earns his bachelor's degree, but his activities as Spider-Man cause him to drop out of graduate school at least three times. Practically speaking, however, he tends to be terrible at conscientious behavior in this sense, particularly when it comes to his interpersonal relationships. He forgets dates, appointments, and birthdays (even his own) with incredible regularity. Spider-Man is too spontaneous (reckless, some might say) and Peter Parker is too unreliable to call him conscientious.

"Though the world may mock Peter Parker, the timid teenager, it will soon marvel at the awesome might of Spider-Man!"[9] Prior to the radioactive spider bite, Peter considers himself a wallflower, a bit of a social outcast at his school. Often buried in his books and having no friends to speak of, he rates low on *extraversion*, the need to be around other people, and therefore high on *introversion*, the need to spend time alone. After becoming Spider-Man, Peter begins exploring his identity more fully and becomes more willing to try getting to know people. He still spends much of his time alone, in his head, web-swinging over the rooftops of New York, and does not prioritize social engagements. He, like most people, over time becomes more of an *ambivert*, someone who enjoys the company of others sometimes and the solitude of being alone at other times.

The friendly neighborhood Spider-Man would rate well in *agreeableness*, a general tendency to be kind, compassionate, and helpful to others. He spends most of his time being altruistic out of a sheer desire to help. However, while he is more agreeable than not, he does have his disagreeable side. He shows the kinds of altruism, compassion, concern, and sympathy associated with agreeableness, but he also utters a lot of insults and does not always make it his top priority to get along with others.

He would rate very highly in *neuroticism*, a tendency to feel anxious when other people in a similar situation would not. Peter Parker, as both himself and as Spider-Man, worries constantly. He worries about his aunt, his friends, his lovers, random citizens, fellow superheroes, sometimes supervillains, and, if he has time, even himself. Peter's high anxiety seems understandable, given his history of caregiver loss at a young age, and it's an element that helps make him so relatable as a character. Human beings worry, often excessively. Some degree of neuroticism is baked into us, but Peter goes beyond the typical recipe. This propensity for perpetual worry may seem to Peter like a hindrance, but to someone with a more optimistic view of his personality, it could be argued as a great strength.

Looking Up
THE OPTIMISM OF HUMANISTIC PSYCHOLOGY

Humanistic psychologists such as Carl Rogers theorized that much of our personality takes shape out of a desire to achieve personal fulfillment and growth by becoming our most idealized self.[10] In humanistic psychology, the *real self* refers to who we actually, literally are. Our *ideal self* refers to the alternate self we wish we were, who we feel we could or should be. The conflict between who we are and who we wish to be is, for most of us, internal. Metaphorical. Psychological. For Peter, it's a conflict he embraces daily. Every time he puts on his costume and becomes Spider-Man, he's weighing his real self against his ideal self. Peter Parker can, occasionally, be ignoble, petty, and clumsy, but as Spider-Man he's daring, heroic, and agile. This conflict between who he feels he is and who he feels he should be is so rampant it's often

Peter's first impulse is to make the choice that benefits him . . . until the Spider-Man side of him steers him back toward nobility. *The Amazing Spider-Man* #5. Art by Steve Ditko.

represented artistically with Peter thinking selfish thoughts while half of his Spider-Man mask appears over his face, representing his desire to be a better person.

Humanistic psychologists often emphasize human potential under the belief that all of us can become our best selves under the right circumstances and motivations. In selflessly choosing to become the superhero Spider-Man, we see the best possible Peter Parker. Had he not made that selfless choice, had he given into anger, revenge, and greed, he would become a *very* different self. Something as simple as a person's motivations can drastically affect who they are.

When Supervillains Besiege the Pyramid
A HIERARCHY OF GREEDS?

Humanist psychologist Abraham Maslow outlined a *hierarchy of needs* in which people's personalities take shape around the prioritization of the most basic, primal human needs over more advanced ones: nutrition before affection, affection before enlightenment, and so forth.[11] This view gained popularity as a model of motivation, despite strong criticism and inconsistency of empirical support,[12] because (1) we like easy diagrams and (2) there is an intuitive appeal to the idea that struggling to meet our most basic needs can get in the way of building relationships, self-esteem, morals, and spiritual growth. It's an idea that matches much of human experience. Maslow felt that criminal behavior and selfish personalities develop when people dwell in baser needs instead of progressing to what he saw as self-actualization.

Physiological Needs

"Nothing matters except the ravening thirst of Morbius!"[13] the so-called "Living Vampire" declares—a clear illustration of Maslow's assertion that the burden of the basest, most urgent bodily needs will distract us from more advanced needs. At the bottom of the hierarchy of needs lie *physiological needs*, physical motivators such as thirst, hunger, and shelter—needs that, as Maslow saw it, must be fulfilled before any other needs can be given consideration. The vampiric Morbius first appears as a tormented, living vampire, cursed to thirst for the blood of the living. The vampiric Morlun (no relation), who consumes the life force of spider-powered superbeings, acts out of his relentless need to feed.[14] While blinded by thirst, both Morbius and Morlun are angry, selfish beings lacking in potentially greater depth of personality.

Safety Needs

Those who are not starving or otherwise overtaken by immediate bodily desires can work on *safety needs*, wherein a person's motivations focus on maintaining long-term physical safety, freedom, and control over their lives. The Shocker, Rhino, and Electro all begin their criminal careers motivated by safety needs. In Shocker's case, he creates his special vibrating shockwave suit to become a better cat burglar so he might never be caught and imprisoned again. After gaining nigh invulnerability and incredible strength, the Rhino decides he's through taking orders from others and vows to use his newfound power to live life as *he* chooses.[15] Because Electro's powers make him more dangerous to be around and complicate his life severely, much of his behavior focuses on finding ways to live safely and comfortably while, curiously, minimizing the harm he causes to others.[16] Keeping himself safe remains his top priority, but this villain with the highly lethal electrical powers does frequently give thought to the safety needs of others, thus moving him closer to the next level up the hierarchy.

Love and Belonging Needs

Love and belonging needs focus on the drive for intimate, interpersonal connections. Professor Miles Warren, better known as the Jackal, inappropriately falls in love with his student, Gwen Stacy, and becomes increasingly jealous of her relationship with Peter Parker.[17] When she dies, seemingly at the hands of Spider-Man, Warren becomes obsessed with cloning her and destroying the person who stole his "love" away. Sandman's criminal origins lie either in his love for a sick daughter who needs money for medical treatments[18] or in high school heartbreak misguiding him into the belief that women are only attracted to men with money.[19] When Morbius has other needs met, he longs to not be alone in his vampirism, and tries to turn the Big Apple into the Bloody Apple by transforming the populace into "living vampires" like himself.[20]

Self-Esteem Needs

Self-esteem needs refer to our need for respect, accomplishment, and self-worth. Some villains first pursue Spider-Man sheerly to prove themselves. Kraven the Hunter, bored of hunting "normal" prey, seeks out Spider-Man as the ultimate test of his self-worth.[21] After every defeat, Kraven finds his self-esteem plummeting to lower levels than before. His entire identity is based on being the world's greatest hunter; with Spider-Man consistently disproving this notion, he becomes lost and obsessed. The Green Goblin also seeks out Spider-Man from the beginning to prove himself. At first, he targets Spider-Man to establish himself as a master criminal to the world at large—similar to the way that many wealthy men will aggressively choose new fields, such as combat sports or aeronautics, to prove their masculinity and self-worth.[22] This villain varies as to whether his Green Goblin persona or Norman Osborn is in charge, but both personalities show some hatred of Peter Parker/Spider-Man. "I wanted to make sure you *knew*," says Osborn to a de-powered Spider-Man, "that you were *nothing* compared to me. Just some dumb kid."[23] Peter Parker's continued success as Spider-Man deals a blow to egomaniacal Osborn's ego: For the billionaire to lose to a working-class kid from Queens is, to him, an insult that engenders a lifelong obsession.

Spider-Man, mouthing off, jabs at villains' self-esteem, which prompts some such as the Kingpin and Venom to attack him over their wounded pride. Wilson "Kingpin" Fisk finds Spidey's antics particularly irksome, often growing increasingly angry during their encounters to the point of blind rage. Fisk derives his sense of self-worth from his accomplishments as New York's "Kingpin of Crime."[24] Spider-Man's constant interruptions of his plans (and remarks about his physique and lack of hair) undermine the decades of work he's put into building his criminal empire. Before Venom becomes a lethal protector, Eddie Brock and the Venom symbiote focus their energy into attacking Peter Parker/Spider-Man, whom both Eddie and the Venom symbiote blame for personal and professional ill fortune.[25] Not until they're able to accept responsibility for their own shortcomings and stop blaming Peter can Brock and Venom move past their villainous origin and become a kind of antihero in the comics.

Self-Actualization

At the top of the pyramid, we have *self-actualization*, becoming the very best version of yourself. Although villains do not fulfill the qualities Maslow perceived in self-actualized people, the drive to self-actualize supposedly exists on some level in everyone. He believed anyone can make progress.

Much of Doctor Octopus's behavior derives from unhealthy efforts to meet his self-esteem needs in what he likely perceives as a warped quest for self-actualization (though self-actualized individuals do not feel compelled to assert dominance over others). He constantly attacks and torments Spider-Man, trying to prove his superiority and seeking revenge for past insults. Otto Octavius feels such a need to prove himself that, after taking over Peter Parker's body, he declares himself the "Superior Spider-Man."[26] Octavius decides he can prove himself the better man by *literally* becoming Spider-Man. He quickly finds that being Spider-Man is harder and more complicated than he imagined. Eventually, his adventures as the self-proclaimed Superior Spider-Man lead to his noblest moment, perhaps one of true self-actualization, in which he realizes that he is not, nor was he ever, the superior Spider-Man, and he sacrifices himself to return control of Peter's body back to him.

More Identities, More Problems, But Also More Benefits

As Spider-Man, Doctor Octopus curses having to maintain a double life. "I'm falling short this time. Why? . . . Perhaps it's 'Peter Parker' holding me back," he ponders (once again the un-actualized Doc Ock finds someone else to blame for his shortcomings).[27] When there's not a mad scientist in control of his body, Peter gains tremendous personal strength and growth from maintaining his double identity. He's a stronger Spider-Man because he draws from the personal lessons and connections he has as Peter Parker, and he's a nobler Peter Parker because of his experiences as Spider-Man. Creating an alternate self allows Peter to grow and explore who he is more fully.

While few of us wear spandex and fight supervillains, we do achieve a similar growth and exploration of self through alternate identities in the form of *online identities*, configurations of defining characteristics of a person in online space.[28] Today, nearly everyone holds some type of double life through their presence in the real world and the online world. There are countless college students with bustling webcam businesses, banal office workers with blogs laser focused on the hobby they secretly love, suburban parents who bring dread and destruction to every battle royale, and so many others. Who we are in reality may not, and often does not, match who we are online in much the same way that "puny" Peter Parker's identity as an everyday guy does not match who he is as Spider-Man.

Online identities often free us to behave in ways we would not in the real world. We can be bolder, be different, freed from the constraints of many real-world consequences. With online identities we can fake new aspects to ourselves, emphasize different real aspects of ourselves, or hide who we are altogether.[29] Online identities allow us to more freely engage in *strategic self-presentation*, shaping others' perception of us for our own benefit.[30] Who we are online is who we've chosen to be online. Through these chosen identities, we can explore who we want to become, or who we wish we could become.[31] And, if we so choose, we can abandon an online identity with ease and start over fresh, free to become whoever we want again. Despite the fact that he might logically continue his superhero career with a different, less controversial name and costume, Peter continues being Spider-Man as a matter of personal responsibility. To abandon the name Spider-Man would mean hiding from his past choices as Spider-Man, something Peter will not do.

That's not to say that he doesn't change who he is over time, or that Spider-Man, the superhero, is static in how he approaches things. Over the years, Peter often explores who he is at any given moment by changing his approach to Spider-Man in much the same way that we engage in self-exploration by adjusting our own online identities.[32] In the black symbiote costume, Spider-Man acts with less forgiveness, tapping into his id and his rage. In the Spider Armor MK II, his bullet-proof body reflects his recommitment to putting himself in the way of any amount of harm to ensure that "Whenever I'm around, wherever I am, no one dies!"[33] Upon joining the Fantastic Four, Spider-Man dons a matching white "Future Foundation" costume, illustrating his new-found willingness to be a real part of a team, a family, of superheroes.[34] This willingness lays the foundation for him to continue opening up to others, and, eventually, finding deeper connections within the ever-growing web of his fellow spider-heroes.

Spiders and Selves Across the Multiverse

Many other spider-heroes swing alongside Spidey over the years, but not many are as active in exploring their own identities as Spider-Gwen and Silk.

Spider-Gwen's background may seem hard to relate to, at first. This version of Gwen Stacy, who debuts as her world's Spider-Woman, hails from an alternate Earth and uses a device to travel the multiverse in order to help other spider-heroes and right other wrongs. In the process, Spider-Gwen discovers that nearly every other universe's Gwen Stacy is dead. Why, she wonders, does she live while other Gwen Stacys do not? Such a question might be best examined through *existential psychology*, a branch of psychology concerned with existence, death, freedom, and meaning.[35] We all must contend with our own mortality. Few of us are presented with as literal reminders of our mortality as Spider-Gwen traveling to parallel worlds where she wasn't bitten by a radioactive spider. Where she doesn't live. She feels frequent *survivor's guilt*, guilt over having lived when others do not, for both her own friends and family and for the other Gwens who died while she lived.

Terror management theory suggests that self-esteem acts as a guard against the terror of our own impending, inevitable deaths.[36] Rather than allowing such stark confrontations with death to cause a lapse in her self-esteem or identity, Spider-Gwen instead grows from it. Seeing the ways in which her life could have gone wrong, or may still go wrong, emboldens her to act quickly, freely, and heroically. "I couldn't save Peter Parker in (my world)," she tells our Peter Parker of Earth-616. "What say we watch over each other?"[37] She's no longer Spider-Woman or Spider-Gwen, instead adopting the new superhero identity of Ghost-Spider to embrace the idea that "Death loves Gwen Stacy."[38] She finds meaning through an examination of her own death and it grants her a renewed sense of self and purpose.

While Spider-Gwen's exploration of her identity comes about as a reaction to her superhero adventures, Cindy "Silk" Moon takes a more active approach to figuring out who she is. After spending a decade locked away in hiding, Cindy feels she's missed out on crucial identity development and spends time in therapy to figure out, among other things, who she is. Spiders, like most animals, do not show a sense of self. Animals with a sense of self can lose it in isolation.[39] Social animals define themselves largely through social qualities. How can you know if you're funny if you're never around anyone else to make them laugh? How do you know if you're extraverted if you're always alone? Cindy has no answers to these questions about herself because she's spent little time around others. She doesn't know what she wants to do with her life or what her hobbies are, and has little knowledge of her family history or Korean heritage.[40] These are things she's working to discover in the way real-world people often do—through concerted effort. She busies herself with work as both Cindy and Silk, tries out numerous hobbies, spends time with her brother, and expands her understanding of Korean language, culture, and history, all in her quest to better understand herself. Ultimately, the thing that provides her the best sense of self is being Silk.

Parallel Selves

For Cindy, Gwen, Peter, and other spider-heroes, their adoption of self-created, alternate identities helps them better understand themselves. In *psychosocial development theory*, adolescents undergo a conflict of *identity versus identity confusion* wherein they struggle to figure out who they are and who they want to be. They're trying to figure out who their real self is and who their ideal self is. In much the same way that most people today begin exploring alternate selves online as teenagers, Spider-Man, Spider-Gwen, and more spider-heroes adopt their own alternate identities while teenagers (or, in the case of Cindy Moon, working through adolescent crises extended by arrested development). What we can learn from their examples is that self-understanding is an ongoing journey rather than a precise endpoint. The process of human development continues ever onward throughout life, and, while these characters by and large don't age, they do grow and change over time. We each exist in a multiverse of our own thoughts, full of the *we* who could be, could have been, and could still become. Peter and his fellow spider-heroes bridge the multiversal gap between the real and ideal self to achieve their best possible selves. The rest of us may not wear masks like the spider-heroes, but we all live multiple lives. In order to live them to the fullest and with the greatest understanding of who we are, we should follow in the footsteps of Peter, Gwen, Cindy, and so many others, and embrace the truth and challenges of becoming the best version of us that we can be.

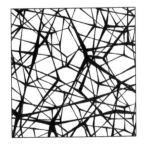

Posttraumatic Growth and Why We Keep Talking About Uncle Ben

People who experience posttraumatic growth may or may not first suffer posttraumatic stress disorder (PTSD),[1] possibly complex PTSD.[2] Even if they do not go through the full disorder, they are likely to experience some posttraumatic stress symptoms.[3] For those individuals, stressors become motivators. They seize their distress and direct into other activities as they find new or renewed purpose in life. For that reason, PTSD symptoms evident among more of those showing posttraumatic growth include *rumination*, dwelling on the traumatic events more than most trauma victims do. People such as Candace Lightner, who founded what was originally called Mothers Against Drunk Drivers after an intoxicated driver killed her daughter,[4] and John Walsh, who hosted *America's Most Wanted* and has advocated for missing children ever since his son's brutal murder,[5] relive the event more than most might. They turned their grief into action. To those whose traumatic experiences drive them to pursue heroic paths, "getting over it" feels like it would be too selfish.

Why do comic book stories keep mentioning Uncle Ben? Why do all three of Sam Raimi's Spider-Man movies include appearances by Uncle Ben even though he dies in the first one? Why do we keep talking about him throughout this book? Because Peter Parker keeps thinking about him. Because Ben's murder prompts Peter to become a hero, and whenever he wants to stop being Spider-Man, he remembers his uncle and puts that mask back on. Remembering Ben does more than remind him of guilt, though. It reminds him of Ben's principles, Spider-Man's purpose, and the good he can do for others.

AUNT MAY: Your Uncle Ben believed he hadn't made much of a difference in this world. If he'd known the hero you'd become because of his death, he'd have been happy he was killed.

PETER: What?

AUNT MAY: He'd have given his life freely without regret knowing New York gained someone like Spider-Man to protect it. So would I.

PETER: But—?

AUNT MAY: This city needs you. Not just another crime-fighter in tights. It needs your heart, your story.[6]

Spider-Man's posttraumatic growth[7] reaches far and wide, beyond himself and his progress. Everyone he helps gets the chance to grow after their own traumas. Anyone who sees him might grow from his example. Uncle Ben lives on through every person his and May's nephew saves or inspires, whether any of them know it or not.

—T.L.

8

Spidey's Sticky Love Life: Relationships

Alex Langley

> "True love—ha! It doesn't stand a chance against reality!"
> —**Mary Jane Watson**[1]

> "Love all, trust a few, do wrong to none."
> —**playwright William Shakespeare**[2]

 Spider-Man answers a phone call from Carlie Cooper while he's chasing down the garbage truck full of his things his landlord has thrown away because Peter's too busy being Spider-Man to earn enough money to pay for the terrible apartment he lives in . . . and he gets interrupted again by the jewelry thieves burning rubber across downtown, so he misses hearing Carlie say she's leaving for a while to "think things over."[3] It's a typical day for everyone's favorite wall-crawler. With a life so over-stuffed with obligations, it's no wonder Peter (and most of his spider-pals) can't seem to maintain relationships, friendly or otherwise.

Most mammals and many other animals are social creatures,[4] with *Homo sapiens* ranking among the most social of them all. Spiders, however, rarely work together, and show little to no social structure.[5] Spider-Man, as both spider and man, desires to establish meaningful connections to others (a *need for affiliation*)[6] while consciously and unconsciously distancing himself from them, paradoxical as that might seem. He wants friends, yearns for romance, wishes he could be nestled into a tight social group, and yet so often chooses to keep others at arm's length—even other superheroes. Spider-Man cameos on the occasional team to handle a *superordinate goal* (problems that require teamwork and cooperation in order to be solved), but even when he's an Avenger, he rarely hangs around long enough to get his photo in the superhero yearbook with them. If he did hang around, he might find that surviving numerous epic crises can help secure his bond with his fellow heroes in the way that real-life first responders and survivors of crises such as natural disasters find themselves similarly bonded.[7]

Given the benefits to social connections (cognitive stimulation, renewed vigor, emotional/informational/social support, to name a few),[8] Spider-Man would do well to allow his social web to spread: to make friends, to connect intimately with others, or to fall in love. But, despite the numerous physical and mental benefits to long-term love,[9] it's something Spidey struggles with. He's a hero who wants what he won't allow himself to have, never realizing that, perhaps by allowing himself to have it, he'll be a better hero (and happier person) in the long run.

A Lot of Swings, Mostly Misses
ROMANCE AND THE SPIDER

One look at Peter Parker's clothes or apartment makes it clear: He's not a rich man.* He also constantly breaks promises, misses appointments, and neglects, well, everything. His manner can be kind and funny but can also be cold, withdrawn, and downright irritable.[10] Outside of his gymnast-like body with chiseled abs and buns of steel, what is it about Peter Parker that makes him attractive to women?

Betty Brant and the Preoccupied-Anxious Relationship
For his first girlfriend, Betty Brant, the answer may lie with her confidence. Her attraction to him begins, perhaps, in part due to seeing him

---

* Save, of course, for the time he briefly becomes a billionaire (*The Superior Spider-Man* #20, 2013).

so consistently as part of their jobs at the *Daily Bugle*—sometimes, just being around the same person or same thing often enough will make us like them because they're familiar (a phenomenon known as the *mere exposure effect*).[11] Once Peter and Betty get past the initial attraction stage, they struggle to achieve intimacy. Betty lacks the self-possession of Peter's later lady friends and frequently stews in jealousy. She's plagued by worries that Peter will leave her for another woman or a more interesting social scene. These fears get exacerbated by Peter's general flightiness and flakiness (not to mention the occasional badly timed visit from his high school friend Liz Allen).[12]

Betty's feelings about Peter exhibit the hallmarks of a *preoccupied-anxious* relationship. According to an adapted *child-parent attachment theory*,[13] which matches early-life family bonds with later types of adult romantic relationships, preoccupied-anxious relationships are characterized by a high desire for interpersonal connection but with low self-esteem. Though Betty craves a stronger connection with Peter, her poor self-worth causes her to feel negatively about herself and internalize his unpredictable behavior. When he misses dates, she thinks he's not attracted to her anymore. When he's exhausted or moody, she thinks she is to blame. She desires frequent reassurance about their relationship status and, simultaneously, readily pushes Peter away so that she is the dumper rather than dumpee. During a moment of personal growth, Betty eventually realizes that Peter's flaky, risk-taking behavior is not healthy for her and moves on to Ned Leeds, a fellow *Daily Bugle* employee who's more stable at the time (long before Hobgoblin's brainwashing destabilizes Leeds).[14]

Gwen Stacy and Attraction by Deprivation

With Gwen Stacy, the reason behind her initial interest in Peter Parker varies wildly depending on the story. In her first comic book appearances, she's equal parts mystified, annoyed, and obsessed over Peter's complete lack of interest in her or anyone else on campus,[15] not knowing the underlying causes of his withdrawn behavior such as his elderly aunt's hospitalizations and his general Spider-Man-related worries. Gwen is an established woman at Empire State University, with good grades, incredible scientific acumen, and the romantic interest of half the student body (and, unfortunately, at least one of the professors). Why, then, would she care if one guy isn't interested? She even asks herself that. Outside of the obvious reason (because she was written that way), the in-story answer could lie in the phenomenon of *attraction of deprivation*, an attraction to individuals whose emotional unavailability is both frequent and apparent.[16]

As time progresses and Gwen gets to know Peter, her attraction deepens—even when he frequently and, from her perspective, randomly, turns cold and irritable. Attractions of deprivation operate on a *variable reinforcement schedule*, meaning they provide meaningful rewards after random amounts of effort or time have been expended. Peter Parker is the relationship equivalent of a slot machine to Gwen: She loses so much more than she wins, but the wins are enticing enough to keep her going. This leads to what is initially a *dismissive-avoidant relationship*, characterized by low interpersonal trust and commitment but high self-esteem. Gwen and Peter keep a distance between them, due to his responsibilities as Spider-Man and her (correct) analysis of Peter's unreliability. Eventually, they do reach a place of greater interpersonal trust and commitment, but if there's something a relationship between two people has trouble surviving, it's having Green Goblin throw one of them off a bridge.

Most modern depictions of Gwen Stacy alter her dynamic with Peter, moving away from the attraction of deprivation/dismissive-avoidant model and instead bonding the two over personal similarities.[17] "Birds of a feather flock together" may be an age-old adage, but it's also supported by mountains of relationship research—people are more likely to enter into romantic relationships with people similar to them and more likely to stay with them.[18] Peter and Gwen are both born-and-raised New Yorkers as well as brilliant students with a love of science and strong moral cores instilled into them by their parental figures. Keeping in mind the *similarity-dissimilarity effect*—general tendency to like when people are similar to us and not actively like when people are dissimilar to us—these commonalities between Gwen and Peter indicate their high compatibility. Had Gwen not been murdered, they likely would have stayed together for the long run—a hypothesis supported by the alternate timeline when Peter gives up being Spider-Man and he and Gwen are married.[19]

Felicia Hardy and the Forbidden Feline

For Felicia Hardy, the Black Cat, her attraction to Spider-Man (and his to her) happens, in part, because of the allure of the taboo. She finds his morality intriguing and enjoys the playful push and pull between them as she tries to pull him into legally and morally dubious activities and he tries to pull her back toward honesty and altruism. Human beings are frequently drawn to secret relationships and infidelity, and oftentimes the harder a person tries to resist their thoughts and feelings, the more often they will have them (a phenomenon known as *ironic rebound*).[20] While Black Cat and Spider-Man's relationship isn't "infidelity" of the typical sense, it is a moral infidelity for Cat and Spider alike. As a costumed thief, her liaisons with Spider-Man will harm her reputation and distract her from her goals. As a costumed superhero who is frequently the subject of front-page news questioning his criminal intent, hanging out with a known thief is, to put it in highly scientific terms, a bad idea.

Being with someone from the other side of the tracks isn't without its non-romantic advantages. For Black Cat, having Spider-Man on her side means she can sneak her way in more easily with him as a lookout, and fight her way out more easily with someone brawling alongside her. Spidey, too, gains the benefit of continued knowledge of NYC's ever-moving criminal underworld. It's an *exchange relationship*, one wherein each member gains benefit from the presence of the other.[21] There are moments when they almost deepen their bond into a *communal relationship*, a relationship where benefits given and received are no longer a factor, but those moments never quite lock into place fully.[22]

With real illicit couplings, eventually the benefits and secret heat are going to run out, or someone is going to desire more than clandestine hook-ups.[23] In this case, it's Spidey. Felicia values her independence too much to allow herself to become deeply attached. Much like the early days of Peter's relationship with Gwen Stacy, Felicia's focus on autonomy and refusal for true intimacy of commitment are indicative of a dismissive-avoidant relationship. In Felicia's case, however, *she* is the flighty and unreliable one. Her unpredictable (to Spidey) behavior leaves him frequently vulnerable and second-guessing himself, and she's often willing to take every advantage her unpredictability grants.[24]

Spider and Cat break up in *The Spectacular Spider-Man* #100 (1985). Art by Al Milgrom, Geof Isherwood, & Vince Colletta.

Even when Felicia truly tries to make their relationship work, her need for autonomy is such that, when Spider-Man finally decides to open up, she's horrified. "S-Spider," she says, still refusing to call him Peter, "y-your mask . . . please. Put your mask back on!"[25] The revelation that he's a poor kid from Queens, living in a shabby apartment, shatters the image she has built up of him as a well-to-do thrill seeker. His removal of his mask and expression of vulnerability is too much for her. Given the tendency for romantic partners to change beliefs and behavior over time to match each other,[26] it's plausible that Felicia, who values financial independence, sees her future changing to match his lifestyle. Rather than surrender her identity for the sake of his, she willingly ends the relationship, storming off the instant he suggests they break up.[27]

Despite periodic hookups, alliances, and skirmishes over the years, the deeper romance between Cat and Spider ends here.

Cindy Moon and Evolutionary Explosions

Cindy Moon, otherwise known as the superhero Silk, feels drawn to Peter for a very "comic book" reason: Because both of their spider-powers come from getting bitten by the same radioactive spider, their bodies emit powerful, synchronous pheromones that cause a magnetic physical attraction between them.[28] For people whose blood isn't radioactively enhanced, pheromones do play a real, albeit significantly smaller, part in attraction.[29] For those who are, however, the results are hard to resist—Peter and Cindy can barely keep their hands off each other.

From an evolutionary psych perspective, many of the reasons behind human romantic behavior stem from a desire to create genetically fit offspring. We're attracted to bilaterally symmetrical faces because they hint at overall health. We tend to desire partners who are youthful, powerful, and resourceful to ensure the survival of ourselves, our offspring, and our partnered caregiver.[30] In the case of Peter and Cindy, the matching pheromones generated by their superpowered bodies plausibly serve the purpose of enticing them to have lots and lots of superpowered babies.

Given that Cindy spends the better portion of her life in a secret bunker hiding away from the spider-hungry vampiric being Morlun, she is uninterested in locking herself into a relationship with Peter Parker and suggests he moves out of New York, possibly to the moon, so that they might better resist their pheromonal attraction.[31] This behavior is in stark contrast to the general tendency for people from isolated, low-population communities to enter committed relationships more quickly than their metropolis-dwelling counterparts.[32] However, given her proclivity toward social anxiety, it may be that she fears entering a deeper relationship with Peter because she feels wary of intimacy. Or perhaps, like many from isolated communities, she fears the social judgment and "gossip" of others over any deeper relationship they might have and so refuses to engage with the idea altogether.[33]

Mary Jane Watson and the Thrill

Mary Jane Watson knows from the beginning (or almost from the beginning) that Peter Parker is Spider-Man.[34] A free-spirited and adventurous young woman, she finds Pete's wild life interesting. As Mary Jane's life is frequently imperiled by virtue of knowing Peter Parker/Spider-Man, she likely experiences an *excitation transfer/transfer of arousal*.[35] Danger causes increased heart rate, blood flow, pupil dilation, and other elements of physical arousal, which then are subconsciously attributed to the person we're with.

Peter and MJ's relationship isn't entirely predicated on thrills, chills, and getting held hostage by supervillains, however. Once the two of them have an honest conversation about Peter's life as Spider-Man, they enter a new, stronger stage of their relationship, one that balances the three elements of the *triarchic theory of attraction*: passion, commitment, and intimacy.[36]

Passionate love refers to physical, lustful attraction, which Peter and MJ have in no short supply: He's a swingin' superhero and she's a swingin' supermodel. *Commitment* refers to a willingness to bond oneself to someone else. When sticky-fingered Spidey isn't in a period of self-inflicted isolation, he has no qualms with committing to a romantic prospect. Mary Jane, at first, prefers to keep her social calendar open, but once she commits to Peter, she commits *hard*. *Intimate love* refers to a willingness to be vulnerable, to express hopes, dreams, fears, and secrets, and it is the type of love with which Peter has the most difficulty.

Women of the Web and the Secure Relationship

Peter and Betty Brant break up because his frequent escapades as Spider-Man draw him away so often that she falls in love with Ned Leeds.[37] He frequently considers explaining his secret identity to her, but ultimately does not. Gwen Stacy dies *because* he's Spider-Man, and he never tells her the truth about himself during their relationship.[38] When Spider-Man finally reveals the Peter Parker beneath the mask to Black Cat, she breaks up with him.[39] When forensic scientist Carlie Cooper figures out Peter Parker is Spider-Man, she also breaks up with him.[40] Mary Jane, however, knows his secret from the beginning.[41] When she reveals this to Peter, she then tells him her own secret history—*reciprocal intimacy* at last. It's an exchange of intimate details more common in the early stages of a relationship but complicated when one person's secrets are greater than the others. Only with Mary Jane does this sort of revelation strengthen the relationship and lead to a renewed connection between Peter and his partner.

Even though it may frustrate her at times, Mary Jane both understands and accepts his life as a superhero. In fact, if the chance or need arises, MJ often embraces the excitement of taking part in superheroics of her own, helping bring peace back to New York with temporary spider-powers[42] or rescuing Peter and other superheroes from captivity by using an iron spider suit.[43] Her relationship with Peter usually embodies *secure attachment*, the healthiest type of adult attachment style, in which there is a high degree of interpersonal trust, individual self-esteem, intimacy, and companionship. Communication, intimacy, and commitment are all strong indicators of the viability of a long-term relationship,[44] and are but a few of the reasons why Peter and Mary Jane's relationship has been so strong that it takes a literal deal with the devil to put a (temporary) stop to it.[45]

Tying Us All Together

Teenagers, twentysomethings, and thirtysomethings are among the loneliest people on Earth.[46] Most iterations of Spidey place him somewhere in his teens or twenties, so rarely does he get to experience the social and emotional benefits of getting older. In the few instances in which we see older Peter Parkers, they tend to either have continued isolating themselves to the point of self-destructiveness,[47] or have achieved a peace with their life and renewed social connections.[48] The more socially connected Peter is to the people in his life, the happier he is and the more effective he is as a superhero. If he were able to tell Carlie Cooper he needs to call her back because he's web-slinging, he'd be able to focus more on catching criminals and not whether she has figured out he's Spider-Man. If he could lean on a domestic partner for stability, he wouldn't be too busy fighting crime to pay his rent and end up with his belongings in the trash. If Peter could get past his fear that connecting with others will bring them more harm than good, perhaps he could finally become the most spectacular Spider-Man he can be.

9

Behind the Mask:
The Web of Loneliness

Janina Scarlet and Jenna Busch

> "I'm lonely. You aren't there for me. I can't do this. It's over."
> —Mary Jane (Kirsten Dunst) to Peter Parker (Tobey Maguire)[1]

> "Loneliness is the subjective feeling that you're lacking the social connections you need. It can feel like being stranded, abandoned, or cut off from the people with whom you belong—even if you're surrounded by other people."
> —U.S. Surgeon General Vivek Murthy[2]

 **W**e are wired to need meaningful connection. And yet, many people are deemed to be "strong" for not showing emotions and are praised for wearing metaphorical "I'm fine" masks.[3] As a result, many people feel *lonely*, sadly detached from other people.[4] After Doctor Strange's spell removes the memory of Peter Parker from the world in the film *Spider-Man: No Way Home*, Peter pretends to be fine when he sees his friends Michelle and Ned talking about getting into college without him. He's heartbroken, likely remembering having a similar discussion with them back when they knew who he was. Peter's metaphorical mask says he's fine, but inside, he must feel lonely without them and hurt from seeing them move on without him. While this is by no means the only time loneliness has posed a problem for Peter Parker in movies, comics, or other media, it may be the most severe: He ends the film utterly alone.[5]

During the COVID-19 global pandemic, the United States surgeon general Vivek Murthy labeled loneliness "an invisible epidemic" and a "public health crisis."[6] In the United States and the United Kingdom, an estimated 20 percent of patients seeking emergency services reported experiencing loneliness.[7] Reaching out in these situations can help. In the comics, Daredevil does this by reaching out to Spider-Man, as his friend and fellow crime-fighter, after the murder of ex-girlfriend Karen Page and the apparent suicide of their mutual enemy, Mysterio. Spider-Man comforts him. The two are then able to bond and feel less lonely in discussing how grief causes them emotional pain and sleep struggles.[8]

Spiking loneliness rates are especially alarming because of the impact that loneliness has on mental health. People who experience loneliness are at a higher risk for anxiety, depression, sleep disorders, and PTSD.[9] Spider-Man struggles with grief and anxiety, keeping his identity a secret, and dealing with the death of loved ones, making him feel terribly lonely.

In addition, people who experience chronic loneliness are more likely to experience inflammation, making them more likely to experience chronic pain and spikes in autoimmune disorders, compared to people who do not feel lonely. In fact, people who feel lonely are significantly more likely to develop cancer, suffer Alzheimer's disease, or otherwise die prematurely compared to people with meaningful social support.[10]

Finally, people who feel lonely are more likely to consider or attempt suicide or engage in risky behaviors compared to people with meaningful social connections.[11] We see the latter when Miles Morales is having issues trying to fit in at his school while also trying to please his demanding father. He seeks out his uncle Aaron, with whom he engages in risky behaviors to paint graffiti in the subway (incidentally leading him to get bitten by the genetically modified spider).[12]

Interconnectedness, a sense of connection and belonging, appears to be essential to our survival and well-being.[13] Interconnectedness can occur when people feel seen, heard, and valued, while loneliness can occur when people feel invisible, unheard, and unvalued. For instance, Miles Morales's difficulties in making friends with the kids at his new school are compounded by his father's work as a police officer who has a hatred and distrust of his alter ego, Spider-Man.[14]

Unseen

The *unseen* subtype of loneliness refers to feeling ignored, isolated, or "ghosted." It also applies to feeling lonely in a friendship or a relationship, as if invisible to the other person.[15] Harry Osborn feels invisible to his father, Norman Osborn, who focuses so much attention on his business and sometimes Spider-Man that he misses the distress this causes his son.[16]

Feeling unseen in this way can activate our nervous system response, the *fight-flight-freeze-fawn* response. Of these, the *fight response* occurs when we feel enraged and demand for the other person to engage with us, possibly to the point of growing combative. The *flight response* occurs when we try to leave the situation. The *freeze response* occurs when we feel too overwhelmed to respond, so we physically do nothing and mentally withdraw. Finally, the *fawn response* occurs when we attempt to use over-the-top people-pleasing as a strategy to get our needs met or to avoid negative consequences.[17] When Peter Parker applies for a teaching job, he ends up in the middle of a school shooting. What he finds out is that the shooter was having a fight response to feeling bullied and unseen.[18]

Feeling excluded activates the same neurological pain receptors as experiencing physical pain, though receiving emotional support can temporarily reduce emotional and physical pain experiences.[19] Furthermore, being emotionally neglected and touch-starved can lead to increased stress, anxiety, and depression, and can negatively impact heart rate, blood pressure, digestive system, and immune system.[20] When Peter and Miles get to know each other in different stories, when three Peter Parkers meet on the big screen, when multiple spider-heroes cross paths while hopping the multiverse, or when Peter meets Cindy Moon (Silk) without crossing universes at all, they are able to discuss the struggles they've all had and to see one another's pain.[21] Because they're able to bond in this way, they each appear to experience a reduction in anxiety and emotional pain.

Humans aren't the only ones who struggle when they experience loneliness. When non-human animals, such as primates, cats, or rats, are caged by themselves and ignored, they begin to self-harm, and in severe enough cases die due to a loss of will to live. In fact, a study from the late 1950s shows that when monkeys are raised in social isolation, they will cling onto anything which resembles the warmth and closeness of a mother, such as a dirty cloth diaper or a stuffed cloth-covered monkey. Given the choice between spending time with a fake wire-mesh monkey that fed them and a soft-cloth fake monkey that did not, the baby monkeys spent the majority of their time (approximately 85 percent) cuddling with the cloth monkey.[22]

Thankfully, the toxic effects of this type of loneliness can often be reversed through meaningful socialization and emotional support.[23] For instance, when Matt Murdock shares his secret identity with his friend Spider-Man, Spider-Man is then able to help open up and console Matt over the loss of a loved one.[24]

Unheard

Whereas the experience of being unseen refers to being ignored, ghosted, or excluded, the feeling of being *unheard* occurs in situations in which we feel invalidated, gaslit, or prejudiced against. While feeling unseen can lead to sadness or depression, feeling unheard often leads to frustration and anger.[25] In one instance, the assassin Elektra breaks up a conversation between Spider-Man and Wolverine. Spider-Man pivots from his discussion and tries everything he can to make Elektra feel comfortable and engage with her. She ignores and disregards him. After several interactions, Spider-Man physically shrinks his posture down in sadness.[26]

In fact, relationships in which one partner frequently invalidates or gaslights the other tend to be more toxic to people's physical and mental health than getting a divorce.[27] Furthermore, experiencing frequent prejudice and microaggressions can also negatively impact our physical or mental health. Feeling unheard in this way raises the likelihood of depression or panic attacks, along with physical issues such as migraines, other chronic pain, high blood pressure, or diabetes.[28] We often see Peter Parker struggle with J. Jonah Jameson for belittling the good work he has done as Spider-Man, especially when one version of Jameson announces Spider-Man's identity and exposes his friends, family, and Peter himself to harm.[29]

Ruptures happen in every relationship, including friendships. However, all parties need to be willing to be open to practice compassionate listening and vulnerable communication skills to repair the rupture.[30] Unfortunately, many people find themselves in situations where they are consistently unheard and, as a result, they might feel unsafe opening up and advocating for themselves.[31] Perhaps Harry Osborn's descent into drugs, darkness, and villainy in comics and movies could have been prevented if Peter had trusted his friend enough to reveal his secret identity as Spider-Man and explain what really happened to his father Norman, the original Green Goblin.[32]

Others, tired of being marginalized or unheard, practice "masking" behaviors to try to fit in. *Masking behaviors* refers to hiding aspects of oneself and/or mimicking aspects of others to try to belong. Masking behaviors are often seen in neurodivergent individuals, such as autistic individuals and people with ADHD. In most cases, masking behaviors lead to exhaustion, frustration, and in some cases, suicidal ideation.[33]

Peter constantly engages in masking behaviors to hide his true self. When Flash Thompson challenges him to a boxing match, Peter hides his extraordinary agility and strength in order to keep Flash from serious harm and to avoid outing himself as Spider-Man.[34] When Betty Brant notices Peter's injuries from Spider-Man's activities, he brushes off the severity of his pain with a joke and a lie, isolating himself without recognizing the strength he gains from his social connections.[35] When Peter gives up his superhero identity because he's trying to fit in and be like everyone else, he ends up not only losing his powers but also enabling the Kingpin to rise to the top of New York's criminal underworld.[36]

Undervalued

Feeling *undervalued*, another subtype of loneliness, refers to feeling like an outsider, like "the other." Many people who feel undervalued experience bullying or overt exclusion for being different and may also become highly self-critical.[37] Once he's outed as Spider-Man, Peter feels singled out by the numerous people who insult him, distrust him, and throw paint on him. He, Michelle, and Ned even get excluded from college, relegated to "outsider" status over their association with Spider-Man—for which Peter blames himself.[38]

Beliefs such as "I don't belong," "I don't matter," and "No one really understands me" are common among those who have been treated this way. Trauma survivors assume that these trauma narratives represent the truth. As a result, they might not tell others how they feel, preventing them from realizing that at least ten percent of people also experience pervasive loneliness.[39]

"In Our Own Way, We Are All Spider-Man"[40]

Cultivating meaningful connections with others begins with cultivating meaningful connections with ourselves. Noticing our thoughts, wants, and feelings, and treating ourselves with compassion can help us to feel seen and less lonely.[41] Even after the world has forgotten who Peter Parker is, just looking at a toy that reminds him of his best friend Ned allows Peter to move forward with his new life in a positive way. Ned might not remember it, but Peter knows just how much their connection allowed him to be true to himself.[42]

In addition, learning to listen to our own needs can allow us to set better boundaries with others and practice self-advocacy skills. Practicing *self-advocacy skills* (abilities to communicate one's needs)[43] can allow us to feel heard, respected, and less resentful, making our needs more likely to be met.[44] Individuals can practice self-advocacy through vulnerable communication and compassionate listening practices. *Compassionate communication* includes listening to the other person without interrupting, trying to understand things from their perspective, and validating their needs.[45] When he takes the time to talk to a grieving Daredevil, Peter creates a sense of connection between them, simply by listening to his friend and letting him talk in the way he needs to.[46]

This is a kind of *vulnerable communication*, communication that includes the expression of one's feelings and making specific requests. A balance of compassionate listening and vulnerable communication skills can allow for all parties involved to feel seen, heard, and valued.[47]

The last component of developing a sense of connection is honoring our core values. Core values refer to our sense of purpose, our moral compass. Helping other people, being a good friend, and helping the environment are all examples of core values.[48] Peter taking the position as science teacher at his old high school after it has fallen into disrepair shows us how his core values are leading him back to help nurture kids in need of guidance.[49]

Part of being a good friend is reaching out. Just as we might be happy to know others are thinking of us, others are also excited to know we're thinking of them. In fact, researchers found that most people tend to underestimate how much their gesture of reaching out "just because" means to others.[50] Spider-Man reaches out to a kid named Tim, who worships him. He shows up in person and reveals his identity to Tim, even telling him the story of how his Uncle Ben died. He makes a connection with him because Tim needs him. Tim is dying of leukemia, and this connection has been what he wanted most in life.[51]

Spiders, Assemble!

As human beings, we are wired for belonging.[52] This is exactly why loneliness causes so many physical and psychological struggles.[53] Spider-Man shows us over and over again that reaching out to friends and having them reach back can change your life. When people feel seen, heard, and valued, that's when they can truly thrive. If people can see and accept one another, then there's no need for metaphorical masks.[54] And when people can see and support one another, then we can keep loneliness at bay. Spider-Man shows us that anyone can be a friendly neighborhood hero for someone else by just being there for them.

 **Janina Scarlet, PhD,** is a Licensed Clinical Psychologist, author, and a full-time geek. The United Nations Association awarded Scarlet the Eleanor Roosevelt Human Rights Award for her work on superhero therapy. She regularly consults on books and television shows including *Young Justice*. Scarlet authored *Superhero Therapy*, *Super-Women*, *Dark Agents*, and *Harry Potter Therapy*, plus chapters throughout this Popular Culture Psychology series. She can be reached via her website at **www.superhero -therapy.com** or on Twitter: **@shadowquill**.

 **Jenna Busch** is a host and writer, covering entertainment. She writes for /Film and Vital Thrills, and Story Attic, a division of The Third Floor. She co-hosted *Cocktails with Stan* with Spider-Man co-creator Stan Lee and hosted *Most Craved*. Busch has appeared in the documentary *She Makes Comics* and as a guest on various news programs and *Tabletop with Wil Wheaton*. Busch co-authored chapters in most books in this Popular Culture Psychology series, beginning with *Star Wars Psychology: Dark Side of the Mind*. Her Twitter handle is **@JennaBusch**.

10

The Grief Goblin: Archnemesis or Greatest Ally?

Benjamin Stover

> "He died because you were too selfish and lazy to prevent it. It was your fault, Pete, and as soon as you accept it, that's when you'll be free of it."
>
> —Peter Parker[1]

> "For the person who seeks to avoid his grief, time is distinctly malignant; it only increases the pressure and strengthens the resistance to healthy mourning."
>
> —psychologist and grief specialist Therese A. Rando[2]

 Spider-Man has been a story about grief and loss ever since the character's first appearance.[3] Numerous comic book stories, motion pictures, and even video games all prominently feature plotlines centered on processing grief and loss.[4] The complicated dynamic of suffering a sudden life-altering loss while simultaneously going through *apotheotic* (divinely strengthening) growth makes a powerful metaphor for the constant cycle of wins and losses, triumphs and sorrows, births and deaths that every living person must endure. Nearly every version of Spider-Man endures deaths, breakups, divorces, loss of identity, loss of safety, friendships ending, firings, and the recurrent problem of friends and mentors losing their sanity from gaining powers and becoming supervillains.

Grief, "the process of psychological, social, and somatic reactions to the perception of loss,"[5] can arise after (or even in anticipation of)

any loss, not just the loss of a loved one. While it is commonly understood that people need to grieve the death of a loved one through a mourning process, many people do not allow themselves to grieve more commonplace losses such as relationships, jobs, or friendships. Grief allows people to *process* the information needed to adjust to a loss—to digest and interpret sensory information from our experiences and to convert it into usable data for future survival.[6] Often, processing grief gets complicated or even blocked by dissociation, guilt, and shame that prevent the brain from moving information from *active memory*, where it is still stored with current emotions, to *long-term memory*, where it becomes a case file stored with processed memories that no longer need emotions attached to them to provide meaning. Spider-Man has quite a few memories that are unprocessed and therefore produce recurring feelings of sadness, failure, and loss.

Spider-Man encounters repeated life-and-death situations that force him to confront the fragility of life. *Existential psychology* teaches that consciousness of our own mortality (our existence) makes life precious because of its impermanence and that our greatest fears all concern loss of life and control. Holocaust survivor and psychiatrist Viktor Frankl, a prominent figure in existential psychology, based his therapeutic modality *logotherapy* on his belief that suffering and loss are an inseparable part of the human experience and that we must be able to *make meaning* of our suffering in order to heal and grow beyond our losses.[7] No matter what normal-life event he may be enjoying, at any second, Peter Parker knows he could get a tingle from his Spidey-sense and have to fend off an attack from members of his prolific rogue's gallery, the police, or J. Jonah Jameson. Even watching the Macy's Thanksgiving Day Parade isn't safe from an attack that requires spider-help![8] The losses Peter incurs, starting with that of Uncle Ben in most versions (or his parents in versions where they disappear when he's old enough to remember them),[9] make it difficult for Peter to make meaning out of being Spider-Man. Several panels in even the early comics demonstrate Peter's difficulty accepting his powers due to the cost of constantly endangering the lives and mental well-being of those he loves most.[10]

Human beings developed methods for coping with and making meaning out of the inevitable suffering caused by death as a biological adaptation out of necessity.[11] All human beings will encounter death and loss. If we were unable to cope with the effects of those losses, we would not be able to adapt and survive. Having the ability to adapt to change does not mean it is an easy thing to do. The grieving process can take time. Getting through the grief process can help reconnect us to the reasons we must go on living and can help us draw on those reasons when we need them most. Frankl highlighted this when he noted wisdom in the philosopher Nietzsche's words: "He who has a why to live for can bear almost any how."[12] Spider-Man has had to dig deep into his psyche to find his "why" to overcome immense pain. In a scene made famous on the big screen, he digs deep to summon everything he has left when stopping a moving train while unmasked, no matter the risk to his own privacy or survival.[13]

The American Psychiatric Association's *Diagnostic and Statistical Manual of Mental Disorders* (DSM) lists several conditions that can occur due to experiencing grief and loss: uncomplicated bereavement, adjustment disorder, and the newly added prolonged grief disorder.[14] *Uncomplicated bereavement*, the expected reaction to encountering loss, lasts for thirty days or less before a return to relatively normal functioning happens. It is listed in the DSM as a *Z-Code*, a method for clinicians to document known stressors that contribute to a clinical presentation but are not disorders by themselves.

Adjustment disorder occurs when a person cannot adjust to a change in their life or the effects of the change after thirty days and develops symptoms of anxiety, depression, or disrupted conduct. Assessing for this diagnosis is difficult, however, with someone like Spider-Man who encounters so many changes, losses, and deaths. A clinician will find it challenging, to say the least, when trying to determine when a clear end to such adjustments and their impact would be "normal." The DSM added *prolonged grief disorder* after many years of research and clinical practice demonstrated a need to cover situations in which a person is experiencing a variety of serious symptoms a year or more following the loss for adults, or six months or more for children and adolescents.[15]

The original 1960s comic books show Peter returning to daily activities and adjusting to the loss of Uncle Ben quickly, albeit with flashes of guilt and shame that appear in Peter's internal monologue periodically. Even though guilt over the loss of Uncle Ben is ever present on his mind, it is likely that the original version of Peter would clinically qualify for the Z-code of uncomplicated bereavement due to the infrequency with which his symptoms of grief prevent him from completing his activities of daily living. To qualify as a mental disorder, the symptoms must significantly impair functioning in one or more areas of life.[16]

The Spider-Man films that Sam Raimi directed in the early 2000s largely mirror the original comics, but the films focus more on exploring the motif of Peter grappling with his guilt and his worry that being Spider-Man endangers his loved ones.[17] As Peter realizes the inseparability of the worlds of Spider-Man and Peter Parker, he experiences increasingly emergent mood and behavior disruptions that would likely result in a diagnosis of adjustment disorder. These films make a pointed effort to show Peter becoming increasingly moody and anxious in the first two installments before some conduct issues emerge due to the aggression amplifying influence of the symbiote suit in *Spider-Man 3*.[18]

The Amazing Spider-Man films,[19] however, show a more tortured version of Peter fixated on his parents' disappearance: moody, isolative, and having difficulty integrating into society even many years after their loss. His symptoms only get worse following the deaths of Uncle Ben, Captain Stacy, and later Gwen herself. The compounding effect that feeling responsible for multiple losses has on processing means that Andrew Garfield's version of Peter would likely qualify for prolonged grief disorder.

The Grieving Process

Regardless of controversies over it,[20] the most famous model on grief, death, and dying is the one developed by psychiatrist Elisabeth Kübler-Ross, the so-called *five stages of grief* (originally stages of dying because she studied terminally ill individuals): denial, anger, bargaining, depression, and acceptance.[21] Even though people often list the stages in a numerical order, grief does not follow a linear or sequential process, and people do not move through the stages in the same order, if at all. Not all need to resolve one phase to move into the next, and likewise moving into a different phase does not mean the previous phase is over forever. The enduring misunderstanding that the process is sequential can distress people. We all grieve in our own ways and in our own time, and we move in and out of stages depending on a number of factors. Spider-Man stories exhibit all these phases at one time or another.

Based on their body language, tone of voice, and facial expressions (collectively known as *affect*), each version of Peter in *Spider-Man: No Way Home* fits a different stage of grief. Tom Holland's Peter-1 and Aunt May both demonstrate *denial*, a state in which people reject the reality of the inevitable death, in the aftermath of the Green Goblin's attack on them. Both Peter and May repeat the phrase, "Just need to catch my breath," due to their emotional need to disconnect and deny the reality that she has been mortally wounded. After she utters her last words (from possibly the most famous text in comic book history)[22] and succumbs to her wounds, Peter is initially unable to accept that she has taken her last breath. He pleads, "Look at me," to her lifeless body. Soon, as he struggles to make sense of a world that has betrayed him and taken much from him despite how much he has given, his *anger* emerges, conflicted and deep. His "It's not my problem, I don't care anymore" speech prompts the other versions of Peter to offer guidance. Andrew Garfield's Peter-3 shares how he tried to rely on *bargaining* by attempting to make a deal with the universe to take away his pain if he kept going like Gwen would have wanted. When that did not work, though, he slipped back into anger before hitting his present stage of *depression* due to turning that anger on himself. While describing how much he gave in to his anger and abandoned restraint, he physically presents disgust: His frown, upturned mouth and nose, and hostile tone all indicate he is still struggling with depression and anger.

Tobey Maguire's Peter-2 demonstrates a calm body with an understanding affect and urges the youngest, newly grieving Peter-1 to find meaning in May's sacrifice, indicating Maguire's version has likely reached a more advanced stage, perhaps *acceptance* as described in Kübler-Ross's original model or maybe something more. Based on the existential work of Viktor Frankl, the Kübler-Ross foundation and grief expert David Kessler later added *finding meaning* as a possible sixth stage.[23] Maguire plays into his role as *wise old man* in this story, gently explaining how his own early anger did not help him make things better and how it took him a long time "to get through that darkness." He urges Peter-1 to understand the importance of May's words and to use them to find meaning by gently saying, "Maybe she didn't die for nothing." Peter-1 is rapidly rotating through emotion states. His affect is distressed. His eyes appear glassy, tearful, and at times unfocused. After feeling seen and supported by others who can prove they know his pain, he manages to get his superheroic side back online and complete his mission.

Complicated Grief

Spider-Man is a character steeped in *complicated grief*, being unable to process a loss fully due to the circumstances surrounding the death and lack of resolution.[24] It is often associated with traumatic circumstances that occur in sudden, unexpected, or accidental deaths due to the amount of dissociation that survivors incur from the shock of the loss.[25] Each version of Spider-Man feels tremendous guilt and shame that their failure to act resulted in the death of a loved one. In *Into the Spider-Verse*, each version of Spider-Man from the multiverse shares their story with Miles Morales in order to help him understand that he is not alone in his suffering following the death of his uncle Aaron.[26] Guilt and shame create what some therapeutic modalities refer to as *blocking beliefs*,[27] which prevent the brain from processing information due to "the suppression of a high level of disturbance."[28] Many authors have compared blocking beliefs in mental wounds to infections in physical wounds due to the pervasive way they prevent healing.[29] Guilt creates a blocking belief by making people feel shame for their failure and believe they do not deserve to heal. This often prevents people from allowing themselves access to the full bandwidth of pain from the loss. This, in turn, also prevents their ability to shift away from the feelings stored during distress and disallows integration of a more rational perspective.

The emotional and rational aspects of the brain can process events differently, even fundamental ideas such as seeing that the world is not safe or fair, bad things happen, and, as Peter Porker says, "You can't

Aerial view of the Brooklyn Bridge, which artist Gil Kane drew as the site of Gwen Stacy's death, although the narrative originally named a different bridge in *The Amazing Spider-Man* #121 (1973).

save everyone."[30] It can be difficult to accept things that are outside of our control. For someone like Spider-Man who can do so many amazing things, it can be even harder to accept such limits.

In one comic book illustration of the power of complicated grief and blocking beliefs even years after the loss occurred, the Chameleon lures Peter to the top of the Brooklyn Bridge by creating an illusion of a kidnapped Mary Jane. He appears to hold her at gunpoint over the spot where Gwen Stacy died, before making a shocking admission and leaping off the bridge to his apparent doom. Witnessing a second death on that spot, even that of an enemy, activates a traumatic *memory network*, "a series of channels where related memories, thoughts, images, emotions, and sensations are stored and linked to one another."[31] Having that memory network activated causes Peter to immediately switch from powerless Peter back into Spider-Man mode, instinctively reacting with the same behaviors he used to try and save Gwen. He grapples with his logical understanding that he cannot save the Chameleon nor is this his fault, and yet his instinctual response is to try to save him.[32]

After he digests what has happened, he begins to re-experience similar losses tied to guilt and shame. He is immediately in pain somatically (bodily) and emotionally. Through a dream sequence, we see Peter processing each loss he still feels responsible for: the Chameleon, Captain Stacy, Kraven, Sandman, Norman and Harry Osborn, his and Mary Jane's own unborn child, Uncle Ben, and finally Gwen herself.[33] The panels brilliantly show Peter working to recontextualize each of the losses in his life and the conflict between the perspectives of his emotional mind and his rational mind. His emotional mind is seeking to self-punish as if that could provide some closure and ultimately relieve the bad feelings, and his rational mind is desperately trying to prove that he did the best he could with what he knew at the time, and it is all right to forgive himself for the impossible.

The Pathway to Meaning

No version of Spider-Man ever allows himself much time to grieve his losses properly. Rarely does more than a day or two pass before a situation with an animal-themed supervillain requires Peter Parker to put personal needs aside and assume the role of superhero. Shifting away from being Peter Parker, teenager/student/photojournalist, into Spider-Man, superhero, enables him to influence the world in ways that were not possible before. Early in his career, though, power and its possibilities make it difficult for the adolescent's developing mind to grow beyond *adolescent egocentrism*, the viewpoint in that stage of life that encourages inflating self-importance, feelings of invulnerability, and sphere of influence. Adolescents do not easily embrace the reality that life will include many losses and that many of them occur due to circumstances beyond our control. The unique combination of having powers that provide a new level of influence on the world while simultaneously still being unable to control everything can complicate grieving. It is likely why Peter Parker defines so much of his identity by losses he failed to stop.

Emotions are often so overwhelming in early grief that people who have experienced a loss may see their own emotion as an enemy. The grieving person often treats their emotions as a villain that needs to be contained deep within the recesses of the mind to protect them from doing further harm. However, this ignores their biological purpose and often prolongs pain rather than providing protection from it. Emotions are the only mechanism we possess to assign relevance to our experiences and learn from them. The grieving process is a complex emotional experience that is painful and can take a long time to complete. However, just because something is painful does not mean it is malicious. Loss is a part of living and having a way to adapt to an ever-changing reality is necessary for survival. Grieving allows us to learn from loss, enabling the brain to feel emotions intensely enough to take meaning from them and accept the unpleasant changes imposed by loss. Without grief, we would not be able to archive the rules that applied to a previous version of reality and would struggle to open our minds to learning the rules of the current version of reality. Pain from loss enables us to make meaningful changes to our lives we would not have done without it.

Without processing his losses, Spider-Man would not be as firmly grounded to his moral foundation to protect others and could have fulfilled the original plan to use his powers to become rich and famous and "let the rest of the world hang."[34] The ability to resist temptation to use his powers solely for his own benefit would be absent without his grief. Knowing the immense pain of losing a loved one to crime drives him to cast aside his desires for fame and wealth to make his life's purpose to use his powers responsibly for the good of others. Despite all the pain it has caused him, grief may be Spider-Man's most important ally as he develops from ordinary teenager to extraordinary hero.

Benjamin A. Stover MA, LCPC, is the Clinical Director at Ardent Counseling Center in Chicago, IL, and a Clinical Therapist for the Chicago Police Department. His clinical focus is trauma, grief, and mood disorders. He is creator and co-host of the podcast *Popcorn Psychology* with Brittney Brownfield and Hannah Espinoza. He has been a participant on several panels at conventions and has contributed to books, podcasts, and blogs. He previously contributed a chapter to *Stranger Things Psychology.*

Postscript

Attachment and Adverse Childhood Experiences

Brittani Oliver Sillas-Navarro

"We bereaved are not alone. We belong to the largest company in all the world—the company of those who have known suffering."
—author Helen Keller[35]

"That's what I want you to do, Aunt May. Let go. Fly. 'Second to the right—
and straight on till morning.'"
—Peter Parker[36]

Spider-Man provides an exemplary example of what it means to live a full life in a short amount of time. This character has to battle not only teenage angst, hormonal urges, and bullying but also bad guys from his and other universes. Loss of loved ones often ranks at the top of stressors that tend to distress people the most, and for younger individuals, losing parents or caretakers tends to upend their lives most severely. Grief changes who we are. For someone like Peter Parker, who experiences grief at such a young age and at such tumultuous times of personal development, the changes he experiences are all the more stark. Spider-Man gives us a glimpse of what it means to be super, even if it's before he can rent a car.

114

Coming Up ACEs

Peter Parker's childhood and adolescence are anything but perfect. In him, we find a hero who faces many challenges along the way due to what psychologists call *adverse childhood experiences* (ACEs). Such experiences include, but are not limited to, situations that challenge typical childhood development, such as the death of a parent, substance use in the home, mental illness in the home, violence, natural disasters, abuse or neglect (psychological, sexual, physical, or emotional), and more prior to the age of 18.[37] An ACE can promote negative emotional functioning due to these negative experiences and can form long-term effects such as difficulty with interpersonal functioning and psychosocial development, health issues, and difficulty in overall functioning.[38] We see this happen with Peter when he is coming of age and attempting to fit in. In his world, as an orphan, he is *othered* by others perceiving and treating him as somehow alien. Being othered or different during this period of development dramatically challenges the norms of his life and not only leads to a social impairment but may also catalyze bullying and create difficulty with social development.[39] It is here where we see a hero who is called to action while undergoing the challenge of reliving his childhood and teenage trauma. As he is called to act, he initially refuses not only because of his level of maturity in the moment but also due to his previous traumas. His ideas of great power and great responsibility become entangled in a traumatic adolescent frame of reference. Therefore his understanding of his uncle's death weighs heavily on someone perhaps too developmentally immature to grasp it all. Although we see his grief and loss of the death of his uncle, we also see the many adverse experiences influencing his decision-making on that night and many others. We also see Peter having difficulty romantically due to some of these ACEs.[40] Had he had a different trajectory in his experiences, he may have had an opportunity to feel more emboldened to be more transparent not only romantically but interpersonally about his trial and tribulations as well as the weight of being a young superhero.

Grief and Attachment, Love and Loss

Grave loss during adolescence may take away the growing individual's sense of security, sense of normalcy, sense of wonder, and sometimes sense of relational dynamics. Losing loved ones at what is already a transitional age can dramatically affect how we relate to one another and how we attach to any other individual.[41] Peter's future relationships with girlfriends, friends, and parental figures from Aunt May to Iron Man are all informed based on his experience of young grief and loss. One of the foundational theorists on attachment asserted that youngsters who experience distress often run to their caregivers.[42] Between his parents and Uncle Ben, Peter repeatedly loses his caregivers, and so he worries greatly about the one who still lives, Aunt May. Without stability in his life (whether financial, parental, emotional, or social), Peter begins to display issues with his ability to attach to others in a secure or healthy manner. Healthy attachment is the result of healthy support systems and stabilized supports throughout one's life, and due to Peter's history of ACEs, he is at risk for future complications in how he maintains or forms attachments.[43] As someone who has experienced difficulty, there is not a question of how such complications will arise but when. When will he set aside his youthful nature to "be a grown up" and when will he struggle under the pressure?

The fact that he achieves so much when he struggles so deeply makes his heroism all the more exceptional. When we connect with such characters, they help us reflect on ourselves and others. We must review and reflect on the complex nature of the adolescent and transitional age youth mindset and give grace when necessary.

Brittani Oliver Sillas-Navarro, MA, AMFT, is the Transitional Age Youth Lead Clinician at Catalyst in San Diego. She obtained her master's degree in family therapy with a clinical focus on grief and bereavement at the University of Houston Clear Lake and is completing her PsyD in couples and family therapy at Alliant International University. She has spoken on several panels at San Diego Comic-Con and Wonder-Con, contributed to books such as *Black Panther Psychology: Hidden Kingdoms* and *Stranger Things Psychology: Life Upside Down*, and participated in various popular culture and athletic podcasts.

Narcissists: Their Own Worst Enemies

The best way to defeat a pack of villains? Set them against each other. Spidey uses that old trick several times over the years, and it always delivers the goods—like when a crash course in ventriloquism is all it takes to send Electro, the Green Goblin, and the Vulture bickering their way back to jail (much to the fury of an invisible man who'd helped them escape).[1] But that's what happens when you challenge a narcissist's self-image.

Narcissism as a personality trait can be a huge burden, both for the "sufferer" and the people around them—never more so than when one of those people dares to challenge the narcissist's dominance. Narcissistic individuals perceive any less-than-aggrandizing interactions as a personal attack, and frequently react with unbridled fury to any threat to their self-image. They are supremely prone to feelings of humiliation and will defend against any sense of inferiority by violently asserting their preeminence. Rather than risk the personal glory by taking down their sworn wall-crawling enemy as a team, for example, they'd much prefer to take it in turn, fight him one-on-one—only to be defeated one *by* one.[2]

Narcissists are wounded individuals whose daily existence, despite their professed awesomeness, is one of emptiness, vulnerability, and a determination to hurt others as much as they've been hurt.[3] And if they can't hurt their enemies, web-slinging or otherwise, they'll settle for hurting their friends instead. Spider-Man knows this, but will the Sinister Six ever learn?

—Daniel Hand

 **Daniel Hand, MBACP,** is an author, historian, illustrator, game designer, and integrative counsellor in private practice. His latest book is *Role-Playing Games in Psychotherapy: Adventures of the Mind*. Visit **monomythcounselling.co.uk** for more information on RPG therapy or to get in touch.

11

Spider-Man, Murder Co-Victim: Guilt, Anger, and Posttraumatic Growth

Shelly Clevenger

"I've worn this suit, gone out there and put my life on the line again and again!
But no matter how hard I try, people die!"
—Spider-Man[1]

"It is important for these unspeakable things to be spoken of, because they actually happened in this world."
—murder co-victim John Walsh[2]

Each murder sends a ripple out into the world, affecting those who care about that victim and causing pain, suffering, and grief. In the United States alone, it is estimated that 64,000 to 213,000 people lose loved ones to murder each year.[3] While the family and friends experience grief and loss similarly to others whose loved ones died, murder victims' loved ones must also deal with the violence of their loved one's death. The violence becomes an additional source of great emotional distress and a hindrance to coping. They also feel the added stress of interacting with the police and court system to try to obtain justice or even just answers to make sense of what happened. This can be very hard for families forced to endure so many meetings, hearings, and trials, often having to repeatedly retell the crime that killed their loved one. In the end, they face the possibility that the person who committed the crime may not be caught or punished in a manner fitting of the crime.

While the term *victim* may not be what first springs to mind when thinking of the character Spider-Man, Peter Parker is a co-victim of murder due to the losses of Uncle Ben, police captains George Stacy and Jean DeWolff, and Peter's girlfriend Gwen Stacy.[4] A *murder co-victim* is an individual who experiences consequences of a loved one getting murdered, which often include psychological distress such as anxiety, panic attacks, depression, posttraumatic stress disorder (PTSD) and often associated physical ailments. Individuals who suffer from PTSD are at risk to develop conditions such as cardiovascular disease, arthritis, asthma, chronic pain and fatigue, diabetes, and gastrointestinal disorders. Co-victims can include family members, friends, spouses, or witnesses to the murder.[5]

Guilt

Because Peter Parker is a toddler (in the original comics) when he loses his parents and grows up before he learns they, too, have been murdered,[6] the first and arguably most influential murder he endures as a co-victim is that of his Uncle Ben. Peter feels self-blame and guilt for his uncle's murder, thinking that if he had just stopped the robber, Ben would be alive—feelings pivotal to his story. He dons the Spider-Man suit to help Aunt May avoid eviction following Ben's murder before working to help save others the way he could not save his uncle, all while his overwhelming feelings of guilt and self-blame motivate him to continue operating as Spider-Man.[7]

Guilt, a self-conscious emotion, affects how we view ourselves or how we think others see us. It includes feelings of failure, shame, and distress, along with an overall negative evaluation of our actions and ourselves.[8] To some degree, this emotion can be important or positive when it helps interpersonal relationships by discouraging behaviors or actions that can sever or harm anyone.[9] Excessive guilt can be psychologically damaging and can produce other negative consequences. A person preoccupied with past mistakes often experiences anxiety, insomnia, crying, panic attacks, muscle tension, loss of interest in things they enjoy (known as *anhedonia*), difficulty concentrating, social withdrawal, and overall sense of inadequacy. The experience can manifest as depression and in some cases be extreme. Individuals who suffer from extreme guilt may punish themselves for mistakes they perceive themselves to have made,[10] which might account for Spider-Man's risk-taking or his self-destructive tendencies in relationships of every kind.

Co-victims often experience guilt, and because it is an emotional response, their reasons behind their guilty feelings aren't always logical. Many blame themselves for what happened, believing it was somehow their fault that a loved one was killed or that they could have changed the outcome. Parents of murdered children are especially prone to such thinking. For example, many mothers whose children have been kidnapped, raped, or murdered reported feeling such extreme guilt that they would punish themselves as they believed they did not "deserve" things that brought them joy, even things that may seem trivial to others such as a latte or chicken pot pie.[11] Guilt can alter behaviors and lives. Like Peter Parker, they may sabotage their own attempts at happiness.[12] The emotional toll can cause individuals to act differently and to punish themselves for the wrongs they think that they committed in letting their loved one be victimized.[13]

Survivor guilt arises among many murder co-victims: negative feelings including guilt and self-blame that a person feels about still being alive after someone else has died.[14] Deaths under violent, traumatic, even catastrophic circumstances tend to produce survivor guilt more often and more severely.[15] Ben's violent murder and the horror of discovering who killed him distress Spider-Man intensely, at least partly because survivor guilt occurs more in individuals directly involved in a traumatic event where a loved one gets harmed. Aunt May, too, blames herself for Uncle Ben's death.[16]

The death of Gwen's father, Captain Stacy, also evokes a great sense of guilt in Spider-Man. Captain Stacy becomes both a supporter of the superhero and a paternal figure to Peter Parker.[17] In a battle between Spider-Man and Doctor Octopus, rubble falls and looks like it will bury a child. When Spider-Man cannot act in time, Captain Stacy rushes to save the child and is fatally wounded in the process. As he is dying, he calls Spider-Man "Peter," telling him to take care of Gwen, revealing he has known the superhero's secret identity. While holding Captain Stacy's body, Spider-Man says, "First I lost Uncle Ben those long years ago! And now the second best friend I have ever had!"[18] Magnifying his feelings of guilt, Spider-Man gets blamed for the death of Captain Stacy by both the public and Stacy's daughter, Gwen. This is the point when Peter Parker's posttraumatic symptoms begin to grow more complex.

Survivor guilt can extend to include guilt that is felt for having stayed safe and unharmed while others suffered. This can be coupled with ruminating thoughts or thinking repeatedly what you "could" or "should" have done to make a different outcome, often to the detriment of personal well-being. Many loved ones of murder victims ask themselves, "Why not me?" or "What could I have done to prevent this?" As a result, many feel responsible for what happened even if they were not there. In most cases, a person could not have done anything to prevent the situation and it was not their fault. Survivor guilt can be impactful and cause psychological issues such as panic attacks, flashbacks, nightmares, as well as ruminations over what happened or whatever you envision happened to the loved one who was murdered. The constant thoughts about how you could have prevented or otherwise changed the outcome often lead co-victims to suffer from irritability and anger and can lead to self-harm behaviors and depression.[19]

After the murder of Uncle Ben, Spider-Man suffers from a great deal of these emotional issues. To cope with survivor guilt, an individual must allow themselves to feel the emotions they are experiencing and to process them and work through it. Peter isolates himself after the death of Ben, which can be a common response to grief and survivor guilt.[20] Withdrawing from others when he needs them most seems habitual for excessively independent Peter Parker. When Mysterio makes him think Aunt May has died, Flash and Harry try to console him but he shrugs them off and marches away.[21] However, staying connected to one's support system is an important part of moving past these feelings,[22] as well as seeking professional help. Doing something to help others can also be a beneficial way to help work through survivor guilt as it redirects your thoughts to alleviating the burdens or suffering of others.

Psychologically, Peter suffers profoundly in the aftermath of his uncle's murder. While he does not seek professional help, he *does* face his sadness and feelings. He continues to go to school and stays (somewhat) connected with his Aunt May and other people. His guilt ultimately leads him to become a superhero, which helps him to process his negative emotions. In taking his heroic turn, Peter is actively trying to change the way he sees himself and others see him. Although people do not know of Peter's double life, doing good deeds and helping people as his alter ego Spider-Man reflects positively back onto Peter and helps him cope with the loss he has suffered. Altruistic behavior can bolster grieving individuals as a coping mechanism.[23]

Rage and Revenge

Uncle Ben's death incites feelings of anger in Peter, which arguably strengthens the feelings of guilt. This may be attributed to his age or the timing of the loss. Developmentally, people have different reactions to loss at different points in their lives. When Uncle Ben dies, enraged fifteen-year-old Spider-Man chases down the killer and captures him but without really hurting him. After Peter spends years ruminating over Ben's murder, Captain Stacy's death provokes great blame and loathing in Spider-Man, but he directs these feelings toward himself rather than at Doctor Octopus.[24] Perhaps this is because Doc Ock kills Stacy accidentally, even incidentally.[25] Intentional murders tend to evoke greater feelings of anger at the perpetrators and often feel more traumatic to survivors.[26] Self-directed anger and inability to forgive oneself will often fester and prepare a person to redirect their anger onto others and even make them more likely to seek revenge over later, perhaps unrelated, events.[27] Ruminating over anger can make a person more prone to desires for revenge.[28] When his girlfriend Gwen Stacy and Captain Jean DeWolff each die during Peter's twenties, a darker side emerges as he acts on his rage and his need and his desire

Gwen's death evokes Spider-Man's fury against the Green Goblin and changes superhero comics forever in *The Amazing Spider-Man* #122 (1973). Art by Gil Kane, John Romita, & Tony Mortellaro.

for revenge. He shouts out that he will kill the Green Goblin for taking Gwen from him. He doesn't pull his punches as much when pursuing criminals while he and Daredevil investigate DeWolff's murder. Both Gwen and Jean die because criminals choose to kill them. Although Spider-Man also blames himself for not saving them, in each case he sees a face at which to direct his fury.[29] Through *projection*, seeing one's own worst qualities in others, and *displacement*, transferring feelings from their original target onto new targets to have those feelings about other people,[30] Spider-Man may channel some of his anger at himself in ways that augment his attacks on others.

The murder of Gwen Stacy, his first true love, is a hard loss for

Peter Parker. Their relationship has previously unfolded as his attempt to have a semblance of a normal and peaceful life outside of his work as Spider-Man, only for Gwen to be targeted and murdered by the Green Goblin *because* of Peter being Spider-Man. This likely contributes to his anger over her murder. After Gwen dies, readers see a seething and unapologetic Spider-Man beat the supervillain brutally. In that moment, Peter embraces his anger and gives in to his desires for revenge. After Gwen's death and the physical act of enacting revenge on the Green Goblin, followed by the Goblin accidentally killing himself, Peter feels washed out, hurt, and empty.

Peter suffers another loss, the murder of Captain Jean DeWolff. Jean, an NYPD detective who becomes a close friend and ally to Spider-Man, is murdered by the serial killer known as the Sin-Eater. The Sin-Eater also murders someone close to Daredevil, leading him and Spider-Man to team up. They uncover the Sin-Eater's identity as a police officer and friend of Spider-Man, Stan Carter. Spider-Man, again filled with rage, also beats Carter violently. Daredevil must intervene and physically pull Spider-Man off Carter, causing Spider-Man to fight Daredevil. We once again see *projection* and *displacement*, with Spider-Man turning aggressively violent against Daredevil, taking out his anger against his ally when he is furious about the death of a friend.

VENOM INSIDE

Revisiting the murders by the Sin-Eater, *Daily Globe* journalist Eddie Brock writes about the man who claims to be Sin-Eater, Emil Gregg.[31] However, Gregg is a compulsive confessor (a poorly understood phenomenon that does happen when certain individuals repeatedly confess to crimes they did not commit, complicating police investigations and criminal proceedings).[32] Once everyone discovers Eddie Brock's mistake and Spider-Man defeats and reveals the real Sin-Eater's identity, Brock loses his job and his wife. Brock blames Spider-Man for the destruction of his life as he captures and reveals the real Sin-Eater. While at a church contemplating suicide, Brock encounters an alien symbiote hiding in the church. The symbiote discovers that Brock shares his hatred of Spider-Man. They bond together to form one of Spider-Man's most notorious antagonists, Venom. Having previously bonded with Spider-Man, the symbiote knows his secret identity, which allows for Venom to torment him.

Brock is displaying *denial*, a type of defense mechanism or unconscious psychological response that protects oneself from feelings of anxiety, pain, threats to self-esteem, or things too hard to handle emotionally. Denial occurs when a person is not able to face the reality of a situation or admit the truth. Eddie Brock is in denial that the things that happened to him, such as misidentifying the Sin-Eater and the dissolution of his marriage, are his fault. He refuses to take responsibility or recognize that his circumstances are the result of his decisions and actions, instead blaming Spider-Man for his own consequences. Eddie engages in both *projection*, seeing his own quality (causal responsibility in this case) in someone else, and *rationalization*, not simply denying the truth but concocting a rational-feeling explanation to make excuses for himself.[33]

This representation of Spider-Man as angry, hostile, and wanting to exact revenge rings true to human suffering. When hurt, people will act out of character and may lash out, even when, under normal circumstances, they would not.[34] Spider-Man's reactions in the aftermath of these murders represents common reactions co-victims experience in a raw way: anger and the desire for revenge. *Anger*—a negative emotion that involves aggressive thoughts or feelings, accompanied with increased heart rate and/or blood pressure, muscle tension, and headaches—can manifest in yelling, arguing, swearing, sarcasm, or cruelty. Anger can also be physically expressed through hitting, breaking things, or retaliatory behavior—all of which we see with Spider-Man. Families who lose loved ones to murder often feel the inclination to take justice into their own hands and harm those who hurt the ones they love. Many murder co-victims seek to deal with their anger or their desire for revenge through punishment of the murderer in the legal system, which can include championing for the death penalty.

Posttraumatic Growth

Posttraumatic growth (PTG) is transformative growth that follows trauma in some people. Factors influencing the likelihood of such growth appear to include *resilience,* the ability of someone to bounce back after a personal difficulty or trauma, often in unexpected ways. A resilient person will not be psychologically altered in the same way as someone who may be less resilient after a trauma. Peter has arguably achieved a degree of posttraumatic growth. While he may never fully accept that a loved one's death wasn't his fault, he eventually moves past the emotional responses he initially experienced in being a murder co-victim and understands his experience better.

Such growth often occurs during great superheroes' origins.[35] PTG often occurs in those who have a traumatic event that challenges them to the core and produces an extreme psychological struggle that often changes or shifts their belief system or view of the world. With PTG, we see individuals experience an appreciation of life, relationships with others, seeing new possibilities in life, and a renewed sense of personal strength.[36]

After each murder discussed (Ben, Gwen, Jean DeWolff), Spider-Man experiences extreme emotional reactions that change his behavior and way of thinking. After processing his guilt or rage, he continues to fight crime and resume his life. He goes on to make new relationships and work with others, which can be viewed as PTG. He has a romantic relationship with Black Cat, the first person he dates as his persona of Spider-Man. They even fight crime together as a costumed pair. He works with the Avengers and has team-ups with other heroes. Spider-Man resolves to not accept "the way things are" in his quest to prevent further loss of life.[37] He expands his world to include others and sees that, although people may be harmed because of his secret identity or the work that he does, it is worth having those relationships and trying to save people as a hero. He is not the loner he once was.

Spider-Man tells Medusa, a leader of the Inhumans, "We're not just our failures. As much as they hurt, we learn from them. Then we go out there and do our best to make up for them, even though we never will. We save people. We save as many as we can to make up for the ones we couldn't. That's all we do."[38] Expressing this shows how far he has come in his growth that he can acknowledge what has happened and embraces his role in working to help save others. Loved ones of murder victims often experience posttraumatic growth similarly to Spider-Man. They may branch out professionally and personally in ways that they would not have before. They may become activists or advocates working to do good and become superheroes in their own way. For example, a group of parents who are murder co-victims, the Parents of Murdered Children, have worked to create laws to help victims' families and support those who have experienced a loss.[39] They were able to transform and grow past their own pain to help others. Some families organize benefits or fundraisers in their loved one's name to help victims and their families. For murder co-victims, this occurs after overcoming a great deal of psychological issues and suffering. While it was not an easy process, they have used their tragedy and trauma to grow and change in a way that would not have been possible previously. It is important to note that PTG is positive in the sense that it helps the individual who is suffering a loss to overcome their psychological and emotional pain or issue, not that losing a loved one because of murder is ever a truly positive experience.

The Spectacular Power

The murder of a family member alters people forever. The way that a person deals with this loss can influence the rest of their lives. Spider-Man provides an example of how trauma and the murder of a loved one can impact a person in surprising ways depending on how they cope and adapt. Guilt can be positive and motivate individuals, as we saw with Peter becoming Spider-Man to help others. But it is important to remember that guilt can be negative if it consumes you and impedes you from living your life because you are so focused on what you feel you did wrong or could have done. Anger, while a natural emotional response to a person you love being murdered, can be destructive when an individual physically lashes out as we see with Spider-Man in the aftermath of Gwen Stacy and Jean DeWolff. Anger can destroy lives. Even though Spider-Man is acting out of what many could consider justified rage, if he gets apprehended for the violence committed against Green Goblin, the Sin-Eater, or Daredevil, he could face criminal charges and incarceration. This can be a real threat to individuals who physically harm those who murdered their loved ones.

In the end, though rage and guilt may eat at Spider-Man, he doesn't let them consume him. Instead, he processes them so that he may continue growing as a person and a superhero. Those who have experienced great tragedy, like Spider-Man, can in turn experience great growth.

 **Shelly Clevenger, PhD,** is an associate professor and chair of the first victim studies department in the nation at Sam Houston State University. She has authored peer-reviewed publications and books on victimization. She uses comics in her courses and volunteers with survivors to create their own comic books to cope with their own victimization. Dr. Clevenger has been recognized with national awards for her teaching and activism to help survivors.

12

Climbing the Walls: Neurosis, Psychosis, and Metamorphosis

Travis Langley

"Spider-Man was the poster boy for the neurotic new hero and it resonated. After all, to put on a mask and go out to fight crime, you have to be a bit crazy."
—comic book writer John Ostrander[1]

"In my dream, I'm Spider-Man, but I'm losing my powers. I'm climbing a wall but I keep falling."
—Peter Parker (Tobey Maguire)[2]

Peter Parker becomes "the poster boy for the neurotic new hero."[3] The Marvel Universe's creators gave their heroes neuroses and their villains psychoses through an endless line of metamorphoses. Pain brought the characters to life. "The more troubled you make a character," Stan Lee told us, "the more interesting he gets to the readers."[4]

Neurosis

"Spider-Man is neurotic. Peter Parker is not a simple dude. He can't just switch off. He never feels like he's doing enough."

—actor Andrew Garfield[5]

Depth psychology, an umbrella term covering several areas of psychology such as Sigmund Freud's psychoanalytic approach, attributes people's behavior to causes deep within the unconscious mind. As early depth psychologists and psychiatrists such as Freud and Carl Jung redefined and popularized the term,[6] *neurosis* covers any mental problems in which the person suffers ongoing distress without losing touch with reality (which would be *psychotic*). Freud saw neurosis as a continuum, not an all-or-nothing state in which a person is either neurotic or not. Nobody handles every stress perfectly and everyone has their quirks. He felt we're all neurotic about different things to different degrees.[7] For that ambiguity and other reasons, such as disagreeing with Freud's view of the unconscious origins, the American Psychiatric Association cut neurosis out of its diagnostic system in 1980.[8] Its editors decided to define mental disorders objectively, to look at empirically measurable actions more than underlying mental issues when possible, as the *Diagnostic and Statistical Manual of Mental Disorders* (DSM) moved from a psychoanalytic model to a medical model.[9] Nevertheless, the World Health Organization (WHO) still finds the term useful for describing many non-psychotic disorders,[10] and the word *neurotic* entered popular language long ago.

When someone calls Spider-Man and other heroes neurotic, they're calling them human. Actor Andrew Garfield, who played the superhero in *The Amazing Spider-Man* movies and returned for a multiverse-crossing team-up,[11] recognized both Peter's neurotic propensity and his humanity when the actor called the character "an over-thinker. It would be much easier if he was a life-saving robot."[12] Calling him the neurosis poster boy, though, says that stress-related difficulties—his angst and worry—distinguish him from his super-peers. If neurosis characterizes who he is as a person, then such feelings do not simply manifest as momentary *states* but instead indicate enduring *traits*, neurotic predispositions that persist and resist change. If his neuroses are pathological, then being human stresses him chronically and in unhealthy ways.

Peter Parker calls himself neurotic. When he wonders why he keeps swinging into action despite public hatred and personal costs, he thinks, "I dunno. It must be a compulsion or something. I guess I'm really hooked on turning into Spider-Man."[13] In one of his earliest conversations with Peter, Captain George Stacy similarly speculates that the masked adventurer "seems driven by some inner compulsion!"[14] A *compulsion*, a behavior a person feels driven to perform in order to reduce anxiety, may go together with *obsession*, a persistent and intrusive thought that produces recurring distress or discomfort.[15] Peter ruminates on many unpleasant things. Arguably, the circumstances of his lifestyle may force him to think about them, but even he feels he overdoes it. He calls himself "Mr. Masochism" for how much he punishes himself.[16]

Spider-Man also calls himself "one of the most depressed people alive"[17] two years after Gwen Stacy's death ("two long, miserable years," according to the Jackal).[18] Full-blown *major depression* could reduce motivation or otherwise keep him from functioning as well as Spider-Man whereas *dysthymia*, milder depression that persists for at least two years,[19] may better fit his frequent affective state. "If things go badly, I'm unhappy," Spider-Man observes, "and if things go well, I'm unhappy, so either way, I just can't win. So much for self-psychoanalysis. Who needs a shrink when a guy has himself to talk to?" In his own answer, he judges himself: "A guy who talks to himself, that's who!"[20]

To some degree, he accepts neurosis as part of his life and self-concept. On the one hand, that can make any effort to achieve greater well-being seem like a futile waste of time. On the other hand, though, it spares the individual from worrying about the worry itself, which may escalate into more intrusive obsessions and panic attacks. At times, though, he does worry his mental state may be in worse shape than that.

Psychosis

"I've always wondered about my sanity. Why would someone normal live this life?"

—Spider-Man[21]

In *The Amazing Spider-Man* #50 (1967), Peter questions his own motives and mental health. Art by John Romita & Mike Esposito (as Mickey Demeo).

Psychiatrist Ludwig Rinehart stops by the *Daily Bugle* to express his interest in Spider-Man. J. Jonah Jameson publishes Dr. Rinehart's assertion, "It is only a matter of time before his id and ego get so confused that he forgets who he really is, and then he will suffer a severe breakdown!" As Rinehart's prognosis weighs on him, Spider-Man starts seeing supervillains who aren't really there. Doc Ock, Sandman, and the Vulture attack only to vanish before his eyes. Spidey thinks he's suffering *hallucinations*, false perceptions out of touch with reality (conjured by the brain either instead of real sensory information or grossly distorting it), as "the start of my crack-up!" Rinehart tells him each hallucination is "another symptom of your schizophrenia!" In the end, though, the "psychiatrist" turns out to be the supervillain Mysterio in disguise. He has created *illusions*, misperceptions derived from real sensory input, to make Spidey doubt his own sanity. Until Jonah intrudes before Mysterio can unmask the hero, the entire ruse fools Spider-Man because it plays on his fears about his own mental state and dangerous potential. "With all my power, if I ever lose my marbles," Spider-Man contemplates, "I really would be a terrible menace to mankind!"[22]

Mysterio uses illusions to make Spidey question his own sanity when he seems to be having hallucinations in *The Amazing Spider-Man* #24 (1965). Art by Steve Ditko.

Spider-Man has seen what happens when previously law-abiding people "go mad" in his world.[23] Even though characters and narrative text both describe supervillains such as Doctor Octopus and the Green Goblin as having "gone insane," the comics rarely connect any villain's supposed insanity to any specific mental illness. Despite the word's use in early psychiatry, *insanity* is not a medical classification or psychiatric diagnosis. It's a legal standard, one that absolves individual responsibility for criminal behavior on the grounds that those who lack rational awareness of the rightness or wrongness of what they're doing need treatment, not incarceration—help, not punishment.[24] When Norman Osborn comes out of his first period of having been the Green Goblin, essentially waking up his true personality, he has no memory from the previous few years. As depicted at that time, the real Norman, though a workaholic and ruthless businessman, has not been a criminal and has no awareness of any crime the Goblin has committed.[25]

Psychosis, the psychiatric term, broadly covers any mental condition, whether temporary state or long-term disorder, in which the person loses touch with reality. The key psychotic symptoms are hallucinations, which Mysterio tries to make Spider-Man think he's seeing, and *delusions*, beliefs that are out of touch with reality. In some instances, Spider-Man does hallucinate but for clear and temporary reasons, usually chemically induced. When the Green Goblin hits him with a psychedelic pumpkin bomb, Spidey hallucinates about the Goblin, other enemies, and his friends.[26] Supervillains and sometimes superheroes get called delusional for how wild and lofty their ideas are, but delusion is more severely disconnected from real life. When a supervillain brainwashes Ned Leeds into thinking he has been the Hobgoblin, that process has induced a delusion in him.[27]

Schizophrenia, the long-term condition "Dr. Ludwig" mentions, includes an assortment of psychotic symptoms that differ from one sufferer to another: delusions, hallucinations, bizarre actions, disorganized speech, or *negative symptoms* (abnormal inactivity or other absence of normal behaviors, defined by what the person is *not* doing).[28] The term comes up in connection with both Norman and Harry Osborn, father and son, and the potential for schizophrenia has a hereditary component. When an identical twin develops schizophrenia, the odds may be about 50 percent or higher that the other twin will develop it, too, only slightly lower if separated at birth.[29] If schizophrenia were totally inherited, the *concordance rate* (how often they match) between twins would be 100 percent, but if genes played no role, odds for that other twin would be no higher than for anybody else.

Writers depict the Goblins' psychosis with inconsistent degrees of accuracy and sometimes confuse schizophrenia with *dissociative identity disorder* (the modern name for *multiple personality disorder*), in this case because of how either Osborn acts when he becomes a Green Goblin. When Norman argues with his own Goblin side or Harry sees his Goblin taunting him from the mirror, is that dissociative or psychotic? The inconsistent depiction makes that hard to answer. When an increasingly paranoid Norman hallucinates Spider-Man crouching on a desk or Harry sees his dead father in the mirror, that is psychotic.[30]

Comics repeatedly refer to supervillains as insane or psychotic without clearly demonstrating symptoms that would clearly show them to be insane or psychotic. Even *delusions of grandeur* (a.k.a. *grandiose delusions*, personal attributions of having great ability, importance, prestige, or power that are out of touch with reality)[31] are difficult to prove when people really have superpowers and sci-fi gadgets. Supervillains may be mentally ill and their narcissism may be way out of proportion to anything they deserve, and yet they may still know what they are doing, recognize the circumstances in which they do it, understand that it is illegal, and distinguish what is real from what is not. Even if the stories would depict the supervillains as more clearly psychotic, that would play into myth that "madness" makes people aggressive. In most cases, the greatest danger they pose is to themselves. Conflating psychosis with psychopathy or violence perpetuates harmful stereotypes.[32] More psychotic individuals become violent than those who are not psychotic, yes, but overwhelmingly *most* psychotic individuals do not.[33] Psychosis appears more likely to bring out violent potential in individuals who are already also *psychopathic*, meaning those who have grown up without empathy or conscience,[34] or when substance abuse complicates their reactions.[35] "Going mad" does not by itself explain the villains "going bad."

Whether a person suffers psychosis or neurosis, beware "the tired trope that severe mental illness = violence."[36] Empirical findings have repeatedly shown that one in five adults suffer mental illness in any given year.[37] We do not see one in five turn into malevolent fiends. Most people with mental disorders, even the more severe conditions, do not commit serious or violent crimes.[38]

Metamorphosis

"The world's changing. It's time we change, too."
—Adrian Toomes, about to become the Vulture (Michael Keaton)[39]

Origin stories for superheroes and supervillains depend on *metamorphosis*, the transformation of a living being's nature whether by natural or supernatural means. It can be physiological, such as when a spider bite transforms Peter Parker's body, or psychological, such as when tragedy changes him from money-seeking wrestler to crime-fighting hero. Without change, there is no origin, no story at all.

Are Spider-Man's foes bad people whose transformations unleash dark potential already inside them, or are they decent people who become villainous only because metamorphosis has reshaped them in both body and mind? Can circumstances turn previously mentally healthy people neurotic or psychotic? Even if they can, is that a separate issue from whether a change in mental state can cast a good person down into the depths of evil?

During Dr. Otto Octavius's radiation research, he uses robotic tentacles to handle components during delicate experiments. After one experiment explodes, fusing the mechanical arms onto Otto's torso, a physician says the man has suffered "an uncertain amount of brain damage. I'm afraid his mind has been permanently damaged!" Narrative text indicates that his ensuing grandiose and paranoid thoughts arise because "the brain which has been damaged by radiation reacts in a bitter way." Within minutes, Octavius escalates from thinking, "They're jealous of me," to deciding that "with such power and my brilliant mind, I'm the supreme human being on Earth!"[40] That does seem grandiose. *Traumatic brain injury* (TBI) can indeed alter how people think, feel, and act, and much research has linked it to violent[41] and other antisocial, criminal, or maladaptive behavior.[42] While the relationship is complex with many other factors possibly mediating the connection,[43] ample evidence indicates that it is possible for brain injury to make *some* people more prone to violence, especially impulsive violence. Injury to the brain's *frontal cortex*, the more advanced area responsible for higher functions such as organized thought and self-regulation, can loosen restraints against acting on impulse. Though Octavius can get angry enough to attack on impulse, especially when Spider-Man goads him, Doc Ock remains capable of analytical reasoning, meticulous planning, and calculated restraint. The first time he goes to prison, for example, he shows self-control sufficient to earn early release for good behavior.[44]

Both Norman and Harry Osborn become Green Goblins after chemically induced changes alter their brains. The Goblin formula and explosion-induced brain damage change Norman.[45] Drug abuse precedes Harry's psychosis.[46] Taking LSD again sends him to the hospital in a state of "total clinical psychosis, what a layman would call schizophrenia."[47] Harry's physician may oversimplify things for that "layman" explanation, and the stories were influenced by "sensational accounts of kids on LSD."[48] The relationship between drug abuse and schizophrenia can pose a chicken/egg riddle: Does abuse of psychoactive substances unleash the psychotic potential some people have already inherited, or does substance abuse as a form of self-medicating lead to early schizophrenic symptoms?[49]

Defense Mechanisms: Fight the Stressor!

Poor stress management defines neuroses and contributes to psychoses. The neurotic individual does not effectively use *defense mechanisms*, the things we do to protect ourselves against anxiety.[50] Use of defense mechanisms may be mature or immature, healthy or unhealthy.[51] Mature, healthy usage can successfully manage stress by transforming unhealthy impulses into healthier activities or by channeling mental energy into better feelings and thoughts about oneself and the world all around. Unfortunately, human beings' direct learning of unhealthy behavior from others and their own trial-and-error attempts at self-regulation may cause them to use defense mechanisms too much, too little, at the wrong times, or in the wrong situations.

Through *sublimation*, one of the healthiest defenses, a person manages distressing impulses by redirecting that energy into more constructive or socially acceptable activity. The person transforms the unhealthy feeling into healthy action. Peter tries this intentionally when feeling utterly alone sometime after Gwen dies: "I thought if I got out in the air, tried my hand at some web-slinging, then maybe I'd begin to get out of this mood."[52] However, when he heads out itching for somebody to punch for his distraction, that would instead be *displacement*, a neurotic defense mechanism that trades one problem for another by transferring a person's feelings away from the real source and onto a safer-seeming (or simply available) target.[53] When villains frustrated by their own failures take their anger out against innocent victims or their own lackeys, they're displacing. In *reaction formation*, another unhealthy redirection of stressful feelings and impulses, the person still directs that mental energy toward the original target but transforms its expression into a different extreme by doing the opposite of what they really want. When the Black Cat attacks Spider-Man because she worries that loving him will diminish her identity and independence, or when Peter pushes away the people he likes and loves because the closeness he really wants also scares him, that's reaction formation.

Altruism, helping others at a cost to oneself, can offset some negative self-evaluations and help the altruist better feel better about life and self. Peter pursues this all the time. *Forgiveness* helps people unburden themselves because the weight of a grudge wears people out. Spider-Man has tried to help many villains leave their pasts behind and become better people. He even tells the guilt-ridden man who really killed Uncle Ben in the movies, "I forgive you,"[54] and says the same to J. Jonah Jameson in comics as the man breaks down in tears over the horrible things he has said publicly and criminals he inadvertently created while haranguing Spider-Man over the years.[55] The problem, though, is that Peter cannot forgive himself.

Peter Parker's most famous defense mechanism is his *humor*, which can be one of the healthier defense mechanisms.[56] *Adaptive humor* helps the person function and adapt to life whether through *affiliative humor*, which enhances how we see and connect with others, or *self-enhancing humor*, which helps us feel better about ourselves without hurting anyone. *Maladaptive humor* instead interferes with healthy life functioning in the form of either *aggressive humor*, which disparages and hurts others, or *self-defeating humor*, which holds us back and can keep us mired in misery.[57] Using more adaptive humor and less maladaptive humor, especially favoring self-enhancing humor over the self-deprecating, predicts greater satisfaction and quality of life.[58] Spidey uses it all. Adaptive humor bolsters him in difficult situations, helps keep him going without collapsing, reassures some of the people he's trying to rescue, and grounds him in the face of intimidation, but his humor can be maladaptive. The kid who gets teased by classmates mentally rehearses biting responses often. The day comes when Spidey gets to hurl sarcasm and mockery against his criminal foes, often to distract them but also to displace his frustrations. However practical that may seem, he antagonizes some people at poorly chosen times. When Dr. Octopus literally extends his hand and offers "to set aside our personal enmity" so they can together save Aunt May from Hammerhead, Spidey rejects his hand, saying, "Okay, I'll work with you, Octopus, but I won't shake your hand. I'm liable to catch something contagious!" Otto makes his response clear: "I won't forget that insult, wall-crawler!"[59]

Although Peter Parker has enough hope to motivate him to persist against great odds and keep trying to accomplish good in the world, he often expects things to go poorly for him. Michelle, the MCU's MJ, expresses the later sentiment at its extreme: "If you expect disappointment, then you can never really get disappointed."[60] *Defensive pessimism*, expecting things to go poorly as a way to reduce anxiety over upcoming events, helps some people anticipate unpleasant events and therefore make preparations for them. Unfortunately, it often serves a *self-handicapping* function by leading individuals to lower expectations, reduce effort, and sometimes create obstacles that will give themselves handy excuses for failure.[61] Michelle interrupts her Peter Parker when he tries to quote her on that, though, when she knows they all need to try their hardest. Defensive pessimism helps her brace herself for circumstances beyond her control, but she sets that view aside when personal effort may still make a difference.

Many more defense mechanisms exist. For example, Eddie Brock utilizes unhealthy reality-distorting defenses that let him blame Peter Parker instead of himself when his life goes wrong: denial, projection, and rationalization (as explained in chapter 11). Freud identified a number of defense mechanisms, without always naming them. His daughter Anna Freud named most and outlined ten. Regarding how many defense mechanisms exist, a later expert said, "As many as the number of angels who can dance on the head of a pin."[62] In addition to preventing neuroses when used appropriately or causing neuroses when not used well, depth psychologists also felt extreme misuse could produce psychosis when the unconscious mind, as desperately as if fighting to survive, makes the person escape stress by escaping reality.[63]

Treatment

Change can be scary, terrifying, even if it's change for the better. Horror stories prominently feature transformation and fear of it, whether physical change such as "becoming a monster" or psychological and spiritual change in tales of losing one's humanity.[64] Mutation injects elements of horror into many a superhero story, at a high rate in Spider-Man tales ranging from his own transformations to those of villains—and some victims—wrapped in animal and Halloween themes.[65]

Not all change is bad, though. Life requires change. Metamorphoses related to neurosis and psychosis are not limited to changes that prevent or produce mental disturbances beforehand. Treatment also strives for change. We hope that changes might all alleviate symptoms and promote growth. People do not typically start going to therapy until after such problems have begun, when they want change for the better in their lives. But that's a topic for chapter 17.

Diagnosis, Prognosis, and the Poster Boy

"Sometimes I look at all the things Peter Parker does in a month, and I have no idea how he gets it all done."

—Daredevil to Captain America[66]

When Norman Osborn finally gets arrested for his crimes as the Green Goblin, reporter Ben Urich writes the story, typing that "Osborn's specific psychosis is known in the medical community as . . ." but readers never see how that sentence ends.[67] Honestly, it is better for the storytellers to assign no *diagnosis* (identification of an illness by giving it a name) than to misuse a real diagnostic label that would mislead the audience, misrepresent real suffering, and further stigmatize real people with the mislabeled conditions. Besides, a diagnosis is just a word, a label, an official concoction of consonants and vowels to summarize a set of symptoms instead of listing them over and over. It does not explain why. The *nominal fallacy* is the cognitive error of thinking that giving something a name inherently explains it—the naming-explaining fallacy.[68]

Given the fact that most supervillains who reform eventually return to crime and most of those who get cured of their transformations such as the Lizard and Morbius eventually change back for the sake of telling new fictional stories, they present a bleak *prognosis*, the professional's estimate for how they will fare in the future. The fiction's emphasis on "cure" may neglect the fact that therapeutic goals emphasize ways to cope with ongoing problems that will not vanish. Human beings are imperfect. Life can hit us hard and then hit us again, and living with mental illness can be an impressive thing.

People facing mental illness may benefit by attending to their strengths more than their weaknesses. People in their lives may enjoy richer relations when they perceive and appreciate the value in those who also happen to be mentally ill.[69] Harry Osborn's challenges make his successes all the more remarkable. Hearing high society guys at Harry's birthday party crack jokes about Osborn's history of mental illness prompts Peter to stick up for his friend. Despite any past troubles, Peter values Harry's friendship and place in his life.[70] Once Harry realizes Peter has stood up for him, he follows Peter away from the stuffy social gathering and suggests they go get pizza. When Peter answers, "That'd be great. I shoved my stuffed mushrooms down that guy's pants," Harry simply responds, "Of course you did, buddy. Of course you did."

Peter rarely shows himself the consideration he shows others. At times he admits, "I need so much therapy,"[71] but does not seek it. Trust is a problem for him: "I've always feared seeing psychiatrists before, lest they discover my true identity!"[72] Admittedly, one psychiatrist turns out to be Mysterio in disguise and another, whom Harry later sees, uses hypnotically uncovered secrets to become yet another Green Goblin.[73] Spidey cannot trust just any therapist. Even so, he knows Doc Samson, who is both superhero and psychiatrist.[74] Cindy Moon (Silk, who got her powers from the same spider that bit Peter) and Ben Reilly (the Scarlet Spider, Peter's clone who shares most of Peter's memories and has even worse trust issues, a.k.a. Chasm after losing many of those memories) see therapists—both regarding their anger and identity issues.[75] Cindy, the one who sees a therapist more consistently and completely by her own choice, benefits more.

Calling Spider-Man "the poster boy for the neurotic new hero"[76] can be a compliment, a badge of honor. A poster child is an inspiration. Putting him on the hypothetical poster says that feelings of anxiety and depression do not make life pointless, that degrees of difficulty and challenge make the heroism part all the more heroic, and that Spider-Man is a model of heroism worthy enough to embody that ideal.[77] Every obstacle he faces both outside himself and within will transform every achievement into an even greater triumph. Despite all his difficulties and his reluctance to help himself, Spider-Man keeps going.

The neurotic hero is a hero.

13

Radioactive Reaction: Anger, Trauma, and Self-Control

Travis Adams, Alex Langley, & Emily Burk

"But at some point, I just—I stopped pulling my punches. I got rageful. I got bitter."

—**Peter 3 (Andrew Garfield) to Peter 1 (Tom Holland)**[1]

"No one heals himself by wounding another."

—**theologian Saint Ambrose of Milan**[2]

Doctor Otto Octavius, in one of his outings after taking control of Spider-Man's body and brain, reacts quickly and punches the Scorpion at his full strength. The punch knocks the man's jaw clean off his body, to Octavius's surprise. This makes Doc Ock reflect on the power Spider-Man possesses and realize that, in every encounter, Spidey restrains his incredible strength to stop his foes without crippling, without killing. Most of us exercise self-control to some degree every day. Few, however, must exercise self-control as much and as often as Spider-Man. Audiences love the web-slinging hero for his quips and everyman qualities, and much like the rest of us, there are times when Spider-Man's patience and self-control are in short supply.

Rage of the Spider

"Whoa, whoa! Man, I was quick to anger!"
—Peter Parker reflecting on his younger self's poorer emotional self-regulation[3]

Self-control, the ability to restrain impulses and command one's own behavior whether overt or covert, emotional or physical,[4] plays a key role in managing aggression. As self-restraint decreases, people grow more likely to aggress. Common factors that deplete self-control include alcohol and hot temperatures,[5] neither of which is particularly a factor for Spider-Man given that he largely avoids alcohol and most of his adventures take place in the perpetually cool pages of comic books. When we use our self-control, we (temporarily) also use some of it up. If we dip too deeply into our limited reservoir of self-control, we can enter a state of *ego depletion* in which we become more impulsive and more susceptible to persuasion.[6]

Serotonin, the complex neurotransmitter that regulates sleep, health, and mood, directly impacts a person's self-control.[7] As our serotonin levels deplete and therefore cannot calm the brain as well, our self-control can deplete with it. Among common causes of serotonin depletion, prolonged stress leads the pack. Spider-Man lives under a level of stress that most people (fortunately) do not, but there are times when the stress of his life begins to wear on him and we see his self-control slip. Feeling depressed after the news of his Aunt May's cancer diagnosis, Spider-Man stops a carjacking by casually, accidentally breaking the young carjacker's arm.[8] Still reeling at the return of Harry Osborn and the danger his return brings to his loved ones, Peter punches a mugger so hard that it nearly kills him in a single blow.[9]

Perpetual stress and trauma beat at the heart of so much of Spider-Man's history. From the loss of his parents[10] to the murder of Uncle Ben[11] to the murder of Gwen Stacy[12] to countless assaults, injuries, betrayals, and near-death experiences, Spider-Man carries trauma with him at all times. Trauma can affect anyone, super or otherwise. When traumatic events linger for longer and with greater intensity than is typical, the person may suffer *posttraumatic stress disorder* (PTSD). PTSD symptoms include drastic shifts in cognition and mood (such as frequent, sudden rage), *anhedonia* (an inability to enjoy previously pleasurable activities), avoidance of reminders of the event, psychologically reliving the event, and *hypervigilance*, excessive alertness to danger.[13]

For many, at the core of their PTSD lies anger.[14] This anger may manifest into aggression, violence, and abuse, whether physical, sexual, or psychological. When anger and aggression become dysregulated, our ability to create and maintain long-lasting meaningful relationships becomes equally impacted. Lack of support (or a perceived lack of support) also exacerbates the risk of trauma-induced disorders.[15] As a primarily solo superhero with a small handful of people who know his secret identity (which for many years had been no one), Spider-Man often allows himself little help. The few times he expects support don't always end well, such as when he saves the *Daily Bugle* from getting robbed by the Vulture and yet finds himself blamed for the entire event.[16] Unsupportive moments like these greatly increase the potential for unhealthy coping strategies.[17]

Anger does not present in the same way for everyone. Some people lash out; others internalize. *Internalizations* of anger (directing anger at oneself instead of outwardly at others)[18] include rumination, self-blame, and self-injury—concepts with which Spider-Man is very familiar. Those who lash out with their anger often do so as a means of seeking protection from being hurt again. By pushing away their loved ones through aggression, they free themselves from the potential of hurt and sorrow. Harry Osborn directs his anger and sorrow over his father's apparent death against Peter and allows his fury to damage their relationship.[19]

Repeated, consistent exposure to trauma can create a state of *survival mode* in which an individual's thoughts, attentions, and actions center on surviving the ongoing stressor no matter the cost to any other aspect of their life.[20] Peter frequently lives at the edge of survival mode. His interpersonal relationships, his finances, his job, nearly everything in his life tend to fall away in service of being Spider-Man. In his case, however, his survival mode tends to focus outward rather than inward. He worries about the ongoing survival of everyone but himself. This concern for people, this perpetual stress over taking responsibility for their well-being and his own, may be exemplified in his spider-sense, his superhuman ability to sense danger.

Spider-Man is the first superhero for whom *worry* is a super-power. The spider-sense helps him survive moment-to-moment danger, but often it stresses him too. The power both helps him avoid danger and prepares him to fight. Sometimes, he can be a lit-tle too prepared to fight. When the stress of life gets to him, he can *regress*, revert to behavior from an earlier point in life—in this case, unleashing the angrier adolescent part of himself. In those mo-ments, a hot-headed web-head may lash out verbally or physically, and he has little difficulty finding targets for his anger. "That's what I love about this city," he muses as he dispatches a group of assailants. "Every time I need to hit someone really, really hard, some jerk steps up and volunteers."[21] For all his heroism, there are times where Spider-Man takes a few notes from the Hulk and be-comes someone whom others wouldn't like when he's angry.[22]

Cause and Effect

Sometimes the reasons for Spider-Man's anger lie within his control—at other times, not. His own *temperament*, his prevailing pattern of emotional disposition, is something he can influence, but it doesn't ex-ist purely as a product of his own making.[23] Individuals whose family members have short tempers are, in turn, likely to have short tempers themselves, whether the reasons may be hereditary or learned environ-mental (nature vs. nurture). A learned propensity for aggression can result from *social learning*, learning through observing others.[24] We see it, we repeat it. Aunt May and Uncle Ben serve as outstanding role models for Peter, particularly when it comes to self-control. And de-spite his parents' absence during his upbringing, their genetics continue to play a part. Given that both are intelligence operatives (a career that requires tremendous precision and self-control), it's no small leap to assume they carry genetic potential that can contribute to the healthy development of self-control.

When we don't get what we want, we feel frustrated. Frustration can beget aggressive feelings and behavior.[25] Peter Parker's adventures as Spider-Man often lead to his own needs and wants getting fulfilled barely, if at all. While he learns to grin and bear it over time, attributing such things to his "Parker Luck" or alleviating his misery by waxing poetic about being a "super-powered sad sack,"[26] moments arise in which his frustrations get to him and his aggressions begin to increase. In those cases, Peter can turn snappy and irritable, bordering on cruel, to people around him.[27] As Spider-Man, personal frustrations can lead him to use dangerous amounts of force, such as on the aforementioned mugger whose arm he broke. He may pick fights with people who don't deserve it, such as the occasional superhero[28] and neighborhood shopkeepers he mistakes for criminals.[29]

Deeper Bites

The pain of social rejection can sting harder than any spider bite, radioactive or otherwise.[30] In Peter's first appearance, in his first comic book panel, students at Midtown High are mocking and excluding him.[31] He's still bold enough to ask a fellow student out on a date soon thereafter, but she, too, rejects him. Peter's teenage years are fraught with social rejection, and this leads to his fantasizing about physically and socially dominating his tormentors—aggressive fantasies common to many who've experienced social rejection.[32] His thoughts of rejection-fueled aggression are brief, however. He quickly stows his anger and instead compassionately takes the perspective of his tormentors to search for the reasoning behind their behavior, or he blames their rudeness on his own flakiness.[33]

Rumination, obsessive thinking over a negative event, correlates strongly with adverse feelings and behaviors including aggression.[34] Peter Parker can ruminate with the best of them. He lives so often in his head, haunted by the ghosts of past events that break his heart and boil his blood. In his case, however, his ruminations more often serve as reminders to stow his aggression and put the needs of others first. The anger he feels is directed less at the robber who murders Uncle Ben than at himself for failing to act in the first place.[35] He channels his ruminations into constructive purpose.

One of the great equalizers in aggression is *provocation*. Spider-Man may provoke his foes with verbal jabs and quips, but, ultimately, *they* are the ones provoking him by engaging in dangerous, harmful behavior. When this behavior extends beyond trying to harm Spider-Man and instead targets his loved ones, Peter becomes his most aggressive self. The Green Goblin taunts his Aunt May, mocking her life philosophies and labeling her as someone who "weakens" Peter.[36] When she dies from the wounds Green Goblin has inflicted, Peter grows enraged, vengeful. It's only with the interceding wisdom and support of the two more experienced Spider-Men that Peter relents from his desire for revenge. In the comics' version, after Peter reveals his identity to the world during the events of the superhero Civil War, an assassin's bullet meant for Peter, ordered by the Kingpin, strikes Aunt May. Peter tracks down the Kingpin in prison and delivers a savage, merciless beating in front of the prison population, one that leaves the once-proud villain physically and psychologically broken.[37]

Wearing Black

"You're quite the bully when you wanna be, aren'tcha, Parker?" taunts rival photojournalist Eddie Brock. He isn't entirely wrong. Having been bullied during his formative years, Peter Parker can carry quite the chip on his shoulder. He mutters to himself about what he could do to school bully Flash Thompson if he really let loose, taunts supervillains with verbal attacks that are both petty and personal, and at times begrudges the sound of police sirens interrupting his life with a call to action.[38] Of course, being Spider-Man, we know that he's never really going to hurt Flash, that his taunts are usually both justified and tactically advantageous (distracting the villains while hiding his own worries), and that he'll always answer the call to action in the end. Part of what audiences love about Spider-Man is that he *has* these moments of petty thinking but behaves nobly despite them. In Freudian terms, his *id*, his drive to behave destructively and selfishly, takes a firm back seat to his *superego*, his conscience. There is, however, one scenario in which his superego gets shuffled to the back and his id is allowed behind the wheel: under the influence of the black symbiote suit.

The black suit enhances Spider-Man's strength, speed, and ability to react to danger far beyond his normal limits, but this living symbiote comes with a side effect that is huge for someone like Spider-Man: It drains his self-control and magnifies his aggression. Wearing it puts him into a state akin to semi-permanent ego depletion. He fights villains such as the Rhino and Shocker with brutality, going so far as to try to torture information out of Rhino and, when that fails, nearly executing him. He lashes out at other heroes who try to help him regain his senses.[39] In *Spider-Man 3*, he's willing to murder Sandman when he finds out he was the man who shot Uncle Ben, and he disfigures Harry Osborn by throwing his pumpkin bomb right back at him.[40]

Under the influence of the symbiote, Peter's willpower weakens and he grows more likely to do impulsive, aggressive things. Mind- and mood-altering substances such as methamphetamines and alcohol can create similar results in the everyday person.[41] Of all the factors that influence violence and aggression, alcohol stands tall as one of the most influential.[42] Fortunately, Peter finds his own version of teetotaling by removing the symbiote from himself and returning to his friendly neighborhood ways. Still, for someone whose life has become inextricably embroiled in aggression, a single gesture like this is insufficient to keep his self-control at full Spidey-strength. He needs to put in the work and then keep putting in the work.

Swinging, Slinging, and Riding the Path to Recovery

"You've lived with this pain for so long, it's comforting. You don't know what you'd do without it."

—Gwen Stacy clone to Peter Parker[43]

Just as traumas differ from person to person, recovery paths may vary. Both traditional therapy and alternative, empirically studied approaches can be beneficial in dealing with trauma and anger.[44] Holistic approaches such as yoga, meditation, and deep-breathing exercises encourage self-exploration and a consideration of how a person interacts with the world around them.[45] Unfortunately, such techniques generally require the person to take a moment and, in one way or another, still themselves (intentionally bring themselves to a state of stillness). If there's one thing Spider-Man isn't, it's still. The X-Men enjoy the odd moment of downtime in the Blackbird, and flying heroes such as Iron Man might be able to meditate during long flights (were they prone to that sort of thing), but Spider-Man is constantly moving, constantly swinging, his mind racing through his own personal problems, superhero problems, and moment-to-moment thoughts about the web-slinging itself. He won't give himself time to be still because, in his mind, if he stays still, others may suffer for it.

AN ANGRY MOON

Cindy Moon, a.k.a. Silk, who gains spider-powers when the arachnid that bites Peter Parker's hand then also bites her ankle, tries to manage her anger issues through traditional *talk therapy*. She becomes the one spider-family member who regularly sees a therapist—a psychiatrist, to be exact. These days, not as many people see psychiatrists as those who see psychologists and other kinds of therapists when they need someone to talk to, someone with professional knowledge and therapeutic experience. Clients mainly go to psychiatrists when treatment needs to include medication. Cindy's psychiatrist, Dr. Sinclair, however, comes recommended by Reed Richards of the Fantastic Four and specializes in clients who "all have secret identities."[46]

Reentering the world after living ten years isolated in a bunker and having missed out on young adult social life and experience since she was eighteen, Cindy finds the world overwhelming. After Dr. Sinclair gets her to acknowledge that the bunker where she previously lived in isolation makes her feel safe, the woman pursues the topic.

SINCLAIR: And expressing that desire for safety—how does that make you feel?

MOON: Angry.

SINCLAIR: Anger. We keep coming back to that, don't we? Can you tell me what makes you so angry?

MOON: That's, uh, that's our time, Dr. Sinclair.[47]

The therapist has run into a *resistance*, something Cindy resists discussing and does not yet feel ready to face.[48]

—T. L.

Although Cindy Moon regularly sees a therapist, Peter Parker does not. He is not one to open up that much. Like many people, though, some alternate-universe versions of him and his friends informally implement therapeutic principles while trying to manage their lives.

In *equestrian therapy*, for example, professionals guide clients through various horse-related activities. This promotes active time outdoors, allowing clients to disconnect from their negative emotions by focusing on the task at hand, and encourages the bond with a nonjudgmental, living thing.[49] Though New Yorker Spider-Man of Earth-616 has no use for a horse, his Earth-31913 counterpart, Web-Slinger, fights crime in an alt-universe wild west with his trusty partner Spider-Horse.[50] Web-Slinger and Spider-Horse, having both been bitten by the same radioactive spider, share a "Rider Sense," a powerful bond between them. This bond provides Web-Slinger many of the same benefits of equestrian therapy as they fight crime in the weird west of Earth-31913.

Spider-Gwen, as drummer for her band The Mary Janes, uses music as both a creative and therapeutic outlet. Drumming helps her to process the guilt, anger, and pain she feels over major losses in her life: the mother she never knew, her best friend Peter Parker who has died in part due to her anger and self-preoccupation, and Billy Braddock, Spider-UK (Captain Britain/Spider-Man) of Earth-833.[51] *Music therapy* offers clients a means of emotional expression and provides clinicians a tool for both assessment and therapy.[52] Though Spider-Gwen

When Spider-Gwen drums furiously, weeping, is she sublimating, self-managing, or turning her rage inward at herself? *Spider-Gwen: Ghost-Spider* #4 (2019). Art by Rosi Kämpe & Takeshi Miyazawa.

isn't experiencing the full benefits of playing with a therapist to guide her, her music is providing a useful emotional outlet to help process her grief and fury.

Self-help versions of therapeutic practices are not limited to alternate universes, of course. They arise in Spidey's life on homeworld Earth-616, as well. *Art therapy*, which allows individuals to express themselves through art,[53] helps process subconscious thoughts and emotions without consciously dwelling on them. When Spider-Man becomes the unwilling recipient of Captain Universe's Uni-Power, he manages the stress of his newfound abilities by experimenting with creating shapes using his webbing.[54] What likely helps him more, however, is his supportive conversation with Mary Jane. Her own experience in therapy, coupled with her full knowledge of Peter's stressful life, make her a powerful ally in his battle against his own negative emotions.

Mary Jane makes use of her therapeutic experience again by later taking Peter to an abandoned theater to help him work through the trauma and anger festering inside after the sudden reappearance of Harry Osborn as the centipede-themed villain Kindred.[55] She encourages him to breathe deeply, to focus on the present and to focus on the physical, which are *mindfulness* techniques encouraging practitioners to center themselves in the moment rather than in past or future worries.[56] From there, she instructs him to pretend that Harry/Kindred is there, in the room, and to say what he would say if Harry really was there. *Psychodrama therapy* puts clients in a safe space, free of judgment, to roleplay and explore their trauma.[57] This approach allows Peter to express his hurt and betrayal over Harry's actions. In doing so, he's able to move forward positively, his mind unburdened by the rage previously growing inside.

Hurt People Help People

Pain. Anger. For better or worse, these concepts inextricably come with being human. Spider-Man's pain forms him no less than his family, friends, intellect, wit, selflessness, and self-control form him. Like any of us, he may hurt or feel anger, but these things do not wholly define anyone. By saving lives and stopping crimes as Spider-Man, Peter wields his self-control to transform his pain and anger into something positive. And by allowing himself the occasional help from a thrill-seeking redhead, a billionaire playboy philanthropist,[58] a guy in the chair,[59] or any of the countless other friends and heroes in his life, Spidey can continue processing that pain and anger to keep being everyone's *friendly* neighborhood Spider-Man.[60]

Travis Adams, LSW, received his MSW from the University of Southern California and is currently a Readjustment Counselor for the VA working with United States military, both active duty and veterans. He is a Marine Corps Veteran who specializes in utilizing various types of therapy to aid veterans in their recovery and has incorporated the use of popular culture in conjunction with standardized treatment models. He has previously authored chapters in *Supernatural Psychology, Daredevil Psychology,* and *Black Panther Psychology.*

Emily Burk, geek, received her BA in Public Relations from California State University San Bernardino and currently works in Digital Asset Management. She has love for all things relating to nerd culture, fandom, and fantasy.

Across Generations:
How Miles Morales Sees
Teen Peter Parker

*U*ltimate Spider-Man co-creator Brian Michael Bendis told us that he learned the most about Peter Parker through the character of a newer Spider-Man, Miles Morales.[1] Even though Parker and Morales spend less time together than Miles might like, Miles learns from his predecessor. Miles sees Peter as a mentor figure, and the original Spider-Man's history, legend, and sometimes notoriety loom over the younger hero's shared use of the Spider-Man name.

BENDIS: Toward the end of my run, we were all offered this opportunity to do a project called *Generations*. I had an opportunity for young Miles to meet young Peter Parker.[2] He's already met adult Peter Parker and has been mentored by him and gotten some wisdom. Now Miles goes back in time [into] a Ditko issue where for Peter, nothing's going well.

Miles visits Peter during and after events of 1966's *The Amazing Spider-Man* #32–33. In the original story, Peter's social life in college gets off to a bad start, Aunt May is on the verge of death, and (as described in chapter 16) Spider-Man strains to heave tons of weight off himself so he can survive to take May her life-saving medication. In the *Generations* story, Pete tells Miles: "Tonight was the first time I really ever thought, 'Oh god, I am done. I'm going to die tonight.'"[3]

BENDIS: Miles, who has both of his parents and a best friend and friends, meets Peter, who has no friends, and people are being viciously cruel to him for just walking by. He's a depressed orphan. This is a depressed child. There's pile of issues going on here. It was then that Miles realized, first of all, how impressive it was that Peter's been able to rise to the occasion of a hero. Miles was able to see that the way he became Spider-Man was almost a privilege in comparison to what happened to Peter and it completely changed *how* he's Spider-Man. I would never have had Miles go back in time to the Steve Ditko days unless an editor said, "We're doing this." When I got there, I found more truth in that one issue than the last hundred that I wrote. Miles saw something that he never would have guessed, and I don't think a lot of the audience perceives Peter back in those days as depressed and neurotic as he is. Yeah, he's guilt-ridden, but the other elements! No one is kind to him. The nicest person to him is Betty Brant, and she's only nice to him a third of the time. His bosses are mean. The audience to this day goes, "Who gets to work at a major metropolitan newspaper at fifteen?" Stan did. He was working where he wouldn't have been at age fifteen, and he was clearly angry about it and wrote it into Spider-Man. He brought truth, and that truth is the thing he's most famous for.

—T. L.

14

Spidery Strengths and Virtues: From Radioactive Bite to Values-Driven Life

Travis Langley

"Peter Parker is such a positive character. He's pure wish fulfillment, an underdog."
—actor Andrew Garfield[1]

> "A hero isn't the one who always wins. It's the one who always tries."
> —Miles Morales (also a Spider-Man)[2]

When we present panel discussions on "Who's the Most Neurotic Superhero?" in front of comic convention audiences, long-time Spider-Man editor Danny Fingeroth quips, "Spoiler alert: It's Spider-Man."[3] The last time we covered this topic in San Diego, *Spider-Man: The Animated Series* showrunner John Semper Jr. disagreed. Spider-Man's guilt and angst may be facets of the character, but John stressed that he is so much more. "That's not what we focused on. We kept him fun. I don't think he is the most neurotic superhero. Batman's way more messed up,"[4] he told us, later adding, "In fact, I never thought my Spider-Man was neurotic at all, really."[5]

In line with Semper's thinking, psychologist Martin Seligman—addressing the American Psychological Association while he was its president—said that psychology as a field has collectively focused so heavily on psychological damage that the discipline has neglected psychological health and that it moved away from improving life for everyone. Overemphasizing the things that can go wrong keeps people from celebrating the ways life can go right. Seligman called for the development of *positive psychology*, "a reoriented science that emphasizes the understanding and building of the most positive qualities of an individual." He felt that "psychology has moved too far away from its original roots, which were to make the lives of all people more fulfilling and productive, and too much toward the important, but not all-important, area of curing mental illness."[6] For that matter, how can we even treat mental illness without better understanding mental health in the first place? What is the better part of human nature, and how much of that does Spider-Man embody?

There is a hero inside Peter Parker, just as there is for Miles, Gwen, Cindy, and others who might not start out planning to follow a hero path and yet they nevertheless do. Sometimes even the super-criminals decide to do right by others. Though guilt over Uncle Ben's loss makes Peter reconsider past choices and discover his heroic purpose in his origin story, pain alone does not make a hero. It could make a villain. It could make a recluse. It could make someone distracted while working on other things. What else goes on inside Spider-Man to make him the guy who will swing in to help others no matter what it costs him?

Character Strengths and Virtues

To understand "what is right about people" and to conceptualize core pathways "that make the good life possible" and meaningful for everyone,[7] Seligman and a colleague searched the world (empirical research from all over the world, that is) to identify character strengths and virtues. They organized information about them into the *Character Strengths and Virtues* (CSV) handbook, an "anti-DSM" or "manual of the sanities"[8] that categorizes and describes qualities associated with productivity, happiness, and mental health,[9] as opposed to the American Psychiatric Association's *Diagnostic & Statistical Manual of Mental Disorders* (DSM), which categorizes and describes mental illnesses.[10]

Across cultures, six *virtues* emerged as core characteristics valued for fostering moral, meaningful, successful, and happy lives—virtues they dubbed wisdom, courage, temperance, transcendence, humanity, and justice to simplify discourse about them. *Character strengths* support and define those virtues. They all involve gaining and implementing the skills and resources that will serve those virtues that will help the individual put their values into action in this life. Peter Parker may not be the happiest person or the most successful in his personal life, but Spider-Man possesses a wealth of character strengths that he puts to work to serve the virtues he finds most important.

Wisdom and Knowledge

Though wisdom and knowledge are two different things, the CSV authors found no single word that adequately encapsulated the virtue that covered interrelated strengths of curiosity, creativity, perspective, open-mindedness, and love of learning.[11] The virtue of *wisdom and knowledge* values smarts of different kinds. A person strong in this area seeks to acquire information and cognitive skills, and to apply them in the service of making life better. Though people may question Spider-Man's wisdom at times, he admires wisdom and unquestionably pursues and reveres knowledge. For Peter Parker, the strength called *love of learning* is one of his defining qualities. In high school, classmates call him "bookworm" like it's a bad thing, but he embraces it. Years later, when Mary Jane expresses dismay that he's reading works by two philosopher/playwrights and the psychiatrist who founded analytical psychology, he embraces that persona.

MARY JANE: Say, do you actually read these monsters?
PETER: When I have the time. These days, I don't have much.
MARY JANE: Yeah, but Sartre, Camus, Jung. How do you relax, Petey?
    By watching educational TV?
PETER: You know me, MJ. My middle name's bookworm.[12]

Drawing upon strengths of *creativity* (which includes ingenuity), *curiosity*, and *open-mindedness* helps him solve many problems. His thinking can be both *divergent* (spreading out to conceive of many options, paths, and possibilities) and *convergent* (narrowing down choices to select which is optimal based on analysis and critique).[13] Repeatedly, he concocts last-second solutions on the fly. Combined with his intelligence and prodigious technical expertise, these strengths enable him to invent the fluid that lets him shoot his distinctive webs and the spider-tracers that help him track criminals down.[14]

Courage

Spidey, his friends such as Miles Morales and Spider-Gwen Stacy (a.k.a. Spider-Man/Spin and Spider-Woman/Ghost-Spider), and other heroes all show great *courage*, exercising the will to pursue goals in the face of opposition. This virtue is central to heroism itself. Strengths of courage include bravery, persistence, integrity, and vitality. The strength of *bravery* is not about fearlessness. Rather, it entails "the ability to do what needs to be done despite fear."[15] Heroes' bravery can, in turn, inspire others to stand up to what they fear too. Though some superheroes face dangerous villains and rampaging monsters more easily than they face interpersonal confrontations in their civilian lives, those threats will not wait. Peter, in particular, postpones important conversations, which can make problems fester.

Temperance

Of the six virtues, he may be strongest in *temperance*, the restraints that protect against excess. Despite some notable exceptions, his lifestyle stays modest. He does not regularly give in to temptation or excess. Despite frequent impatience, his temperate strengths are many.

Spider-Man shows great *mercy* toward others, as reflected by how often he tries to help villains reform or heal and actively works to spare enemies' lives (while also pointing out the impracticality of killing enemies when they'll keep coming back from the dead angrier than ever before).[16] Peter stops one alien invasion by showing the Tinkerer empathy and mercy instead of continuing a fight.[17] Norman Osborn gets a chance to be a better man purged of his past sin, and Peter decides to help. Speaking to a likeness of Gwen Stacy about why he'd work with Osborn, Peter says, "He's trying to be a good man. The way I see it, it's my responsibility to help him. It's my responsibility to keep from becoming the man who killed you."[18] When Spider-Man finally reveals his true identity to J. Jonah Jameson, it is not to help himself. It is an act of mercy, one taken at great risk. Seeing Jonah broken, mired in self-loathing, feeling unloved and alone, Peter unmasks to show him someone cares, to give him a chance to escape his own hate: "I told you I do this to save lives. And if telling you this, breaking this cycle, helps save yours . . ."[19]

Despite the fact that he performs his good deeds at the sacrifice of Peter Parker's reputation, Peter perceives himself as being weak in *humility* or *modesty*. He chastises himself for moments his ego gets the better of him. He is humble,[20] and his own humility keeps him from recognizing that. The glory hound he worries about becoming would not cover every square inch, even his eyes, in a full-body costume. His difficulty integrating his own contradictions provides part of the character's appeal.

And, reckless as he can be, he does not show the kind of temperate preparation or caution associated with the strength of *prudence* as often as he perhaps should. When Dr. Octopus takes control of Peter Parker's body and brain, Octavius reflects in amazement over how poorly Peter Parker plans.[21] Years of relying on his spider-sense to detect danger and possessing the power to face almost anything that comes up,[22] as noted in chapter 4, may atrophy some measure of his caution. He grows accustomed to solving problems off the cuff.

BLACK CAT (regarding the villain Queen Goblin): She is not like any Goblin you've ever faced before. Saving me is one thing, but are you sure you're ready for her?

SPIDER-MAN (recently waken from a coma): That's my secret, Cat. I'm never ready.[23]

During one of Otto Octavius's first outings as the self-proclaimed Superior Spider-Man, however, he discovers Parker's greatest strengths of temperance to be his *self-regulation* or *self-control*. When Otto as Spider-Man fights the Scorpion, in one punch he knocks his opponent's jaw off. Stunned at this unexpected result, Octavius thinks, "Never knew this body held so much power. All these years, Parker must have been holding back."[24]

Self-control can show up in supervillains too. As Electro, Max Dillon has the power to electrocute entire crowds and yet he does not. Despite all the times he threatens to kill, he refrains. Once, Electro loses control and his power kills only because Doc Ock (while still playing Spider-Man) conducts experiments that destabilize the electrical powers.[25] Dillon cautions Francine Frye, a groupie who idolizes supervillains and prefers to live dangerously, "My power's been acting up. You should probably keep your distance"—and yet she kisses him, only to suffer unintended electrocution.[26]

Transcendence

The virtue *transcendence* reaches beyond mundane existence "to embrace all or part of the larger universe."[27] Feeling connected to things greater than ourselves and vaster than our surroundings can help provide a sense of meaning in life. This may make some feel distant, disconnected from those right around them, yet help others feel more human and fully alive.[28] Spider-Man is not a "big picture" guy. Meditating in contemplation of the cosmos would make him impatient to get out there, swinging around the city in search of people to help and dangers to combat.

Similarly, the transcendent strength *appreciation of beauty and excellence* matters to him. Excellence in scientific achievement impresses Peter. As a youngster, he finds himself starstruck upon meeting accomplished scientists. Although appreciation of aesthetics falls to the back burner when crisis looms, it manifests every time he feels a sense of awe—when the normally chatty Spidey finds himself stuck for words or gazes at the vastness of space and utters, "Wow!"

Certain transcendent strengths help Spider-Man persevere and overcome obstacles. He has *hope* that his efforts will do some good. For him, hope is active. He does not simply wish for things to be better; he works to make things better. When he contemplates his own life and purpose during his many depressed moments, though, he often feels pessimistic, "bewildered, confused, and bitter."[29] He can show *gratitude*, although he rubs many the wrong way when he seems ungrateful.

The transcendent strength of *humor* emerges as one of Spider-Man's better-known features. Cognitive behavioral therapist Homaira Kabir observes, "From calming the vascular system and reducing depressive symptoms, to enhancing relationships and providing a greater purpose in life, humor is a primary contributor to a well-lived life." She adds, though, that "humor can also bring tears of irritation or outbursts of anger."[30] Spidey makes jokes. As Peter Parker, he makes fewer. Wearing the mask frees him to share what amuses him or simply to vent. Before he gains his powers, he laughs easily with Uncle Ben and Aunt May, but laughter among his peers makes him feel bad. "Someday I'll show them," he sobs to himself. "Someday they'll be sorry—sorry they laughed at me!"[31] It's the kind of remark comic book villains utter. Even after he gains his powers, the most humor in his thoughts about peers tends to be sarcastic. That tendency lessens some, though, as he and his peers mature, as time helps them heal.

As a transcendent strength, humor can help the person to appreciate life and rise above strife, to manage difficulties without letting them feel overbearing. Spider-Man's humor does not simply rile and distract foes. It helps and reassures others, as he explains to Jonah when the two finally have their revelatory conversation: "I joke to put people at ease, to counter the mask I need to wear!"[32] Chapter 5 describes his use of humor as a powerful defense mechanism, and this current chapter will come back around to look at how Spider-Man might better exercise this essential strength.

Humanity

Interpersonal strengths that involve befriending and taking care of others make up the virtue *humanity*. Spider-Man will fight to protect people. Peter Parker can be a great friend and he goes to great lengths to support the aunt who raised him, but he can also be a forgetful, negligent, inconsiderate friend and nephew. Even when he has not forgotten about them, he prioritizes the needs associated with other virtues over his *affiliative needs* (needs to affiliate, to connect with others). Though rushing out to save someone's life is urgent, to be sure, he also sabotages himself. Despite how much he yearns for love and appreciation, he does not always feel he deserves them.

Love, which includes the sharing of aid, comfort, and acceptance, lies at the foundation of deep relationships and drives so many human endeavors.[33] Relationships between people help us feel human and alive. Love takes many forms. While he has little family, his *familial love* runs strong for the uncle and aunt who raise him. In his youth, he aches to know *romantic love*. Most deeply, he will love Gwen Stacy and, after Gwen, Mary Jane Watson. Others date him along the way, but Gwen and MJ are the great loves of his life. Other forms of love manifest as he cares deeply for friends, and his concern for the welfare of humankind keeps him out there aiding and comforting strangers. He often feels unworthy of love and other happiness.

Kindness, more complex than merely acting nice, includes compassion and concern for others' well-being.[34] *Altruism*, performing acts of self-sacrifice, is a hallmark of niceness, and Spider-Man makes one self-sacrifice after another. At times when personal guilt drives him more than concern for others, his motivation is not as inherently kind, but it is in there often. Empirical research shows that love, kindness, and helpfulness not only make life nicer for others but also bolster the person who does them, girding the person against a range of emotional difficulties (e.g., depression, anxiety) and cognitive decline.[35] Spider-Man's depressive tendencies may originate in how lonely and unwelcome he felt among peers as a child, and as an adult, he sometimes thinks of himself as "one of the most depressed people alive."[36] Exercising his strengths of humanity may keep clouds of gloom from engulfing him.

The CSV's authors had trouble deciding whether *social intelligence*, *emotional intelligence*, or *personal intelligence* best fit the strength that essentially boils down to *people smarts*. (They went with social intelligence while acknowledging the other parts.) Peter Parker has his charm, but not enough. If he were stronger in this area, he would not regularly disappoint and anger those close to him and he'd be better at smoothing things over—which is not to call him utterly inept by any means, but this is not his strongest suit. Many times, his quickness to irritation leads him to walk out on people who'd been on the verge of mending fences with him.

Despite his shortcomings in maintaining the balance between his life as Peter Parker and life as Spider-Man, that ongoing effort reinforces his humanity and makes him a stronger person. When Andrew Garfield's grief-gripped version of Spider-Man decides he "has no time for Peter Parker stuff," he becomes more rageful and violent as the vigilante. He feels inspired by Tobey Maguire's Parker who, despite some ups and down in his personal life, including the romantic side with Mary Jane, somehow "makes it work." When Garfield's version wants Tom Holland's Peter to follow a better path, he is acknowledging that his own path should be better. Helping his fellow Spider-Men save others (not only five villains from other worlds but also the younger Peter's girlfriend Michelle) helps Garfield's Spidey work on his own redemption.[37]

Miles Morales demonstrates great humanity from his first appearances. The moment his number is drawn, giving him the opportunity to attend a charter school that can give him a chance at a better life, Miles demonstrates his empathic nature: His first thought is not to celebrate for himself but instead to sympathize for teary-eyed peers whose numbers were not drawn.[38]

The most psychopathic criminals lack empathy, compassion, and love.[39] When some criminals do feel motivated by love of family, they may do so to the exclusion of others, narrowly restricting their strengths of humanity. Some, on the other hand, will sacrifice any individuals as collateral damage for the sake of what they see as the greater good, though often driven more by their own egotistical desire to be the one who makes the decisions for everyone else. At times Spider-Man shakes his head at many supervillains' lack of humanity, baffled by their selfish, petty motives and their waste of great gifts and skills. He says as much to the villain Sauron (a vampiric pterodactyl man who drains the life force of others and has named himself after "that dark lord who personified evil"[40] in *The Lord of the Rings*).

SPIDER-MAN: You can rewrite DNA on the fly, and you're using it to turn people into dinosaurs? But with tech like that, you could cure cancer!

SAURON: But I don't want to cure cancer. I want to turn people into dinosaurs.[41]

Justice

Of the virtues outlined in the CSV, one goes to the heart of super-heroism more than any other: *justice*, the pursuit of what is right, fair, and equitable for everyone. No Marvel superhero has stayed busier or participated in more published adventures in the pursuit of justice than Spider-Man has. The person who prioritizes this virtue, not content to assume that justice will happen on its own, will take action to see it manifest.

To make sense of injustice, especially when tragedy challenges your worldview or how you see yourself (as happens during Spider-Man's origin), you may draw one of three global conclusions: (1) People will get what they deserve (the *just-world phenomenon*[42]) through *natural justice*, (2) there is no justice, or (3) justice happens but people must help make it happen. People who believe in natural justice suffer less stress and depression because the world feels safer to them and they don't feel pressure to make things right.[43] The need to believe in a just world can lead people to make some unjust decisions: The crueler the fate, the more harshly they blame and demean its victims.[44] They *rationalize*, make up rational-feeling explanations, as their own way to cope when faced with unjust situations.[45] This perspective feels reassuring to the person who holds it because most people, even the worst, think of themselves as basically good and deserving of fair treatment. Even criminals may use this argument to derogate their own victims and resent law enforcement for trying to stop them.[46] When Spider-Man tries to stop villains' crimes, they blame him for spoiling their fun and everybody else for driving them to antisocial actions, not themselves for committing crimes. At the other extreme, believing there is no justice, while a depressing view that renders the world bleak and miserable, also lets many feel unpressured to work to make things better because "What's the point?"

Rejecting those justifications for inaction, Peter Parker repeatedly reminds himself of the most active position: that justice exists if people help and work to make it exist. Those who pursue *restorative justice* actively work to reestablish justice after injustice has already occurred. Such efforts can feel empowering and reassuring, and they can be productive.[47] Even though he cannot save Ben, Gwen, or other victims who have already died, saving others helps Spider-Man feel that some measure of justice has been restored overall. Some, though, seek revenge more than repair—*retributive justice*.[48] The Punisher wages his war on crime, destroying criminals because the system has failed to stop them—but more so to take out his anger at them all.[49] Revenge regularly motivates the villains, so they keep attacking the same heroes. Revenge is a complex thing. Many victims' families need to know that perpetrators have been punished. They feel as though such punishment may help them move forward, and for some, it does. The principle of fairness, one of the CSV's justice strengths, focuses more on restoration than retribution when dealing with offenders, differing along dimensions of punishment, compensation, and rehabilitation.[50]

Peter varies in his justice-related strengths. *Citizenship*, feeling connected and obligated to the common good, and *fairness*, treating others in equitable ways, matter a great deal to the friendly neighborhood Spider-Man. These, he can pursue by himself or briefly during his hundreds of single-adventure team-ups with other superheroes, essentially superhero hookups. Although he is capable of both *teamwork*, working together with others, and *leadership*, the power or ability to direct groups, these are not his strengths. Despite many team-ups and stints, he tries to work alone and is commonly perceived as a loner—which makes some fans object when he joins the Fantastic Four briefly or the Avengers for a longer run.[51] When sometimes-girlfriend Felicia Hardy, the Black Cat, works with him, the partnership falls apart after he judges her priorities and they disagree over which laws they should or should not break.[52] When three Peter Parkers from different universes try to fight enemies together, they fare poorly at first because they do not know how to pull together. Andrew Garfield's Peter says outright, "I don't know how to work as a team," and Tobey Maguire's version concurs.[53] Whenever Spider-Man does work with a team, he may offer ideas on what they need to do but tends to defer to others such as Cap, Iron Man, or Luke Cage to take the lead.

The pursuit of justice fills Spider-Man's days and nights. For its sake, he will sacrifice his own security, happiness, and relationships. In terms of his own inclinations in this regard, though, Peter Parker's behavior has been ambiguous at times. In the first version of his origin story, he has no clear reason to allow the burglar to get away, not even annoyance at the person who's getting robbed. He simply does not feel like it. Only after he later he realizes that same burglar is the one who murders Uncle Ben does Peter feel the weight of that decision.[54] Ever since, he keeps reminding himself of that event to make himself keep going. Sometimes, to serve his top values, he has to remind himself of them.

The Value of Values

The CSV authors developed the Values in Action (VIA) inventory,[55] a test to identify which strengths a person values most: the *signature strengths* each individual finds most important and those that come most naturally.[56] Humor, for example, seems one of Spider-Man's signature strengths, even if he sometimes should use it in healthier, more affirming ways. Peter Porker (Spider-Ham—in comics, an anthropomorphic, spider-powered pig that had been a spider until bitten by an irradiated pig)[57] considers humor a defining quality in any universe's spider-hero: "Sometimes this life we've chosen can take a toll on you. But it isn't always just 'great power and great responsibility' that makes a Spider-Man. It's the ability to crack jokes in the face of impossible odds."[58]

Exercising strengths builds them up.[59] Much as we might like to fortify ourselves in every area where we're weakest, research shows that people tend to become happier, more productive, and more successful when they focus on a few where they're already stronger, such as the five ranked highest on the VIA. In Spidey's case, he might try to increase how often he uses healthier humor and to use it more freely in the Peter Parker part of his life. Not only does exercising valued strengths and using them more creatively help them flourish, it also makes individuals conscious of their own priorities. It can be too easy to lose sight of the things that mean the most to us. Whether they do so naturally or by making themselves stay mindful, people who live a *values-driven life* stay more conscious of their core values and live better lives.[60]

Short-term needs can get in the way of long-term priorities. Sometimes we have to keep reminding ourselves of what's truly important.

Mindfulness, the state of focusing attention to stay conscious of something specific in the present moment, does not always come naturally. People may learn tricks and techniques through *mindfulness exercise* to help them become more aware in the moment.[61] A specific phrase, song, image, or memory may help. Reminding himself of specific failures, especially the deaths of Uncle Ben and Gwen Stacy, prods Peter Parker to remember his own values because neglecting them may have gotten his uncle killed.[62] Mindfulness can help people enrich strengths by finding more ways to use them. For example, Spider-Man can remind himself to appreciate other people's humor. Instead of telling Deadpool to shut up when the guy keeps cracking jokes while they're tied up,[63] a mindful Spidey might broaden his strength of humor by sharing

When his crime-fighting campaign and public scorn exhaust him and make him want to quit, remembering those values keeps drawing him back in. *The Amazing Spider-Man* #50 (1967).

someone else's laugh, his patience by accepting Deadpool's need, or his social intelligence by sympathizing when the other guy takes his turn yammering away in the face of danger the way Spidey often does.

Every live-action Spider-Man in the twenty-first century has moments when he needs to be reminded. The versions played by Tobey Maguire and Andrew Garfield each quit when frustrated by failures, only to rush back into the fray once reminded of their purpose and upon seeing emergencies arise.[64] When they lose sight of their greater purpose, they engage in *self-alienation*, the opposite of *authenticity*. "We can improve well-being by identifying and removing ways that we alienate ourselves from our beliefs or ideals," says writer Jan Stanley, noting that empirical research "suggests that looking for ways we can be more aligned with our values, ideals, and images of our true selves is a route to greater well-being."[65] Though stepping away from being Spider-Man momentarily lifts a weight off their shoulders, it does not make either version of him happier overall when he's not being true to himself.[66]

The younger Spider-Man played by Tom Holland loses sight of his core values after Norman Osborn's Green Goblin persona gleefully commits murder. Even as Aunt May staggers, dying, she stresses that saving Osborn and the other criminals is still the right and responsible thing to do. Enraged over the murder, he means to kill Osborn with the Goblin's own glider. Maguire's Spidey reminds him—without a single word, with only a look shared between two men who are alternate versions of the same person—that this is not the way. Reminded of the values his aunt has taught him, Holland's Spider-Man instead injects Osborn with a cure to clear the man's mind and thus finishes the process of saving them all.[67]

If Not a Full Life, Perhaps a Life Well Lived

"The happiest people are those who experience engagement, meaning, *and* pleasure—what we call a full life. Superheroes do not have the fullest possible lives," the CSV's lead author and a colleague observed,[68] noting also that the villains have more fun. They saw that while superheroes epitomize many great strengths and virtues, "everyday people seem *more* likely than superheroes to have *strengths of the heart* that connect them to specific other people: love, kindness, gratitude, and humor." Despite demonstrating one of the better-known senses of humor out of all superheroes, Spider-Man is weaker than many at maintaining stability in his connections to specific others. Through his secret identity, he does stay more involved with everyday people than do many other superheroes, who mainly hang out with detectives, spies, journalists, and fellow supers, but spreading himself thinly between social worlds makes all his relationships lack stability and depth. Through most of his career, not even his best friends among superheroes, such as the Human Torch, know his real name.

The Green Goblin taunts Peter for "struggling to have everything you want while the world tries to make you choose. Gods don't have to choose."[69] These are the words of a villain. They may seem hypocritical coming from a man who, as Norman Osborn, neglects the son he loves in order to build his business, but the point is that when he turns into the Goblin, he feels no love. He mistakes morality, sympathy, and concern about others for weakness, calling Peter "strong enough to have it all, too weak to take it!" The person who lives "the good life," as positive psychologists see it, promotes well-being, builds happiness, and makes the world better for all—for themselves as well as others. Spider-Man chooses the harder path in order to do the most good.

After psychologist Todd Kashdan shifted from simply studying a negative aspect of life (anxiety) to studying how it combines with a positive strength (curiosity), he better understood positive psychology's key principle: Any examination of the worst in life falls short without also considering the better. He also found purpose beyond that. His research "has made me realize that the fundamental objective of my life is not to be happy or have a high frequency of positive emotions, but to have a rich, meaningful existence. That's what I want to inspire in other people as well. In such an existence people are going to have an abundance of both positive and negative experiences. If you don't make mistakes and have moments of intense anxiety, it means you're not taking risks. When you are trying to avoid threats, you can't discover your strengths and figure out how to use them in your life. So for me, it's a shift from looking for the positive to looking to live a life that matters."[70]

Whereas villainy chases self-interest before all others, heroism sacrifices personal interest for the sake of others. Heroism involves doing the right thing at the toughest time, helping and protecting others at great risk or cost to oneself.[71] Much as Spider-Man might like to "have it all" in every area of his life, he voluntarily suffers so that others might not. He draws upon many strengths to try to live up to the values he has been taught by Ben and May and to serve the virtues that he hopes can make the world a better place, that can make the neighborhood a friendlier place to live.

Many might call that a life well lived, a life that matters.

"I needed Spidey in my life as a kid, and he gave me hope . . . He made me, Andrew, braver. He reassured me that by doing the right thing, it's worth it. It's worth the struggle, it's worth the pain, it's worth even the tears and the bruises and the blood. He saved my life."

—actor Andrew Garfield[72]

15

Daring to Dream the Myth Onward: The Persistence of Archetypal Themes in Spider-Man

Kevin Lu

"We, the voice of evolution, the weavers of the web of time, the voice of history, speaking through you, must not be suppressed again. Accept us. Accept who we are. Accept who you are. The man who dreamed of being a spider and the spider who dreamed of being a man . . .

Be the man you are but now, at last, embrace the Other."

—The Other to Peter Parker[1]

"Conscious and unconscious do not make a whole when one of them is suppressed and injured by the other. If they must contend, let it at least be a fair fight with equal rights on both sides . . . Consciousness should defend its reason and protect itself, and the chaotic life of the unconscious should be given the chance of having its way too—as much of it as we can stand. This means open conflict and open collaboration at once."

—analytical psychology founder Carl Gustav Jung[2]

 A storyline that would pave the way for later Spider-Verse epics[3] introduces some unique twists to the Spider-Man mythology: A character called Ezekiel believes that the origins of Spider-Man's powers are more mystical than Peter would care to admit.[4] Ezekiel claims Peter is the current bene-factor in a historical lineage of individuals representing the spider *totem* (primal symbol) and that he has been chosen to bear the responsibili-

ties of this mantle. Because the story reflects the archetypal nature of the totem concept, the theories of Swiss psychiatrist and psychoanalyst Carl Gustav Jung may shed light on the psychological implications of Ezekiel's revelation.

A totem is usually an animal that acts as a guide and guardian, one that is revealed for the first time to those undergoing initiation rites. Your totem tells others to which clan you belong and is also a potential source of superhuman power.[5] Ezekiel explains to Peter:

> Who and what you are bridges the gap between spider and man. But you're not the first. There are totemistic powers that go back to the dawn of time. Their presence remains with us almost like a race memory. Ask a shaman or an Egyptian priest. Ask Eve when the snake spoke to her and offered her a great deal on produce. We tell stories, put on masks, build statues and say prayers to a memory. The memory that once, when the world was new, great forces walked the earth. Forces that bridged the gap between humans and other species.[6]

What Ezekiel offers here fits an accurate definition of Jungian archetypes. The similarity with one of Jung's own definitions is striking: There is a thinking in primordial images, in symbols which are older than the historical man, which are inborn in him from the earliest times, and, eternally living, outlasting all generations, still make up the groundwork of the human psyche. It is only possible to live the fullest life when we are in harmony with these symbols; wisdom is a return to them.[7]

Jung's psychology has undeniably penetrated the mainstream. Concepts such as *introversion/extraversion*, *psychological types*, and *individuation* all stem from analytical (Jungian) psychology. His approach to psychotherapy and the early studies he conducted intuited what are now "norms" of training and standards of practice in diverse fields. For example, Jung's *word association* studies laid the foundation of the so-called lie detector test.[8] The notion that a therapist should sit across from their patient as an equal (rather than having the patient lie down), the practice of writing down your dreams, and the necessity of a therapist undergoing their own analysis are Jungian innovations.

Jungian ideas have inspired comic writers and artists. Jung's *Red Book* may, in fact, be read as a graphic novel—a combination of text and image detailing a personal battle with the unconscious.[9] Whether the use of Jungian concepts by writers and artists is intentional,[10] employing a Jungian lens can heighten our appreciation of psychological themes in comics.

Not only is Spider-Man a typical (archetypal) hero, but the suggestion that there are both chosen representatives of, and pretenders to, various totemic thrones exemplifies the relationship between *archetypes* and *archetypal images* (any images that function as *symbols* representing the archetypes). The development of the totem concept in subsequent storylines—in particular, through the monologue of the Other[11]— illuminates the arduous process of individuation: the need to strip back the public mask (the archetypal *Persona*) to be reborn as a more integral version of who one truly is (the *Self*). Individual consciousness and free will are of the utmost importance when facing aspects of oneself that have been deliberately hidden or of which one is blissfully unaware. Peter's battles with the vampiric villain Morlun provide, when read symbolically, excellent examples of the centrality of consciousness to personality development.[12]

A Hero Is a Hybrid

Have you ever wondered what makes a hero a hero? In his book, *The Hero with a Thousand Faces*, author Joseph Campbell details the so-called *Hero's Journey*, the typical pattern of encounters and challenges that heroes symbolically face.[13] Through a comparative approach, Campbell argues that the cycle constitutes a recurring pattern that is the bedrock of all hero myths and stories. Irrespective of historical time and geographical space, the points that make up the larger pattern consistently reappear. Accordingly, even though Campbell was not strictly Jungian, this pattern may be deemed *archetypal*.

In the totem storyline, for example, Spider-Man ventures forth into a region of supernatural wonder (Peter's increasing involvement with Dr. Strange) where fabulous forces are encountered and decisive victories are won (evidenced by the number of supernatural foes Spider-Man has recently defeated including Morlun, the Shade, Shathra, Dormammu, and Morwen).[14] Spider-Man then returns from these adventures to benefit humanity. After his encounter with the Other, Peter finds a renewed sense of purpose, begins to awaken the untapped power of the spider totem, and saves several innocent people from a collapsed apartment block in the process.[15]

Equally and in parallel with Campbell's hypothesis, have you noticed that most heroes are rarely conceived of as "pure"? Most find themselves caught between opposing realities, and their heroism stems precisely from how they deal with the tension that arises when caught between polarities. This sense of being caught "betwixt and between" has been dubbed *liminality*, the feeling that one inhabits an indeterminate state.[16]

Another way to frame the "in-betweenness" of heroes is by describing them as hybrids. Hybrids do not fit easily into any given category yet are uniquely positioned; they belong to multiple realms while trying to carve an identity that transcends the pigeonholes into which others may fit them. If an attempt is made to locate examples of this motif by engaging in what Jung called *amplification*—uncovering parallels that enhance the theme being investigated—the most illustrious heroes emerge at the front of the line. Alongside Campbell's description of the Hero's Journey, hybridity is an equally important indicator of an archetypal hero. Unsurprisingly, Spider-Man embodies this very hybridity.

While Ezekiel declares Peter to be a direct successor receiving instinctual spider-powers (a pure source of totemistic forces that have existed since the dawn of time), vampiric antagonist Morlun, who would benefit most from feeding on Peter's timeless essence, is not so sure. He confesses to his servant and prisoner, Dex, that there is something "wrong" about Peter.[17] Peter, in turn, never truly embraces Ezekiel's explanation of Peter's proximity to this totemistic source because he knows that he is "impure." The spider that bit him, whether by accident or fateful design, was subjected to a massive dose of radiation. Even if the spider possessed powers before being experimented on, the act of experimentation inevitably changed the spider's nature. Peter's guess is that intensifying those aspects of himself that are "impure," by injecting himself with radiation (to which he has developed some resistance given his original ordeal), will weaken Morlun. It is this very "impurity" at the heart of Peter's embodiment of the spider totem that saves him; it gives him a fighting chance to defeat a nemesis the likes of whom Peter has never encountered. While pulverizing the weakened Morlun, Peter thinks to himself that "the spider and the radiation met in the lab, got hitched in the test tube, and together they produced me. A child of the spider. First cousin to the atom."[18] Peter's hybridity is not a weakness. Rather, it is a potent source of strength. But why is it important to understand hybridity as a trait of the archetypal hero? What does Jung's archetypal theory tell us about Spider-Man's enduring legacy?

The Old and the New

"Whatever the source of your power, you are tied to the spider. It is your icon, your totem, the template for your identity. When you follow the spider, you inherit the ways of the spider. Its natural powers—and its natural enemies."

—Dr. Strange[19]

Spider-Man and the stories we tell about him endure because they reveal insights about human nature, observations that often lie hidden "beneath the surface." At times, readers are challenged to reflect on what is really going on behind the explosions, action sequences, and crumbling buildings. One explanation, from a Jungian perspective, is that the characters and stories touch upon either a universal truth or fundamental experience: They get to the core of what makes us tick. The relatively new, historically speaking, stories about Spider-Man, his allies, and foes may, in fact, be retellings of older stories. Given this historical connection and the symbolic significance attached to it, the Spider-Man mythos provides insight into our humanity: where we have come from, where we have been, where we are right now, and where we are going. After all, humans created these stories about superhuman beings, and knowing something about the motivations driving our storytelling reveals insights into who we are.

Think of this realization—that the contemporary stories we love are rooted, both symbolically and psychologically, to previous ones—as being akin to holding up a mirror to ourselves. The mirror reflects an image of us, but also magnifies details that are easily missed: the wrinkles, scars, blemishes, and canyons running through our skin that may tell a remarkable story. The totem storyline symbolically holds this mirror up to readers. Ezekiel compels us to consider the connection between Peter Parker and the West African/Caribbean spider god, Anansi. Spider-Man is not a character without precursors. By extension, stories about Spider-Man are also connected to the stories of his forerunners. What the totem storyline does so well is to present Spider-Man as a new manifestation of an older god and to connect Spider-Man's legacy to a larger cultural and archetypal history of the human species.

Archetypes and Life's Goal

What makes a human life "human"? What are the events and situations that distinguish a human life from all others?[20] While on the surface, cultures around the world celebrate difference, Jung was more interested in unearthing cross-cultural similarities. For example, most cultures celebrate the birth of a new child and mourn the death of loved ones. The way these rituals are conducted changes, but the psychological need to perform them remains. We inherit a bare-bones scaffolding, rather than any specific memory or way of doing things.[21] That is why Jungians often say that an archetype itself is unknowable (as an underlying, unconscious theme) and that only aspects of it become known through archetypal images or symbols.[22] (The Hero archetype, as an abstract and inherited motif, manifests through Spider-Man, King Arthur, and countless other heroes who symbolize that underlying pattern—the "thousand faces" of Campbell's book title.)[23]

The psychological goal in life is to become more aware of these often darker, hidden aspects of our personality, what Jung terms the *process of individuation*. The more that is known about the unconscious, the lesser the likelihood it will take on an uncontrollable, monstrous form when it seeks acknowledgment and attention. Individuals can engage these archetypal figures/totems, talk to them, and negotiate a way forward that neither jeopardizes everyday reality nor neglects the unconscious aspects of personality. For Jung, individuation is a heroic call to arms that should not be ignored. (The psychological process of understanding one's own public Persona, private Shadow, and other archetypes correspond with steps in individuation.) Disregarding this call can have disastrous consequences, which Peter learns all too well when he meets the Other.

Persona, the Self, and Individuation

Peter's confrontation with the Other is a prime example of the need to enter a constructive dialogue with internal figures/totems. The Other imparts to Peter some valuable advice if he is to continue being Spider-Man or, from a psychological perspective, if he is to follow his own path of individuation with honesty, sincerity, and authenticity.

His spider-powers may represent instincts that are embodied (for example, his spider-sense). There is always a lingering possibility, from the very conception of our friendly neighborhood hero, that he represents something larger, and that some *thing* is "alive" in him. Through Ezekiel's revelation, Peter is catapulted into a process of self-discovery, retrieving memories of when the spider bite happened and trying to come to terms with the more mystical and "irrational" explanations of his power's origins. These explanations sit in tension with his logical, scientific mind. Although Peter is not on intellectual par with Reed Richards, he is no slouch either. Through an analysis of Morlun's DNA, Peter deciphers a working hypothesis and hatches a plan that allows him to defeat Morlun. This tension between the rational and irrational, the scientific and mystical, reflects and amplifies the psychological and existential struggle with which Peter is grappling: Who is the man and who is the spider? In Jungian psychology, if an unconscious aspect of an individual is not made conscious, if the person makes no attempt to come to terms with their hidden dimensions of depth, they are in danger of losing the balance between their conscious and unconscious lives. When this imbalance occurs, the psyche gives us nudges and clues in the form of bodily symptoms, dreams, and even fantasies. For Jung, these symptoms are not entirely negative. While they may portend the negative consequences of being stuck in old patterns of interaction, they are equally invitations to change our current condition—an opportunity to do things differently, to turn our lives around.

After Peter emerges (barely) from his fateful meetings with Morlun and Shathra, still reeling from Ezekiel's betrayal, he does not yet fully embrace his connection to the spider totem. Consequently, the ultimate manifestation of a bodily symptom afflicts him: Peter is dying. That which has stricken him deteriorates his body, and nobody—not even Mr. Fantastic, Iron Man, Black Panther, and Dr. Strange combined—can find the underlying cause of Peter's ailment. From a Jungian perspective, what afflicts Peter is not something physical, but psychological. The symptoms are both a wakeup call and an invitation to learn more about himself—to accept those parts of his personality he has denied.

The reincarnation of Morlun constitutes the return of an archetypal figure from Peter's past with which he has not sufficiently dealt. Symbolically, something needs to "die" in Peter, be it either an old perspective or psychological defense preventing him from integrating the lessons learned from previous (psychological) battles. The Other declares that what needs to die in Peter is his dogged attachment to a Persona:

> The spider was just a piece of cloth. An empty husk, from which you could emerge human, normal, as though the spider was not still inside you. Putting it on meant that you could take it off. But now the spider has taken you off . . . You did not look too deeply into what you had become or what you could do. You committed the crime of superficiality.[24]

The Persona, according to Jung, is the social mask one wears to operate and survive in society. Everyone can, and should, have multiple masks. Depending on the situation, people can choose which mask they wear to perform the task at hand. The Persona, therefore, is connected to *decorum*, the ability to act in an appropriate manner given the circumstances in which individuals find themselves. For Jung, there is nothing wrong with the Persona per se. Psychological difficulty occurs when the ego over-identifies with a particular mask—believing that a person's identity only amounts to *this* role and nothing more.[25] The crime Peter commits is resigning himself to the comfort of mediocrity. He decides to play it safe and therefore remains stuck to the cloth mask he wears, but one that barely scratches the surface of his true potential. Individuation, however, cannot be attained without taking a risk. In "rolling the dice," Peter may either achieve his fullest potential or he may fall flat on his face. But what matters is making the decision to "show up," to take the risk, and to place the bet.

Peter has over-identified with the outward Persona of the spider but this is merely a façade and an excuse to ignore the big "S" Spider within—an image of his true capacities, what Jung terms the archetypal *Self*.[26] Rather than taking the time to dialogue with his totemic source, Peter chooses to indulge the more trivial aspects of his power, stopping short before anything more exciting or disturbing could be discovered. Disregarding a vocational calling to become more than what he is not only leads to debilitating symptoms, it also invites the manifestation of Peter's undeveloped *Self* in a most terrifying form—the pure spider essence that awakens to feed on Morlun.

Before Peter is invited, through dream, to dialogue with the neglected Other, a sacrifice is demanded. Much like Odysseus who sacrifices his best lamb to Tiresias before seeking his counsel, Peter needs to give up a part of himself prior to meeting the Other within. Like Luke and Anakin Skywalker losing hands, Peter loses an eye. Having paid the necessary price, he is ready to be initiated into his physical death and psychological rebirth. He is chided and reminded, in equal measure, of his responsibility to cultivate his connection to his Spider (archetypal) side.[27]

The rebirth motif is a central metaphor Jung uses to describe both individuation and the necessity of coming closer to realizing our fullest potential.[28] The story of Peter's death, rebirth, and confrontation with the Other not only lends itself to Jungian interpretation, but it also deepens our awareness of how significant these psychological events are and that they should not be ignored. While the Other leaves no doubt regarding the arduous path that lies ahead, it remains Peter's prerogative to choose. The unconscious will only give so many warnings. The rest is up to Peter.

Coming Full Circle
HYBRIDITY, CONSCIOUSNESS, AND FREE WILL

Is Peter the human "husk" who dreams of a Spider, or the Spider that dreams of becoming conscious in man? Whether Peter will ever realize the full extent of his powers is not the point. What can be appreciated, from a psychological perspective, is Peter's right to choose. This touches upon an often overlooked but central principle in Jungian psychology—the most significant factor in psychological development is not the unconscious, but consciousness.

Everything that resides in the unconscious lies in potential. It is the task of individual consciousness to make that which is unconscious, conscious. Stated another way, it is an individual's prerogative to choose how they live the ancestral energies, patterns, and instincts that constellate throughout life. One can do this in either a constructive or destructive manner. Peter chooses the former, which is why, as a hybrid comprised of both god-like qualities and human fallibility, he becomes the perfect vehicle for the spider totem's continuance and vitality.

The spider totem selects Peter to house and mediate its energies. He, in turn, exercises his own free will. His decision to use his powers in the service of good is what saves him, both from Morlun and, eventually, Ezekiel and a character known as the Gatekeeper. Peter—the human, individual spark of consciousness—is just as important as the totemic power with which he is entrusted. Peter is, according to Ezekiel, "the real deal," not merely because he is closer to the instinctual, archetypal source of the spider, but because Peter chooses to live out that energy ethically and in line with his own values (as addressed in chapter 14). Humanity chooses what to do with the power it is given.

Morlun, being a combination of every type of cell and possessing one of the purest forms of DNA, logically should have killed Peter during both their encounters. Morlun does a surprisingly effective job of beating Peter within an inch of his life. But psychologically, Peter wins because his ethics and values ensure his survival and, by extension, the endurance of that instinctual energy with which he has been gifted. Pretenders to these archetypal thrones—including a host of animal-inspired villains Peter has fended off—only mimic archetypal truths "to get a momentary taste of totemistic force."[29] They can don the Persona, but they cannot get to the numinous essence of the totem itself.

What sets Peter apart—aside from the cheekiness, occasional silly joke, and cheesy one-liners that are part and parcel of any Trickster—is his integrity. And that is something you cannot fake; that is not something you can pretend to be. Peter is perfectly imperfect. He is a representative of the spider totem and a contemporary archetypal image that tells us as much about Jung's archetypal hypothesis as he does the human condition.

Kevin Lu, PhD, is a tenured professor and head of the department of psychosocial and psychoanalytic studies, University of Essex. His publications include articles and chapters on C. G. Jung's relationship to the discipline of history, Arnold J. Toynbee's use of Jungian psychology, critical assessments of the theory of *cultural complexes*, sibling relationships in the Chinese/Vietnamese diaspora, racial hybridity, and Jungian perspectives on comics and film. Originally from Toronto, Canada, Kevin now resides with his family in England.

16

You'd Think Having Superpowers Would Make Life Easier

David Schwartz

"Fate gave me some terrific super-powers, and I realize now that it's my duty to use them."

—**Peter Parker**[1]

"Life is never completely without its challenges."

—**Stan Lee, Spider-Man co-creator**[2]

If you suddenly found yourself with superpowers, how would you use them? Perhaps you'd think about how you could make some money or become really famous and popular. Maybe you'd want your own TV series. All logical thoughts. Probably not at the top of your agenda would be becoming a crime-fighter. What could possibly motivate you to wear a costume, chase down supervillains, and risk your life every day? After all, unless you're invulnerable, being a superhero is pretty risky. Even if you have the powers of Spider-Man, for example, with super-strength and agility, you're still mortal. You can still be hurt or even killed! The odds might be with you, but that doesn't mean you're always going to win. No matter how you look at it, being a superhero is dangerous.

What would be some of the factors that could cause someone to go into this line of work? People who are intrinsically drawn to help others might see a new ability as a gift that allows them to do so. However, when you factor in the risks and dangers involved, it would take someone fully committed to the idea of helping humanity to make that leap into the superhero business.[3]

Another type of person who might feel drawn to becoming a superhero could be a *thrill seeker*. Psychologically speaking, a thrill seeker might be enthusiastic about the idea of pursuing risk or danger for the sheer rush,[4] but not all of us are thrill seekers.[5] Someone who scores high in *thrill seeking*, which is one form of *sensation seeking*, would likely revel in the exciting opportunities afforded by superpowers and show greater risk-taking in applying them.[6] This might be amplified during adolescence,[7] but anyone gaining great powers would likely think long and hard about the best ways to use them. After all, the police and the public at large may not be admirers of a do-gooding vigilante. Authorities may be distrustful and suspicious. Yet, in Spider-Man's case, he risks his life day after day after day for little or no reward. The big psychological question is, why?

The Original Motivator

Young Peter Parker is not a thrill seeker by any stretch of the word. He is not interested in being a do-gooder or receiving praise from the public. His first thoughts after becoming Spider-Man are to benefit financially for himself and his family.[8] Only after a personal tragedy does he feel driven to fight crime. He is not instinctively drawn toward it.

Spider-Man's first appearance is a modest beginning for a character who would become one of the most popular comic book characters of all time, if not *the* most.[9] When looking for a strong protagonist, it would be hard to find someone more relatable than Peter Parker. He is young, insecure, and an underdog who people can root for and care about.[10] Much research has shown that people appreciate someone who struggles to achieve their success. Under certain circumstances, they find them more attractive for making the effort to take on opponents who seem to have an unfair advantage over them.[11] Many people feel inclined to adopt the underdog's emotional perspective,[12] perhaps feeling some affinity because of a tendency to think they themselves deserve better in their lives. Personal feelings of *relative deprivation* may thus incline people to empathize with the teenage orphan and the hero who keeps facing uphill battles.

Few comic book heroes struggle as much as Peter. He is a put-upon, ridiculed, and unpopular person. He is also a favorite target of the school bully Flash Thompson. Flash acts like a typical high school bully, who sees someone's weaknesses and takes advantage of them.[13] He belittles Peter in front of classmates,[14] calls him names,[15] and threatens his safety.[16] Over time, this type of bullying can cause someone to retreat from social interactions.[17] The bully's victim may tend to withdraw emotionally as it can feel unsafe to express who they really are.[18] By hiding their own desires and feelings, they may detach emotionally to protect themselves.[19] While this emotional shield can help protect them from being emotionally hurt, it can also shut down their feelings. Over time, this can lead to depression, less connection with others, and self-isolation.[20]

Peter Parker recognizes his unpopularity. He knows that he's seen by his classmates as someone they've mostly written off and this produces its own scars on his emotional makeup. He is living many of our worst fears. He is the underdog we want to see succeed, the underdog many of us have felt like at one time or another.[21] These weaknesses make him more relatable. To one extent or another, too many people have experienced what Peter goes through, and can therefore relate to his struggles.

The Relatable Superhero

While many superhero comic books at the time (during Spider-Man's earliest years of publication) focused primarily on the action taking place, Spider-Man stories would focus just as much on characterization. A slew of supporting characters with developed personalities populate his world. J. Jonah Jameson, Peter's boss and newspaper publisher, constantly criticizes Spider-Man and spends his time trying to turn the public against the hero. Peter's girlfriend in the early comic books is Betty Brant, Jameson's secretary, which creates for Betty a rivalry with Peter's classmate Liz Allen. As the series progresses, the triangle romance between Peter and his love interests changes to Gwen Stacy and Mary Jane Watson, but still maintains the soap opera elements between the characters. It is these interpersonal relationships that help the reader relate to Peter's struggles and make Spider-Man feel even more real.[22] It is also these relatable situations that help people accept the supernatural elements in the stories. After all, if the reader believes in the reality that's been created, it's easier to suspend disbelief for the fantasy elements.[23]

Another relatable aspect of Spider-Man was that he isn't perfect. While other superheroes seem more confident and surer of themselves, Spider-Man often messes up.[24] He doesn't always fit in or say the right thing. He may jump the gun and interfere with would-be criminals before they've committed the crime.[25] He may become overconfident and let his ego put him in danger.[26] He may even lose his temper and lash out at other superheroes who are trying to help him.[27]

Spider-Man's early episodes are filled with struggles that readers can relate to and understand. He has to ask permission from his aunt to travel to Florida to fight the Lizard.[28] The dangers he faces as Spider-Man drive a wedge between him and his girlfriend.[29] He worries he is losing his grip on reality.[30] When he tears his face mask, he has to choose between capturing the supervillain and protecting his secret identity.[31] These internal and external conflicts are some of the things that have always endeared Spider-Man to readers. From the beginning, readers could feel his pain. We could identify with his struggles. Even though he has extraordinary powers, he still has to deal with life's setbacks just like the rest of us.

When Superman fights some giant gorilla or alien monster, it may be an exciting adventure, but it doesn't necessarily grab us emotionally. When Spider-Man pushes himself and strains to lift tons of machinery under which he is trapped, literally lifting a weight off his back so he can secure the medication he needs to save his Aunt May's life, readers not only care about his efforts, they care about both of the characters involved because of their struggles.[32] Spider-Man feels like a friend, which helps the reader become invested in his success.

We can also relate to Peter Parker's world. Many of us know first-hand the difficulties he faces. We understand that teenagers can be cruel, cliquish, and self-centered. Teens are figuring out who they are and, as such, don't always give others a lot of thought. They can be self-focused and so absorbed in their own needs that they think mostly of themselves and not the other people in their lives.[33] While this can be true regardless of a person's age, it can be especially true of teenagers.[34] The lack of consideration he has received from many of his peers has led to Peter having quite a large chip on his shoulder.[35]

Peter sees his new powers as a gift that will enable him to live a more exciting life and to take care of himself and his family. Typical of self-focused teenagers, he does not see a larger picture where he would have a responsibility to use his powers to help people. On the contrary, he does not believe he owes anybody anything. He initially wants to use his powers to make money. The fame and adulation are merely by-products of his desire to help his family financially. He spells it out quite clearly in his origin, thinking about the love he has for his aunt and uncle who raised him: "I'll see to it that they're always happy, but the rest of the world can go hang for all I care!"[36] These are the thoughts of a teenager who has been emotionally hurt by his peers. He sees his newfound powers as a means to take control of his life and concentrate on the people who have been there for him. He doesn't see any reason to help anyone but his immediate family.

The Driving Force

To one extent or another, Spider-Man has spent decades haunted by the death of his uncle and the guilt he feels because of it. It is this incident that turns him from a self-serving teenager to a driven young man, determined to stop crime. His original desire to make money (*extrinsic motivation*, driven by ulterior purpose) shifts to an intrinsic need to take care of others (*intrinsic motivation*, driven to perform an action for its own sake). He determines that no one else will suffer due to his inaction. Peter is gripped by an obsessive need to protect people from danger. This is not something he has chosen freely. It is something he feels compelled to do because of the guilt he feels from his previous inaction—a guilt that now controls him. From this moment onward, every criminal he stops is part of a greater effort to reduce the weight of responsibility he feels for his uncle's death.[37] This compulsion no longer allows Peter to lead a normal life. When he becomes aware of someone in trouble, he will leave his school studies, become unreliable with his friends, and lose many nights of sleep due to his strong urge to stop crime.

Spider-Man creators Stan Lee and Steve Ditko's master stroke in creating the character was giving him as strong a motivation as any in the Marvel or DC universes. His momentary failure to stop the criminal who ultimately kills his Uncle Ben has been directly responsible for creating his psychological compulsion to help others.[38] He consistently runs toward whatever danger appears and rarely thinks of his own safety. The needs of anyone in danger take priority. He is on what appears to be a lifelong treadmill of being controlled by his sense of responsibility to others. Clearly, this pressure would take a strong psychological toll on anyone, especially a teenager.

Peter's Aunt May

Though Aunt May has gotten progressively younger in the blockbuster Spider-Man movies, she is initially introduced as a frail, older woman. Aunt May has health problems from nearly the start of the series and is one of the reasons Peter Parker wants to keep his identity a secret. At first, he fears that if he were arrested, it would break his aunt's heart,[39] and as her health worsens, he worries that her heart might not be able to handle the shock of learning he is Spider-Man.[40]

While Aunt May's health problems are of primary concern, she also contributes much wisdom to the teenage Peter Parker. She has been an instructional and positive inspiration to Peter throughout the series. For example, when Peter's concern for his aunt's health causes him to stop pursuing his adventures as Spider-Man for fear she couldn't handle the shock if he were injured, it is his Aunt May who shows him the importance of standing up for what you believe in and not being a quitter.[41] She helps to strengthen his confidence and sense of family.

Clicking a Switch

Over the years, Peter Parker has found ways to compartmentalize his guilt to be able to maintain friendships and connections with people. This enables him to live what appears to be a normal life with his friends and family. However, when he learns of someone in trouble, it's like a switch clicks and everything else falls by the wayside. He is driven to deal with the danger at hand. This proverbial switch controls his actions. He is not in a position to choose; he only reacts. How many of us understand what it's like to be controlled by things that happened in our past? How many times have we responded to situations automatically because of our past experiences? For many of us, when our emotions become activated, they control our actions.

With this understanding, Spider-Man can be viewed as a tragic figure. He exudes good spirit and energy, jokes around with people, and seems to not have a care in the world. However, beneath the surface, he is living a life of compulsion. He stays on a continuous treadmill trying to make right a situation that can't be fixed. His guilt and sense of responsibility compel him to fight crime day after day, year after year, no matter how it affects the rest of his life.

Courting Danger

One of the downfalls of living a life where you chase danger is that it can bring danger toward the people you care about the most. By constantly putting himself in the path of everyday criminals and supervillains alike, he also places the people in his life at risk. Over the decades, this has resulted in the deaths of his beloved Gwen Stacy,[42] her police captain father,[43] and major villains such as the Green Goblin.[44] While Spider-Man does not cause their deaths directly, their proximity to his orbit becomes a factor in them. This means that even as Spider-Man may someday be able to emotionally heal from his uncle's death, there are fresh losses that reinforce the initial trauma and help keep him on the treadmill of fighting crime.

J. Jonah Jameson admits to himself that petty motivation drives his attacks against Spider-Man in *The Amazing Spider-Man* #10 (1964). Art by Steve Ditko.

While Spider-Man fights tirelessly for people in need, not everyone sees his efforts as heroic. For example, Peter's newspaper boss, *Daily Bugle* publisher J. Jonah Jameson, bears a strong hatred for Spider-Man for many years.[45] This means that even as Spider-Man risks his life to save people, he is rarely hailed a hero. Jameson's motive is revealed as extreme jealousy in an early comic book issue. Jameson says to himself, "Spider-Man represents everything that I'm not! He's brave, powerful and unselfish. The truth is, I envy him!"[46] Due to Jameson's jealousy, the *Daily Bugle* regularly attacks Spider-Man and fosters distrust by the public. There are times he's even labeled a criminal. Yet, even when he is vilified and misunderstood, Spider-Man maintains his resolve to help others.

The Journey Continues

Over the decades, Spider-Man has traveled into outer space,[47] had a symbiotic being overtake him then become a life form of its own,[48] and grown from his high school years into adulthood. With all these experiences, at his core he is still working through the trauma faced by a teenage boy whose inaction inadvertently causes the death of his uncle. The psychological stress, guilt, and shame that this event causes in his life helps form the impetus that turn him into a crime-fighter, and endures as the main motivating factors in his life.

"As Peter Parker, I was just a helpless, confused school kid! But as Spider-Man, things are gonna be a lot different."
—Peter Parker[49]

David Schwartz, MS, LMFT, is a Licensed Marriage and Family Therapist (LMFT #87261) in Southern California. Earlier in his career, he was an animation writer working on numerous television programs, including *DuckTales*, *Jonny Quest*, *The Addams Family*, and many others. David has been a comic book fan and collector since he was eight years old, with his first Marvel comic being an early issue of *Spider-Man*.

When artificial influences alter good people in ways that unleash the worst parts of themselves, Spidey tries to restore them to who they really are. Like real people whose body chemistries have been altered, not everyone will recover, but some will.

Dr. Curt Connors experiments on himself, trying to regrow his missing arm. It comes back, but he transforms. The Lizard's debut back in 1963's *The Amazing Spider-Man #6* ends with Spidey curing the reptilian villain, who transforms back into Connors (for a while). Art by Steve Ditko.

Lily Hollister accidentally knocks over Green Goblin chemicals, which change her into the supervillain Menace. After Peter returns, Spidey injects her with a cure that brings Lily back in *Superior Spider-Man #31* (2014). Art: G. Gamuncoli, J. Dell, & T. Pallot.

Time and time again, Spidey seeks to save people, including metamorphed foes. The next chapter takes a deeper dive into Peter's belief in in recovery and redemption. The guilt-ridden hero needs to believe.

—T.L.

17

The "Cure" for Spider-Man: Therapy Offers an Alternate Way Home

William Sharp with Eric D. Wesselmann

"I've been working on curing super-criminals and reforming them. Time to put my money where my mouth is."
—Peter Parker[1]

"Where once psychoanalysis freed people to be ordinary—to suffer common unhappiness—now it frees them to become what was once the privilege of the gifted and reckless few."
—psychoanalyst Adam Phillips[2]

 ans associate Spider-Man stories with the themes of personal responsibility, hope for positive change, and redemption. Peter Parker, though often written as a tortured do-gooder who can never seem to catch a break, is ultimately a character of optimism committed to seeing the best in people and thus helping reform those who have lost their way. Even when the odds are against him, he asserts that "the decency in a single human heart" can overcome an onslaught of supervillains and that the love expressed in second chances has the power "to shake the world!"[3] What makes Peter such a compelling character might be "his unwavering belief that all life—even that of the vilest supervillain—is worth saving."[4] Spider-Man stories in every medium show examples

of Peter giving criminals and supervillains second chances to reform their lives, often at his own risk.[5] At one point, he even shows compassion to unapologetic mass-murderer Carnage, suggesting that the lifetime of physical and psychological abuse that Carnage suffered should evoke understanding rather than punishment from others: "In his own fashion, he just may be the most innocent of all!"[6] Curing supervillains who have turned to villainy largely because of accidents or addictions becomes a key plot element in the film *Spider-Man: No Way Home*. In some ways, Peter may be seen as a superhero equivalent of a therapist or other mental health worker. But what does it mean to "cure" in psychology? Who gets to decide what healthy or better living looks like?

What Is "Cure"?

When you are having a heart attack, there is a clear treatment protocol. If your arm is broken, there is an idea about what cure looks like. But what is a cure in psychotherapy? If you are depressed, does a cure mean you are less depressed? Free of depression? Ecstatically happy? Some patients come into the consulting room with an idea about why they are coming, but others are not sure. They may have an idea that they want to change, but goals may evolve through the course of treatment. Sometimes the patient may be replacing one problem for another. One good thing to do as a therapist is to ask questions: What does the patient want? How do they think they can get it? And what do they feel gets in the way of doing what needs to be done? When the therapist forgets to ask these questions, and when Peter Parker goes into action trying to fix supervillains without finding out what they want, there is no alliance to build the work on. Should Spider-Man send all the deviant villains back to their own universe? Or should he save them from their own destruction? Peter Parker's adventures as Spider-Man can be a metaphor for the treatment process. His own struggles around what to do with Doc Ock, Green Goblin, Electro, Sandman, and other villains lead us back to a repeating question: *What is cure?*

Spider-Man and therapists alike struggle with the concept of "curing" someone. Denial and repression can work against certain goals. Building therapeutic alliances and identifying good guys from bad guys are all part of the work of both psychotherapist and web-slinger alike. Things get even more complicated as we consider players from beyond the consulting room that get drawn into our worlds of therapy, for example, medical versus social models of mental health, insurance companies, and well-meaning families. These can all feel like they are from other universes and make any progress toward cure difficult.

Alleviating Symptoms vs. Going on an Adventure?
Spider-Man and Dr. Strange

> "Cure. Cure some ass."
> —Tobey Maguire's Peter Parker[7]

"An extraordinary aim for psychoanalysis [is] to be on better terms with one's primary process."
—psychoanalyst Adam Phillips[8]

Some believe that to *cure* is to have a problem removed. Peter has tried to give up being Spider-Man multiple times from the start of his hero career[9] in various iterations of the character, but the experience usually does not meet his expectations and he returns to leading his dual life.[10] This should be a clue that sometimes the first solution isn't always the obvious. The psychoanalyst Adam Phillips writes that sometimes we think about "change" but in the end, the life you want "is an odd, surprising compound of the life you thought you wanted and the life you discovered you wanted; of the life you have and the life you aspire to."[11] After Peter realizes they brought villains to his universe, Dr. Strange quotes the old adage, "Be careful what you wish for."[12] The same could be said of starting therapy: Sometimes the outcome is different than imagined and the old life you had looks appealing again. Characters looking for cure find this out the hard way sometimes; for example, Dr. Connors experiments on himself to regrow his missing arm and instead mutates into the Lizard.[13] Michael Morbius tries to cure himself of a rare, fatal blood disease and instead turns himself into a vampire-like creature, cursed with a primal need for blood.[14]

The many forms of therapy approach cure differently. Some approaches follow manuals with defined goals, steps, and protocols for conducting each session.[15] These therapies attempt to change thoughts and behaviors, with the belief that feelings will naturally follow or don't matter. There are a number of published workbooks and treatment planners a therapist can buy to map out how to treat a problem, regardless of the patient. But getting these goals from a book does not acknowledge the unique and complex human before them, a person with a history and *will to meaning* (the will to seek meaning in life).[16] Dynamic therapies such as psychoanalysis, humanistic, expressive, and art therapies, to name but a few, focus more on feelings and as such get difficult to define and measure objectively. There is no manual. Many therapists employing manual techniques ultimately extend treatment beyond the twelve sessions the approach calls for, finding themselves engaging in a talking process and building an alliance with their patient even though it is not part of the "how to" manual. Surely, this is a sign that, in the end, we all realize there is a human being behind the mask the patient presents wearing.

To the therapist, insurance companies and managed care can feel like invading villains from some other universe as well. Too often the relationship between therapist and patient gets discounted as the insurance company seeks protocols based on short-term and therefore cheaper costs. Some see alleviating the symptoms as "cure" enough ("The person is depressed, so help them get out of bed and out to work. That's living."). There is a danger, though, when people besides the client determine the goal of treatment. Ultimately a judgment is being made. That judgment can be based by the majority or those in power—either within a moral or medical model—and not right for the individual patient. People don't fit nicely into one diagnostic category or approach from a book. For a therapist employing a personal model, cure is something much more individualized and a product of the universe created between therapist and patient, without invaders from the multiverse of madness.

Dr. Strange, trained as a surgeon, comes from a medical model. If there is a problem, directly alleviate it. Before seeking treatment, a common attempt at cure for some patients involves avoidance or "forgetting." It is no wonder, then, that when Peter Parker approaches Dr. Strange, he wants a quick fix and Dr. Strange helps in the way he was originally trained. He performs a spell of forgetting from the Runes of Kof-Kol. It doesn't work as intended and, as in our universe with patients, this hasty, initial treatment makes things worse. For Peter and Dr. Strange, they fracture the borders between universes. For patients, the "spells" cast are powerful defense mechanisms, namely *denial* (refusing to recognize a disturbing truth) and *repression* (locking away a disturbing memory, feeling, or thought).[17] They can lead to similarly fractured and incomplete lives for patients. These defensive spells may not do what they expected. The problem comes from not looking for the root causes, and that oversight can lead to a multiverse of problems. It is important to remember to treat and not just to cure.

Enter Sigmund Freud, founder of psychoanalysis. He proposed that our personalities were collections of reactions to our early life situations. They emerged as defense structures built to deal with conflict and frustration and they served a purpose. In the present, they become neurotic patterns of having or avoiding feelings. These side effects are what people call *symptoms*, but they are a part of everyone's character and not necessarily a problem to be fixed. So, what is cure in this approach? What does "cure" mean? It goes back to working with the patient to find out what they are seeking. Do they want better relationships? Do they want to be more assertive when pursuing a promotion? The psychoanalyst, like Peter Parker, has to be open to the twists and turns of an adventure and sometimes the dangers of exploring what a supervillain or patient may seek.

Therapists coming from dynamic approaches start with exploratory questions and are supposed to be free from any preconceived ideas about what a person should be doing. Psychoanalysis is an analysis of the psyche, an attempt by the analyst to understand but not necessarily change anything for the patient, although once understood the patient may have an insight about themselves and seek change. Any change in behavior, thought, or feeling is a side effect of the work. Psychoanalyst and essayist Adam Phillips writes, "One of the things psychoanalytic treatment can do is enable people to actually explore the nature of their wanting, because their objects of desire may have been foisted upon them, as opposed to being ones that they discover."[18]

Such may be the case with the cat burglar, Felicia Hardy, the Black Cat. Hardy begins her reformation process when she first becomes attracted to and then partners up with Spider-Man. However, she often struggles with defining her own moral convictions and self-concept of heroism.[19] Peter regularly serves as an inspiration and moral exemplar for her, continuingly motivating her to grow as an individual. For example, when Peter decides to reveal his secret identity publicly during Marvel's *Civil War* arc, he exposes himself and his family to constant danger simply because he was following his moral code. Because of this, the Black Cat again gets inspired on her journey of self-knowledge and notes how he has reminded her that "it's never too late to figure out who you really are."[20]

Exploring the Multiverse: What's Up?

"Now all we gotta do is lure these guys someplace, right? Try to cure them, while they try to kill us."
—Andrew Garfield's Peter Parker[21]

"The pluralistic universe—the title of one of William James's books—was what he called a 'multiverse' of unpredictable variety and possibility."
—psychoanalyst Adam Phillips[22]

When Peter Parker mentions fixing the multiverse trespassers, Doc Ock says, "Fix? Like a dog?" and the Lizard chimes in with "Trust me, Peter, when you try to fix people, there are always consequences." And in some ways, this is the problem when the "cure" is coming from outside the unique goals of the patient. It is pointed out to Peter that his so-called helping is strong-arming: You either get fixed or return to your point of origin to meet your fate. Adam Phillips writes, "It is possible that the analysis can only begin when the patient (and the analyst) have acknowledged what their concept of cure may be a refuge from."[23] A good exploratory question at intake is "What's up?" It can be invaluable to get the patient talking. The invitation is for the patient to bring whatever *they* want to their session. Freud cautions against wishes, predictions, or desires coming from the psychoanalyst.[24]

Dr. Otto Octavius, a.k.a. Dr. Octopus or simply "Doc Ock," is the first villain to appear in the film *No Way Home*. When nanotechnology from Peter's suit infiltrates Octavius's octopus arms, Peter can slow down his rampage. The therapeutic alliance that builds up is important in treatment and is best when mutually worked on and agreed to over time. Eventually, that feeling of being with the therapist can be internalized so the patient carries some nano-like aspect of the treatment in their own mind. The patient can start asking themselves, "What would my therapist say?" and then devise their own plan from there.

The second villain who appears, Green Goblin/Norman Osborn, is reminiscent of the cases presented in psychoanalyst Brett Kahr's book *Bombs in the Consulting Room*.[25] In both *Spider-Man: No Way Home* and Kahr's book, we meet characters that are truly in need of our understanding and help, but who have some explosive quality to their character. Norman Osborn shows up at FEAST, the shelter where Aunt May works, because he has seen a sign and wants some help. "He's lost," May describes him. "I don't just mean in the cosmos. In his mind."[26] Here May challenges Peter's plan to just send the multiverse trespassers home without any intervention. After Peter contends, "Sending them home is the best thing we can do for them," May points out that the plan might the best thing for himself but not necessarily for the "villains." May says, "This is what we do. We help people."[27]

Aunt May is like a therapist's supervisor who points out that when in the room with patients, the work has to go at the patient's pace and attend to their needs and what they came for, not those of the insurance company or well-meaning families, and certainly not out of the therapist's desires. Kahr's cases reveal how much he would have liked to discharge or even blame the patient for their problems—sending them back to the referral source so they could be someone else's problem, but Kahr has come to learn that clients reveal much through nonverbal communication, and so he reminds us again that all behavior is an attempt at communication. Aunt May gets this and it is why she wants Peter to think of alternative ways to "cure" the problem and not to just take the path that is easiest for him.

The Lizard/Dr. Curt Connors offers a darker perspective on "cure" when he develops a megalomaniacal idea that "everyone should just be like me," essentially deciding he should cure people of their own humanity and its associated woes in the film *The Amazing Spider-Man*.[28] Dr. Connors's idea to turn everyone into a lizard needs to be checked in the same way that all therapists need to check their own wishes and goals for patients at the door if they truly want to allow the patient to determine their own path, uniqueness, and eventual individualization.

For Electro/Max Dillon, the new world he finds in *No Way Home* seems better than the one he came from, offering him both corporeal form and a tantalizing source of power.[29] An escape into illness may sometimes be an attempt at cure for some patients (trying to flee from life's stressors but trading one set of problems for another). Psychoanalysts will often allow a patient their defenses because they served a purpose—they helped the character survive an ordeal. However, those defenses prevent them from getting other things that they might want, or from doing things in an easier fashion. In today's modern psychoanalysis, *joining* is a therapeutic technique to working with resistances in which the analyst "goes with or sides with" the patient's conscious lived experience. Freud wrote that sometimes a real cure feels dangerous and so the unconscious convinces the conscious mind that what is in the here-and-now is better than a cure, "The consequence is that the ego's attitude to the cure itself is that of defense against a new danger."[30]

Sandman/Flint Marko, who eventually helps the Spider-Man of his universe, is a good example of the importance of the relationship between therapist and patient, or the *therapeutic alliance*. As mentioned earlier, the therapeutic alliance is when the therapist and patient can use each other in supportive ways to answer the questions: What do you want, how can you get it, and what might get in the way? Marko is the character with the most desire for a cure—what does he want? To get back to his daughter. How can he get it? For Marko, it is by any means possible, and we see him side with both the villains and then the

Spider-Men of *No Way Home*. What gets in the way? The ambivalence might be an issue for Flint. It might cause him some other issues later, but of the "villains" he is one that has set his own goal.

Beyond the Villains
BACK TO PETER PARKER AND STEPHEN STRANGE

> "You were just trying to fix things.
> And so, maybe just run it by us next time, you know?"
> —Michelle "MJ" Jones-Watson[31]

"Implicit in psychoanalysis is an ethic of assertion—of the unconscious, of wishes, longings, and fantasies, of truth and freedom. Action is selected after taking both parties into consideration with respect for the patient's transference."
—psychoanalyst Elizabeth Dorsey[32]

Remember, identities as heroes and villains might depend on which side you are fighting for. Both Peter Parker and Dr. Strange have been changed—one by a radioactive spider, the other by a transcendental voyage of self-exploration.[33] Strange tries to cure Peter of his desire to rehab the villains. Dr. Strange clearly shows the problems of imposing a cure when he says of the mirror dimension, "I'm in charge."[34] Luckily, like an astute patient, Peter can advocate for himself in treatment. Peter recognizes his own "order" in the mirror universe, the Archimedean Spiral, and says, "You know what's cooler than magic? Math!"[35] Peter has broken free of what the well-meaning Dr. Strange was trying to impose on him. It is what Adam Phillips intimates when writing about psychoanalyst Marion Milner's ideas, "Psychoanalytic treatment is an antidote to indoctrination; it is an enquiry into how people influence each other, into the individual's history of living in other people's regimes."[36] Freud himself said as much when writing his paper on whether there is ever an end to a psychoanalysis, "Instead of inquiring how analysis effects a cure . . . we should ask what are the obstacles which this cure encounters."[37]

The Peter Parkers of *No Way Home* are all *wounded helpers*. They have slightly different stories and challenges but are works in process themselves. Tobey Maguire's Peter Parker has dealt with a case of impotence when he lost his powers. Andrew Garfield's Parker talks about his anger issues when he admits he found himself no longer pulling his punches. Tom Holland's Parker struggles with the adolescent issue of a secret and exposed identity. All the Peter Parkers grow, however. Holland's Parker has changed by the end of *No Way Home*. He has learned lessons from his adventure—ones he didn't plan to initially. In the epilogue scene, he visits MJ.[38] He has rehearsed and written down what he is going to say, a far cry from earlier impulsiveness. He has matured.

As an alternative to cure, according to psychoanalyst Adam Phillips, Freud settled on free association as a "way of transforming oneself and others without mastery."[39] Many dynamic mental health treatment providers want a person to find their own goals and work toward them. Talking helps and is the royal road to exploring the adventures posed by our unconscious parts of character.

In the Spider-Man multiverse Marvel has created, we see many metaphors for the processes involved in therapy, but we also see how the concept of cure is explored and it is not as cut-and-dried as first thought. So, whether you desire homecomings of a sort, being far from home, or feeling there's no way home, you might want to seek out the help of your friendly, neighborhood therapist.

 **William Sharp, PsyaD,** Certified Psychoanalyst, is an associate teaching professor at Northeastern University in Boston, a practicing psychoanalyst in Brookline, and the director of the Masters in Clinical Mental Health counseling program at the Boston Graduate School of Psychoanalysis. He has contributed to Popular Culture Psychology books on *Doctor Who* and *Daredevil*, and written on psychotherapeutic treatment in *The Joker Psychology: Evil Clowns and the Women Who Love Them.* You can follow him on Twitter: @WilliamSharp

Eric Wesselmann's biography appears at the end of chapter 2 on page 19.

Life Lessons from the Hero Overhead:

The Unsung Hero with the Famous Song

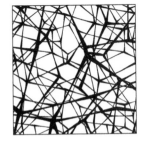

"Here comes the Spiderman!"
—Spider-Man in his first appearance (before adding the hyphen)[1]

Everyday people "can become the most inspirational heroes, especially if they remain hidden and humble. We call these heroes the *unsung heroes*."[2] A superhero as renowned as Spider-Man may not seem unsung, especially when literally sung about.[3] Somehow the original cartoon theme song that celebrates his heroism even pops up within the comics, becomes a ring-tone in one movie, and gets performed in all three Sam Raimi *Spider-Man* movies by street performers and a marching band.[4] As the song points out, though, he does not perform his good deeds in pursuit of fortune or fame. Spider-Man may be famous, but within the fiction, Peter Parker normally is not.

His comic book adventures see more than twenty years of publication before Spider-Man finally shares his dual identity with anyone who will remember, and even then the Black Cat rejects the amazing hero's ordinary alter ego.[5] Felicia Hardy adores the fantasy of Spider-Man. In comics and film, cruel consequences befall those around him when the world learns he is Spider-Man.[6] In each medium, magic makes the world forget but at a great personal sacrifice no one else will know Peter made, and yet he makes such sacrifice for the sake of those he feels should not have to suffer for knowing him. In no story is he less famous—ergo, more unknown and alone—than when the world forgets Peter Parker existed.[7] J. Jonah Jameson condemns Spider-Man as a "coward" for hiding behind a mask, the irony of which is that the MCU's Peter Parker has just performed his bravest act by relinquishing all recognition, accepting absolute anonymity so he might save the entire world. No one will know what he gave up for them. No one will know who he is or ever was. They still know Spider-Man,[8] the public persona, but they do not know the true hero behind the mask, the man who chooses to swing through the city saving people in the first place.

When someone steps up from the crowd to oppose tyranny, shields a bystander with their own body, helps a person escape a burning building even though the helper's own fate and name remain unknown, or simply helps a stranger get up after falling down, these acts inspire us because they seem truly altruistic, performed with no interest in wealth, fame, or other *extrinsic* (external) reward.[9] Even if action itself somehow provides Spider-Man with *intrinsic* (internal) reward, satisfaction for doing something for its own sake and not for ulterior purpose, that still sends a good message—that it's great to be the hero. While we admire Peter Parker for his heroic sacrifices and relate to him for all his human worries, we also enjoy how much he makes heroism look like fun.

"You inspire people as Spider-Man and Peter Parker."

—long-lost sister Teresa (Durand) Parker

—T. L.

Final Word
Choices
Alex Langley

Spider-Man exists because Peter Parker makes a choice.

With Spidey, there's no heroic destiny granting him superhuman power by birth, no desire for vengeance to fuel his dark nights, no desperate need to protect his vulnerable people. On a selfish whim, he lets a small-time crook pass by undeterred, and an innocent man dies. But if Peter doesn't make that selfish choice that leads to Uncle Ben's death, he doesn't become a superhero.[1] If we don't make the choices we've made, we don't become the people we are.

There's no boss telling Spider-Man what to do, or, rather, what he *should* do. He has never had his own Professor Xavier teaching him how to be a responsible part of community or a Nick Fury always telling him when to spring into action. Some of us may be lucky enough to have a Professor Xavier or Nick Fury providing mentorship and guidance, but many don't. And even those who do know that, ultimately, decisions on what we each do with our lives are made by us and us alone. Spider-Man's selfish choice affects his life and the lives of others in ways he never imagines. This, in turn, leads to an altruistic choice to become a hero, and it is a choice Peter Parker continues making every time he puts on that costume.

We all choose to don our own costumes every single day. Some days, we become our best selves, our spectacular spider-selves. Other days, when we get too bogged down with life annoyances or exhaustion, we become Peter throwing his costume away in an alley, feeling passively resigned to lives we'd regret, or Spider-Man in the black-suited symbiote, our worst and most id-driven selves poised to make selfish choices we'll wish we could undo. But to err is human[2] (or superhuman, as the case may be). Errors are unavoidable, and, in the words of Uncle Ben, "maybe even necessary."[3]

One of the beautifully human things about Spider-Man is that, just like the rest of us, he sometimes makes the wrong choice. He has angry thoughts and petty impulses. He often considers abandoning being Spider-Man entirely. When life gets hard, he feels frustrated by the knowledge that it doesn't have to be so hard. These imperfect, ignoble thoughts and impulses define us all as humans just as much as does the capability for quick action, steadfast nobility, compassion, curiosity, and selflessness. When Spider-Man extends compassion to others, even villains, it's partly because he knows what it's like to make a choice you regret. Every time he stops to deal with the "small things"—the muggings, the bullyings, the kids with cats stuck in trees—it's because he has seen the avalanche that results from letting the small things slide and snowball. Every time he stays out well past his bedtime even though he knows he's going to be exhausted at work the next day, it's because he feels that maybe, just maybe, he can save someone from pain if he just tries a little harder.

Like all of us, Spider-Man *chooses*. He chooses to be the hero he is just as we choose to be who we are. We may not have the proportionate strength and agility of a spider like Spider-Man, or have a unique blood composition that can save lives like James Harrison, or have vast fortunes from war profiteering that we can use to save the lives of Jewish people like Oskar Schindler. But Spider-Man (and his amazing friends) show us that, whether we're a shy bookworm from Queens, an artist from Brooklyn, or a drummer from another dimension, one person really can make a difference."*[4]

They show us that we can all be Spider-Man.[5]

We can all keep swinging ahead by making the selfless choice

---

* 'Nuff said.

no matter how tempting the selfish one may be. We can remember our loved ones and our heroes, real and imagined, to help us find the strength to lift that waterlogged rubble. We can help those who need it—friends, strangers, and villains alike. We can continue on and resist giving up because that next choice we make could be the best choice we've ever made.

"When I think of Spider-Man? I think, no matter what, he's never going to stop trying."

—*Peter Parker, the Spectacular Spider-Man*[6]

Notes

Acknowledgments: Our Amazing Friends

1. Fingeroth (2004).
2. Examples: Fingeroth (2007, 2011, 2019).
3. It's spider-sense. Robbie Thompson's *Silk* scripts answer the last part about the Spidey variant: Because fellow spider-hero Cindy Moon calls her trouble alert her "Silk-sense," that makes Peter Parker's Spidey-sense with a capital S. Yes, we know Aunt May calls it something else in 2019's *Spider-Man: Far from Home*, which one universe's Peter also calls it in the comics *Spider-Man* #2 (2023).
4. Fingeroth (2004), p. 22.
5. A reprint of the story from *Marvel Team-Up* #1 (1972).
6. *Spider-Man* (1977 motion picture); *The Amazing Spider-Man* (1977–1979 television series).
7. *Star Trek II: The Wrath of Khan* (1982 motion picture).
8. Lee (2016, 2018).
9. *Into the Spider-Verse* (2018 animated motion picture).

Introduction: "A Really Tough Life" and "the Real Pain"

1. Lee (2016), p. xiii.
2. *Fantastic Four* #1 (1961).
3. As early as *Fantastic Four* #4 (1962), Johnny Storm the Human Torch gets mad, quits the team, and physically fights the Thing, fire vs. rock.
4. Batchelor (2017); Fingeroth (2019); Hatfield (2012); Tucker (2017).
5. *The Amazing Spider-Man* #1 (1963b): Peter sobs, "I wish I had never gotten my super powers!" #2 (1963a): He thinks, "I don't think I'll ever stop getting a charge out of it!"
6. Ostrander (2013).

7. Established in their origins: Superman—*Action Comics* #1 (1938); Batman—*Detective Comics* #33 (1939); Spider-Man—*Amazing Fantasy* #15 (1962).

8. According to She-Hulk, superheroing is for "billionaires and narcissists—and adult orphans, for some reason." *She-Hulk: Attorney at Law*, episode 1-02, "Superhuman Law" (August 25, 2022).

9. Langley et al. (2021).

10. Keat (2012); Polák et al. (202); Prokop & Tunnicliffe (2008).

11. Quoted by May (2004).

12. *Amazing Fantasy* #15 (1962).

Part I. Swinging into Action

Chapter 1. Why Does He Keep Doing What a Spider Can?

1. *The Amazing Spider-Man* #53 (1967).

2. Quote attributed to Abraham Maslow, but unconfirmed.

3. *Amazing Spider-Man Annual* #15 (1981).

4. Norris (2021).

5. *The Amazing Spider-Man Annual* #5 (1968).

6. *The Amazing Spider-Man* #122 (1973).

7. *Spider-Man 2* (2004 motion picture).

8. *Marvel's Spider-Man* (2018 video game).

9. *The Amazing Spider-Man* #10 (1964).

10. *The Amazing Spider-Man* #153 (1975).

11. Omoto & Snyder (1995).

12. Ebstein et al. (2010).

13. *The Amazing Spider-Man* #4 (1963).

14. *The Amazing Spider-Man* #50 (1967).

15. *The Amazing Spider-Man* #70 (1969).

16. Levine et al. (2008). Editor's note: Not my own view. I love New York and New Yorkers—T.L. Co-editor's note: Agreed!—A.L.

17. *Spider-Man* (2002 motion picture).

18. Barnes et al. (1979).

19. *Spider-Man: No Way Home* (2021 motion picture).

20. Machluf & Bjorklund (2015).

21. Shepela et al. (1999).

22. *Amazing Fantasy* #15 (1962).

23. *The Spectacular Spider-Man Magazine* (1968).
24. Batson et al. (1991).
25. *The Amazing Spider-Man* #19 (2016).
26. Losing memories leads to Reilly's descent into more ruthless activities under the pseudonym Chasm—e.g., *The Amazing Spider-Man* #93 (2022); *Dark Web Finale* #1 (2023).
27. Latane & Darley (1968); *Amazing Fantasy* #15 (1962).
28. *Free Comic Book Day (Secret Empire)* (2017).
29. Yerkes & Dodson (1908).
30. *Peter Parker: The Spectacular Spider-Man* #310 (2018).
31. Karns et al. (2017).
32. *Schindler's List* (1993 motion picture).
33. Criss (2018).
34. Roberts (1996).
35. Criss (2018).
36. *The Amazing Spider-Man* #1.5 (2014).

Chapter 2. Why Do Heroes Stick? The Social and Psychological Functions of Hero Stories

1. *Spider-Man 2* (2004 motion picture).
2. Rosenberg (2013), pp. 14–15.
3. *Spider-Man 2* (2004 motion picture).
4. Allison & Goethals (2016); Kinsella et al. (2015a, 2015b).
5. DeMatteis (1994).
6. Allison (2016), p. 5.
7. DeFalco (2001), p. 9.
8. Graham et al. (2001); Sullivan & Venter (2005).
9. Contino (2002), p. 7.
10. Fiske & Linville (1980).
11. Kinsella et al. (2015b).
12. *The Amazing Spider-Man* (2012 motion picture); *Spider-Man 2* (2004 motion picture); *Spider-Man: Far from Home* (2019 motion picture).
13. Becker & Eagly (2004); Staats et al. (2009).
14. *The Amazing Spider-Man* #381 (1993).
15. Skitka (2012).
16. *The Amazing Spider-Man* #33 (1966).
17. *Amazing Fantasy* #15 (1962); *The Amazing Spider-Man* #378–380 (1993); *Spider-Man Unlimited* #1 (1993); *Web of Spider-Man* #102 (1993).

18. *The Spectacular Spider-Man* #201 (1993).

19. Monin & Merritt (2012).

20. "Hero in Crisis" DVD bonus on *Spider-Man 2* (2004 motion picture).

21. In his first two issues alone, he thinks both "I wish I had never gotten my super-powers!" (*The Amazing Spider-Man* #1, 1963b) and "I don't think I'll ever stop getting a charge out of it!" (#2, 1963a).

22. *Spider-Man 2* (2004 motion picture); *Spider-Man: Homecoming* (2017 motion picture).

23. *Spider-Man: The Animated Series* episode 2-07, "Neogenic Nightmare Chapter VII: Enter the Punisher" (November 4, 1995); *Spider-Man: No Way Home* (2021 motion picture).

24. Batson et al. (2014); Dovidio et al. (2006); Pfattheicher et al. (2022); Singer & Klimecki (2014).

25. Director Sam Raimi, cited by Cotton (2004).

26. *Spider-Man* #26 (1992).

27. *The Amazing Spider-Man* #79 (1969), #377 (1993), #7–8 (2014); *The Spectacular Spider-Man* #202 (1993); *Spider-Man Unlimited* #2 (1993); *The Sensational Spider-Man* #34 (2007).

28. Ho (2004), p. 42.

29. *Ultimate Avengers vs. New Ultimates* #4 (2011).

30. Frimer (2016); Kinsella et al. (2015a); Klapp (1954).

31. Allison & Goethals (2011).

32. Rubin (2013); Rubin & Livesay (2006); Scarlet (2017).

33. Van Tongeren et al. (2018).

34. Coughlan et al. (2019); Green et al. (2016); Kinsella et al. (2019).

35. *The Spectacular Spider-Man* #200 (1993), #220 (1995).

36. Worthington & Allison (2018).

37. Exline & Geyer (2004).

38. Worthington & Allison (2018).

39. LaBouff et al. (2012).

40. *The Amazing Spider-Man* #532–533 (2006).

41. Worthington & Allison (2018).

42. Johnson et al. (2010); Ronay et al. (2017).

43. Silverman et al. (2012).

44. *Spider-Man: Homecoming* (2017 motion picture).

45. *The Amazing Spider-Man* #121 (1973).

46. *The Amazing Spider-Man* #122 (1973); *The Spectacular Spider-Man* #211 (1994).

47. *Captain America: Civil War* (2016 motion picture).

48. Lewis (1995).

49. *The Spectacular Spider-Man* #189 (1992).

50. *The Spectacular Spider-Man* #206 (1993).

51. Two examples from among the many: *The Amazing Spider-Man* #378 (1993); *Spider-Man Unlimited* #2 (1993).

52. Cotton (2002), p. 29.

53. Thomas (2008).

54. *The Sensational Spider-Man* #34 (2007).

55. *The Amazing Spider-Man* #7 (2014).

56. Allison (2016); Franco & Zimbardo (2006).

57. Izadi (2015); Jewers (2021).

58. DeMatteis (2004).

Chapter 3. Reweaving: How Those Great Powers Alter a Young Hero's Sense of Self and World

1. Quoted by McGreal (2012).

2. *Spider-Man Special: Black & Blue & Read All Over* #1 (2006).

3. Peter—*Amazing Fantasy* #15 (1962); Cindy—*Silk* #4 (2015); Miles—*Ultimate Spider-Man* #1 (2011).

4. Laird (2017); The Take (2018).

5. Peter—*Amazing Fantasy* #15 (1962); Miles—*Ultimate Spider-Man* #1 (2011); Gwen—Cindy—*The Amazing Spider-Man* #1–2 (2014); *Silk* #1 (2015). Jessica Drew (an earlier Spider-Woman) gets them in childhood but skips adolescence, spending it in suspended animation.—*Spider-Woman* #1 (1978), #7 (2020).

6. In *Spider-Gwen* #34 (2018), she finally calls herself Spider-Gwen, but later replaces that with Ghost-Spider (*Spider-Gwen: Ghost-Spider* #10 (2019)).

7. Erikson (1959, 1968); Erikson & Erikson (1998).

8. Moore (2013); Zaikova (2022).

9. Schouten (1991); Wall & Ferguson (1998); 1 Corinthians 13:11.

10. *Amazing Fantasy* #15 (1962).

11. The first of many mentions.

12. Term first suggested by linguistic anthropologist Manesi (1994).

13. *Silk* #4 (2015).

14. Bull (2021); Hale et al. (2021); Johnson et al. (2020); Newcomb et al. (2018).

15. *Spider-Gwen: Ghost-Spider* #10 (2019).

16. *Ultimate Comics Spider-Man* #14 (2012).

17. Which contributes to the Punisher mistaking Nightcrawler for Spider-Man in the shadows in *The Amazing Spider-Man* #161 (1976).

18. *The Amazing Spider-Man* #78 (1969).

19. Freud (1936).

20. Folgey (2019).

21. Shi et al. (2021).

22. Starting with *Spider-Man* (2002 motion picture); discussed with other Spideys in *Spider-Man: No Way Home* (2021 motion picture).

23. *Amazing Fantasy* #15 (1962).

24. Sternberg (1994).

25. *Ultimate Spider-Man* #6 (2001). *The Amazing Spider-Man* (2012 motion picture).

26. Gibson (1979).

27. *Spider-Man 2* (2004 motion picture), among a thousand more.

28. Van Rens & Heritage (2021).

29. Biswas & Visell (2021).

30. Nelson et al. (2019).

31. Ki (2022); Momi et al. (2019, 2021); Takeuchi et al. (2016).

32. Unclearly in *The Amazing Spider-Man* #1 (1963b), more clearly in #2 (1963b).

33. *Amazing Fantasy* #15 (1962).

34. *The Amazing Spider-Man* (1977 motion picture); *Ultimate Spider-Man* #1 (2000).

35. Di Silvestro (2020).

36. *Silk* #1 (2015).

37. *The Amazing Spider-Man* #656 (2011).

38. Gresh & Weinberg (2002); Kakalios (2009); Kelly (2021).

39. Howze (2016).

40. Examples: Wolverine—*Ultimate Spider-Man* #66 (2004); Deadpool—*Deadpool* (2016 motion picture).

41. Both *Spider-Girl* and *Spider-Man* #1-5 (2020). An extracted eye stayed gone until the Other cocoon grew him a whole new body.

42. *The Amazing Spider-Man* #175 (1977).

43. *The Amazing Spider-Man* #195 (1979).

44. Broken in *The Amazing Spider-Man* #194, healed in #199 (both 1979).

45. *The Amazing Spider-Man* #113–115 (1972).

46. *The Amazing Spider-Man* #425 (1997), 25 years after the original duodenal ulcer.

47. *Amazing Fantasy* #15 (1962).

48. Bartholomaeus (2012); Connell (2005); Smith (2014); Soulliere (2006).

49. *The Spectacular Spider-Man* #21 (2005).

50. *Ultimate Spider-Man* #1 (2011).

51. *Spider-Man* #1 (2022).

Web File I. Before the Bite: Psychosocial Stages of Parker Development

1. *Civil War* #2 (2006).

2. Erikson (1959, 1968); Erikson & Erikson (1998); Henschel et al. (2020).

3. Kesavelu et al. (2021); Knight (2017).

4. *The Amazing Spider-Man Annual* #5 (1968); *Ultimate Spider-Man Super Special* #1 (2002).

5. McCabe (2006).

6. Etemesi (2022); Hurych (2020).

7. *The Amazing Spider-Man* #200 (1980).

8. Bergman et al. (2017).

9. Originally written and drawn more like 17, but later stories retroactively establish the age as 15.

10. Kentor & Kaplow (2021).

11. Freud (1905).

12. Erikson (1959, 1968); Erikson & Erikson (1998).

Part II. Weaving

Chapter 4. Along Came a Spider-Mentor

1. *The Amazing Spider-Man* #49 (2003).

2. Harvard T. H. Chan School of Public Health (2002).

3. Eby (1997).

4. *Amazing Fantasy* #15 (1962).

5. *The Amazing Spider-Man* #50 (1963).

6. *The Amazing Spider-Man* #3 (1963).

7. *The Amazing Spider-Man* #59 (1963); #71 (1969).

8. *The Amazing Spider-Man* #49 (1999).

9. *Amazing Fantasy* #15 (1962).

10. Kram & Isabella (1985).

11. LaFleuer & White (2010).

12. *The Amazing Spider-Man* #18 (1964).

13. Bowlsby & Ainsworth (2013); Bretheron (1992).

14. Collins & Feeney (2000).

15. Sandler & Gaffney (2021).

16. *The Amazing Spider-Man* #54 (1967).

17. *The Amazing Spider-Man* #536 (2006).

18. *The Amazing Spider-Man* #18 (1964).

19. *Superior Spider-Man* #4 (2014).

20. *The Amazing Spider-Man* #1 (1963).

21. *The Amazing Spider-Man* #1 (1963).

22. Aron & Aron (1986).

23. Aron et al. (2004).

24. *The Amazing Spider-Man* #1 (1963).

25. Bozeman & Feeney (2008).

26. Lankau & Scandura (2002).

27. Mitchell et al. (2015).

28. *Ultimate Spider-Man* #4 (2000).

29. *Marvel's Spider-Man* (2018 video game).

30. *Spider-Man 2* (2004 motion picture).

31. *The Amazing Spider-Man* #529 (2006).

32. *Captain America: Civil War* (2016 motion picture).

33. *Civil War* #2 (2006).

34. *The Amazing Spider-Man* #500 (1999).

35. *The Amazing Spider-Man* #641 (2010); *Spider-Man: No Way Home* (2021 motion picture).

36. Leidenfrost et al. (2014).

37. *Incoming* #1 (2019).

38. Little et al. (2010).

39. *The Amazing Spider-Man* #28 (2001).

40. *Spider-Man and the X-Men* #1 (2015).

41. Holbeche (1996).

42. *Peter Parker, the Spectacular Spider-Man* #110 (1985).

43. *The Amazing Spider-Man* #396 (1994).

Chapter 5. From a Leap to a Spark: Miles Morales and the Coming-of-Age Experience For Latinx and Black Heroes

1. *Spider-Man: Into the Spider-Verse* (2018 animated motion picture).

2. Jaye (2020).

3. *Amazing Spider-Man* #365 (1992).

4. *Spider-Man* #2 (2016).

5. *Spider-Man* #3 (2016).

6. Ortiz (2020).

7. Humphrey & Bliuc (2021).

8. *Ultimate Comics Spider-Man* #1 (2011).

9. Jefferson as S.H.I.E.L.D. agent, explained in *Miles Morales: Ultimate Spider-Man* #8 (2015). Aaron, first appearance as Prowler: *Ultimate Spider-Man* #1 (2011). Aaron as Iron Spider: *Spider-Man* #234 (2018).

10. Boyd-Franklin (2003); Miville et al. (2017).

11. *Miles Morales: Ultimate Spider-Man* #1 (2014).

12. *Spider-Man* #2 (2016).

13. Lee (1960).

14. *Spider-Man* #1 (2016).

15. Barton (2020); Rodriguez & Morrobel (2004).

16. Bronfenbrenner (1979).

17. Huerta (2018).

18. Richards et al. (2014).

19. Huerta (2018).

20. Fergus & Noguera (2009).

21. Freud (1905/1960); Martin & Ford (2018).

22. *Miles Morales: Spider-Man* #2 (2019).

23. *Spider-Man* #3 (2019).

24. Boyd-Franklin (2003).

25. *Ultimate Fallout* #4 (2011).

26. Adame et al. (2022).

27. *Ultimate Comics Spider-Man* #1 (2011).

28. Huerta (2018).

29. Wassertheil-Smoller et al. (2014).

30. Arciniega et al. (2008).

31. *Spider-Man: Miles Morales* (2020 video game).

32. *Spider-Man: Into the Spider-Verse* (2018 animated motion picture).

33. *Ultimate Comics Spider-Man* #1 (2014).

34. *Spider-Man: Into the Spider-Verse* (2018 animated motion picture).

35. Fuller & Cole (2010).

36. *Miles Morales: Ultimate Spider-Man* #2 (2014).

37. Laurie & Neimeyer (2008).
38. Phinney (1989).
39. Development Services Group (2022).
40. Western & Pettit (2010).
41. Sanchez et al. (2017).
42. Arciniega et al. (2008).
43. Arciniega et al. (2008).
44. Weiston-Serdan (2017).
45. MBK Alliance (n.d.).
46. Diemer & Blustein (2006).
47. *Miles Morales: Ultimate Spider-Man* #1 (2014).
48. *Spider-Geddon* #1 (2018).
49. Sue et al. (2019).
50. Meléndez et al. (2021).
51. Taylor et al. (2015).
52. Sue et al. (2019).

Chapter 6. Finding Your Inner Superhero: Adolescent Moral Identity Development

1. *Miles Morales: Spider-Man* #1 (2019).
2. Ellison (1952).
3. Casey & Galván (2016); Coleman (2021); Doumas et al. (2022); Fernandez-Kranz & Nollenberger (2022); Harris et al. (2022); Zhang & Chen (1990).
4. Arain et al. (2013).
5. Arnett (2000); Tanner & Arnett (2016); Zarrett & Eccles (2006).
6. Forest Hills first gets mentioned in *The Amazing Spider-Man* #7 (1963). Burstein (2006) shares insights regarding the friendly neighborhood and what it means for Peter Parker.
7. *The Amazing Spider-Man* #8 (1964).
8. *Spidey: School's Out* (2018).
9. Kohlberg & Kramer (1969); Kohlberg (1971).
10. Griffin et al. (2019); Jinkerson (2016); Litz et al. (2009).
11. *Amazing Fantasy* #15 (1962).
12. Malti (2016); Malti et al. (2021).
13. *The Amazing Spider-Man* #13 (1964).
14. Armstrong-Carter et al. (2021); Do et al. (2020); Sasse & Baumert (2022).
15. Duell & Steinberg (2020).

16. Armstrong-Carter et al. (2022).
17. Erikson (1968).
18. Marcia (1966).
19. *The Amazing Spider-Man* #24 (1965).
20. Kohlberg (1976).
21. Steinberg (2009).
22. *The Amazing Spider-Man* #31 (1965).
23. Bryant (2019); Demby (2014); Gonzales (2021); Owens (2017).
24. *Spider-Man* #2 (2016).
25. Kohlberg (1971).
26. Du Bois (1969).
27. Hoggard et al. (2015); Sellers et al. (2003).
28. Spencer & Spencer (2014); Velez & Spencer (2018).
29. *What If...? Miles Morales* #4 (2022). Regarding the author's apology: Mercado (2022); Johnston (2022).
30. Malti et al. (2021).
31. *Miles Morales: Ultimate Spider-Man* #1 (2015).
32. *Miles Morales: Ultimate Spider-Man* #10 (2015); *Miles Morales: Spider-Man* #11 (2019).
33. *Miles Morales: Ultimate Spider-Man* #1 (2015).
34. *Miles Morales: Spider-Man* #17 (2021).
35. Ballard (2016); Hope (2016); Hope et al. (2020).
36. Hope et al. (2020).
37. *Miles Morales: Spider-Man* #3 (2020).
38. Roy et al. (2014).
39. *The Amazing Spider-Man* #1 (1963).
40. Epstein et al. (2017), p. 4.
41. Burton (2007).

Chapter 7. Into the Spidentity: The Multiverse of Personality and Identity

1. Stevenson (1886).
2. Gandhi (1993).
3. *Amazing Fantasy* #15 (1962).
4. Cattell (1943).
5. Baumeister (1999).
6. Mischel (2009).

7.   Kassin (2003).
8.   Costa & McCrae (1992); McCrae & Costa (1987).
9.   *Amazing Fantasy* #15 (1962).
10. Rogers (1959).
11. Maslow (1943, 1971, 1996).
12. Acevedo (2018); Geller (1982); Soper et al. (1995).
13. *The Amazing Spider-Man* #101 (1971).
14. *The Amazing Spider-Man* #30 (2001).
15. *The Amazing Spider-Man* #41 (1966).
16. *The Amazing Spider-Man* #9 (1964).
17. *The Amazing Spider-Man* #149 (1975).
18. *Spider-Man 3* (2007 motion picture).
19. *Friendly Neighborhood Spider-Man Annual* #1 (2007).
20. *Spider-Man*, episode 2-6, "Neogenic Nightmare Chapter X: The Immortal Vampire" (October 28, 1995).
21. *The Amazing Spider-Man* #15 (1964).
22. *The Amazing Spider-Man* #14 (1964).
23. *The Amazing Spider-Man* #28 (2017).
24. *The Amazing Spider-Man* #50 (1967).
25. *The Amazing Spider-Man* #300 (1988).
26. *The Amazing Spider-Man* #700 (2013).
27. *Superior Spider-Man* #15 (2013).
28. Kim et al. (2011).
29. Hu et al. (2017).
30. Baraket-Bojmel (2016).
31. Hu et al. (2015).
32. Ruyter & Conroy (2002).
33. *The Amazing Spider-Man* #655 (2011).
34. *FF* #1 (2011).
35. Frankl (1956/2006).
36. Greenberg et al. (2012).
37. *The Amazing Spider-Man* #11 (2014).
38. *Spider-Gwen: Ghost Spider* #4 (2019).
39. Gallup (1977).
40. *Silk* #1-2 (2022).

Web File II. Posttraumatic Growth and Why We Keep Talking About Uncle Ben

1. LaRocca & Avery (2020); Palgi et al. (2020); Su & Chow (2020); Weber & Schulenberg (2022).
2. Dagan & Yager (2019).
3. Ferris & O'Brien (2022); Garcia et al. (2022); Tomich & DiBlaso (2022).
4. Fell et al. (2016); Lerner (2011); Mothers Against Drunk Driving (n.d.).
5. Walsh (2008).
6. *Spider-Man Special: Black & Blue & Read All Over* #1 (2006).
7. Clyman (2012); Rendon (2015).

III. Threads

Chapter 8. Spidey's Sticky Love Life: Relationships

1. *The Amazing Spider-Man* #259 (1984).
2. Shakespeare (1623/1982), p. 264.
3. Not a specific issue, just the kind of thing that happens to Spidey all the time.
4. Latané & Walton (1972).
5. *Web Warriors* #1 (2015).
6. McAdams (1989).
7. Schachter (1959).
8. Hill (1987).
9. Chin et al. (2017).
10. *The Amazing Spider-Man* #37 (1966).
11. Zajonc (1968).
12. *The Amazing Spider-Man* #17 (1964).
13. Hazan & Shaver (1987).
14. *Spider-Man: Hobgoblin Lives* #2 (1997). See also *The Amazing Spider-Man* #68 (2021).
15. *The Amazing Spider-Man* #31 (1965).
16. Page (2011).
17. *The Amazing Spider-Man* (2012 motion picture).
18. Byrne et al. (1966).
19. *Peter Parker: The Spectacular Spider-Man* #304 (2018).
20. Wegner et al. (1994).
21. Clark & Mills (1979).
22. Clark & Mills (1979).

23. Foster & Campbell (2005).

24. *Peter Parker: The Spectacular Spider-Man* #300 (2018).

25. *Peter Parker, the Spectacular Spider-Man* #87 (1983).

26. Halnon (2022).

27. *Peter Parker, the Spectacular Spider-Man* #100 (1985).

28. *The Amazing Spider-Man* #4 (2014).

29. Verhaege et al. (2013).

30. Vashi (2015).

31. *The Amazing Spider-Man* #9 (2014).

32. Leonhardt & Quealy (2015).

33. Johannesdottir et al. (2021).

34. *The Amazing Spider-Man* #257, #259 (1984); *Marvel Graphic Novel* #46 (1989); *Untold Tales of Spider-Man* #16 (1995).

35. Dutton & Aron (1974).

36. Sternberg (1986).

37. *The Amazing Spider-Man* #18 (1964).

38. *The Amazing Spider-Man* #121 (1973).

39. *Peter Parker, the Spectacular Spider-Man* #87 (1983).

40. *The Amazing Spider-Man* #673 (2011).

41. *The Amazing Spider-Man* #257 (1984).

42. *The Amazing Spider-Man* #673 (2011).

43. *The Amazing Spider-Man* #15 (2017).

44. Karimi et al. (2019).

45. *The Amazing Spider-Man* #544 (2007).

46. Peplau & Perlman (1982).

47. *Into the Spider-Verse* (2018 animated motion picture).

48. *Spider-Man: No Way Home* (2021 motion picture).

Chapter 9. Behind the Mask: The Web of Loneliness

1. *Spider-Man 3* (2007 motion picture).

2. Murthy (2020b).

3. Brown (2015).

4. Murthy (2020a).

5. *Spider-Man: No Way Home* (2021 motion picture).

6. Scheimer & Chakrabarti (2020).

7. Murthy (2020a).

8.   *Daredevil* #8 (1998).
9.   Cacioppo et al. (2014); Murthy (2020); Shevlin et al. (2015); Stickley & Koyanagi (2016).
10. Coan et al. (2006); Eisenberger (2012); Epel & Lithgow (2014); Friedman et al. (2006); Hawkley & Cacioppo (2003); Tate (2018); Wilson et al. (2007).
11. Murthy (2020a); Stickley & Koyanagi (2016).
12. *Spider-Man: Into the Spider-Verse* (2018 motion picture).
13. Brown (2021); Scarlet (2023); Xu & Roberts (2010).
14. *Spider-Man: Into the Spider-Verse* (2018 motion picture).
15. Emoto (2011).
16. *Spider-Man* (2002 motion picture).
17. Walker (2018).
18. *The Amazing Spider-Man* #31 (2001).
19. Bach et al (2019); Chu (2017); Coan et al. (2006).
20. Moller-Roth (2021).
21. Three Peters—*Spider-Man: No Way Home* (2021 motion picture). Miles—*Spider-Men* #1–5 (2012). Group—*Into the Spider-Verse* (2018 animated motion picture). Cindy—in time after they meet and she becomes Silk in *The Amazing Spider-Man* #4 (2014).
22. Harlow (1959).
23. Reinhardt & Rossell (2001).
24. *Daredevil* #8 (1998).
25. Brown (2021); Scarlet (2023); Tawwab (2021).
26. *Savage Wolverine* #6 (2013).
27. Waldinger & Schulz (2010).
28. Menakem (2021); van Der Kolk (2014).
29. *Spider-Man: Far from Home* (2019 motion picture); *Spider-Man: No Way Home* (2021 motion picture).
30. Brown (2015); Scarlet (2020).
31. Brown (2015).
32. *The Amazing Spider-Man* #96–98 (1971), #136 (1974); *Spider-Man 2* (2004 motion picture); *The Amazing Spider-Man* (2013 motion picture).
33. Miller et al. (2021).
34. *The Amazing Spider-Man* #8 (1963).
35. *The Amazing Spider-Man* #33 (1966).
36. *The Amazing Spider-Man* #50 (1967).

37. Gilbert & Irons (2009); Scarlet (2023).

38. *Spider-Man: No Way Home* (2021 motion picture).

39. Beutal et al. (2017).

40. *Spider-Man: No Way Home* (2021 motion picture).

41. Borawski & Nowak (2022).

42. *Spider-Man: No Way Home* (2021 motion picture).

43. Daly-Cano et al. (2015).

44. Tawwab (2021).

45. Engel (2010).

46. *Daredevil* #1 (2022).

47. Brown (2015); Scarlet (2020).

48. Wilson & Murrell. (2004).

49. *Spider-Man: No Way Home* (2021 motion picture).

50. Liu et al. (2022).

51. *The Amazing Spider-Man* #248 (1983).

52. Brown (2015).

53. Murthy (2020a).

54. Murthy (2020a); Scarlet (2023).

Chapter 10. The Grief Goblin: Archnemesis or Greatest Ally?

1. *Webspinners: Tales of Spider-Man* #12 (1999).

2. Rando (1984), p. 114.

3. *Amazing Fantasy* #15 (1962).

4. *Spider-Man: Into the Spider-Verse* (2018 animated motion picture); *Marvel's Spider-Man* (2018 video game); *Marvel's Spider-Man: Miles Morales* (2020 video game); *Spider-Man: Far from Home* (2019 motion picture); *Spider-Man: No Way Home* (2021 motion picture).

5. Rando (1984), p. 15.

6. Shapiro (2001).

7. Frankl (1956/2006).

8. *Spider-Man* (2000 motion picture).

9. Ben—*Amazing Fantasy* #15 (1962), among many others. Parents—*The Amazing Spider-Man 2* (2014 motion picture).

10. *The Amazing Spider-Man* #1 (1963b), #4 (1963), #17–18 (1964); *The Amazing Spider-Man Annual* #1 (1964).

11. Averill (1968).

12. Frankl (1956/2006), p. 9.

13. *Spider-Man 2* (2002 motion picture).

14. American Psychiatric Association (2022).

15. American Psychiatric Association (2022).

16. American Psychiatric Association (2022).

17. *Spider-Man* (2000 motion picture); *Spider-Man 2* (2002 motion picture); *Spider-Man 3* (2006 motion picture).

18. *Spider-Man 3* (2006 motion picture).

19. *The Amazing Spider-Man* (2012 motion picture); *The Amazing Spider-Man 2* (2014 motion picture).

20. Corr (2020); Retsinas (1988); Roos (2012, 2013).

21. Kübler-Ross (1969).

22. *Amazing Fantasy* #15 (1962). See Draven (2021).

23. Kessler (2019).

24. Rando (1984).

25. Rando (1984).

26. *Spider-Man: Into the Spider-Verse* (2018 animated motion picture).

27. Shapiro (2001).

28. Shapiro (2001), p. 198.

29. Fisher (2021); Rando (1984); Shapiro (2001).

30. *Spider-Man: Into the Spider-Verse* (2018 animated motion picture).

31. Shapiro (2001), p. 33.

32. *Webspinners: Tales of Spider-Man* #11 (1999).

33. *Webspinners: Tales of Spider-Man* #10–11 (1999).

34. *Amazing Fantasy* #15 (1962).

Postscript: Attachment and Adverse Childhood Experiences

35. Keller (1929), p. 1.

36. *The Amazing Spider-Man* #400 (1995), quoting Barrie (1904).

37. Karatekin et al. (2022).

38. Hays-Grudo & Morris (2020).

39. Juvonen & Gross (2005).

40. As early as the first pages of *Amazing Fantasy* #15 (1962).

41. Sochos & Aleem (2022).

42. Bowlby & Ainsworth (2013).

43. Hays-Grudo & Morris (2020); Juvonen & Gross (2005); Karatekin et al. (2022).

Web File III. Narcissists: Their Own Worst Enemies

1. *Spider-Man*, episode 1-19, "To Catch a Spider" (January 13, 1968).
2. *The Amazing Spider-Man Annual* #1 (1964).
3. Shaw (2014).

IV. Tangles

Chapter 11. Spider-Man, Murder Co-Victim: Guilt, Anger, and Posttraumatic Growth

1. *The Amazing Spider-Man: Soul of the Hunter* (1992).
2. Walsh & Schindehette (1997), p. 1.
3. Center for Victim Research (2019).
4. Respectively, *Amazing Fantasy* #15 (1962); *The Amazing Spider-Man* #90 (1970); *Peter Parker, the Spectacular Spider-Man* #107 (1985); *The Amazing Spider-Man* #121 (1973).
5. Stretesky et al. (2010).
6. *The Amazing Spider-Man Annual* #5 (1968).
7. *Amazing Fantasy* #15 (1962); *The Amazing Spider-Man* #1 (1963).
8. Tangney et al. (2002).
9. Erb et al. (2022); Taihara & Malik (2016); Tangney (1994); Tignor (2017).
10. Tangney et al. (2002).
11. Clevenger (2016).
12. Barlé et al. (2017); Carveth (2006).
13. Tangney et al. (2002).
14. Hutson et al. (2015); Kreitler at al. (2013).
15. Cassell et al. (2013); Fimiani et al. (2021); Juni (2016); Valent (2010).
16. *The Amazing Spider Man* #38 (2002); *Spider-Man 2* (2004 motion picture).
17. Fettinger (2006).
18. *The Amazing Spider-Man* #90 (1970).
19. Miranda et al. (2003).
20. Murray et al. (2021).
21. *The Amazing Spider-Man* #196 (1979).
22. Murray et al. (2021).
23. Berzoff (2011); Gaab (2012).
24. *The Amazing Spider-Man* #91–100 (1970–1971) and beyond.
25. *The Amazing Spider-Man* #90 (1971).
26. Asaro (2001).

27. Barber (2018); Barash & Lipton (2011); Bartolomé (2021). See also Besharat & Shahidi (2010); McCullough et al. (2007).
28. Contreras et al. (2020); Crostley (2010); Crowe & Wilkowski (2013).
29. *The Amazing Spider-Man* #121–122 (1973); *Peter Parker, the Spectacular Spider-Man* #107–110 (1985).
30. Barash & Lipton (2011); Milburn & Liss (2008); Sjöström & Gollwitzer (2015).
31. *The Amazing Spider-Man* #300 (1988).
32. Williams (2016).
33. Freud (1924); Vaillant (1977).
34. *Peter Parker, the Spectacular Spider-Man* #107–110 (1985).
35. Moore (2021).
36. Tedeschi et al. (2018).
37. *The Amazing Spider-Man* #655 (2011).
38. *All-New Captain America Special* #1 (2015).
39. Clevenger et al. (2018).

Chapter 12. Climbing the Walls: Neurosis, Psychosis, and Metamorphosis

1. Ostrander (2013).
2. *Spider-Man 2* (2004 motion picture).
3. Ostrander (2013).
4. Lee (2018), p. xii.
5. Sherwin (2014).
6. Freud (1917/1920, 1924/1963); Jung (1915, 1953/1959).
7. Edwards (2019).
8. American Psychiatric Association (1980).
9. American Psychiatric Association (1980). See Horwitz & Wakefield (2007); Wilson (1993).
10. World Health Organization (2022).
11. *The Amazing Spider-Man* (2012 motion picture); *The Amazing Spider-Man 2* (2014 motion picture); *Spider-Man: No Way Home* (2021 motion picture).
12. Sherwin (2014).
13. *The Amazing Spider-Man* #96 (1971).
14. *The Amazing Spider-Man* #59 (1968).
15. American Psychiatric Association (2022).
16. "Yeah, that's me—Mr. Masochism, 1974!" *The Amazing Spider-Man* #139 (1974).
17. *The Amazing Spider-Man* #141 (1975).

18. *The Amazing Spider-Man* #146 (1975).
19. American Psychiatric Association (2022).
20. *The Amazing Spider-Man* #139 (1974).
21. *The Amazing Spider-Man* #100 (1971).
22. *The Amazing Spider-Man* #24 (1965).
23. Wahl (1995).
24. Eigen (1995); Fersch (2005); Moran (1981).
25. *The Amazing Spider-Man* #39–40 (1966).
26. *The Amazing Spider-Man Annual* #9 (1973).
27. *Spider-Man: Hobgoblin Lives* #2 (1997).
28. American Psychiatric Association (2022).
29. Cheung et al. (2012); King et al. (2010); Rutter (2006).
30. Norman—*The Amazing Spider-Man* #121 (1973). Harry—*Spider-Man 2* and *3* (2004, 2007 motion pictures).
31. American Psychiatric Association (2022).
32. Kaufman (2011).
33. Douglas et al. (2009); Naudts & Hodgins (2005).
34. Bo et al. (2021); Engelstad et al. (2019); Krakowski & Czobor (2018).
35. Mulvey & Fardella (2000).
36. Barrett (2020). See also Wedding et al. (2010).
37. National Alliance on Mental Health (n.d.); National Institute of Mental Health (n.d.).
38. Eriksson (2022); Naudts & Hodgins (2005); Tengström et al. (2004).
39. *Spider-Man: Homecoming* (2017 motion picture).
40. *The Amazing Spider-Man* #3 (1963).
41. Clark et al. (2020); Colantonio et al. (2014); Gordon et al. (2017); Ineson et al. (2022); Jansen (2020); Raine (2013); Williams et al. (2018).
42. Bogner et al. (2020); Cornelius (2013); Elbogen et al (2015); Galovski et al. (2021); Scott et al. (2015).
43. Bonow et al. (2019); Brewer-Smyth et al. (2015).
44. *The Amazing Spider-Man* #11 (1964). Admittedly Octavius promptly pursues revenge when he gets out.
45. *The Amazing Spider-Man* #40 (1966).
46. *The Amazing Spider-Man* #96–98 (1971).
47. *The Amazing Spider-Man* #121 (1973). *Schizophrenia* had recently replaced *schizophrenic reaction* in the DSM-II (American Psychiatric Association, 1968).
48. McNally (2016, quote from book abstract).

49. Chen et al. (2004); Di Forti et al. (2007); Tucker (1994).

50. Freud (1936).

51. Vaillant (1977).

52. *The Amazing Spider-Man* #123 (1973). A strict Freudian might not consider that to be a defense mechanism at work when he deliberately web-slings for this purpose, *consciously* rather than *unconsciously* pursuing stress relief, but swinging around the city has become such a part of him that there would be times when he does this without thinking about why.

53. Vaillant (1977).

54. *Spider-Man 3* (2007 motion picture); *Spider-Man: No Way Home* (2021 motion picture).

55. *The Amazing Spider-Man* #10 (2022).

56. Freud (1905/1960; 1928); Vaillant (1977).

57. Kuiper & Leite (2010); Neziek et al. (2021); Schermer et al. (2021).

58. Oostthuizen (2021); Schall (2021).

59. *The Amazing Spider-Man* #159 (1976).

60. *Spider-Man: No Way Home* (2021 motion picture).

61. Ferradás et al. (2017); Norem & Cantor (1986). Cramer (2010) equated defensive pessimism and self-handicapping with defense mechanism strategies.

62. Vaillant (1977), p. 79.

63. Freud (1924).

64. Fry (2019); Marano (2006); Nesseth (2022).

65. Hick (2006).

66. *The New Avengers* #5 (2004).

67. *The Pulse* #5 (2004).

68. Remedios (2018); Levy (2019).

69. Rosenhaft (2020).

70. *The Amazing Spider-Man: Extra* #1 (2008).

71. *Spider-Man/Deadpool* #1 (2016).

72. *The Amazing Spider-Man* #24 (1965).

73. *The Amazing Spider-Man* #180 (1978).

74. *Marvel Team-Up* #102 (1981).

75. Cindy—*Silk* #7 (2015). Ben—*The Amazing Spider-Man* #75–88 (2021–2022). In #88, Ben's therapist also turns into a supervillain, the Queen Goblin, but not by choice and not because of mental problems. The Beyond Corporation forces her transformation. Ben adopts the name Chasm in *The Amazing Spider-Man* #93

(2022). The Queen Goblin is not to be confused with the Goblin Queen, Jean Grey's clone Madelyne Pryor, who conspires with Chasm to "take back" lives they feel robbed of (*The Amazing Spider-Man* #14, 2023; *Dark Web Finale* #1, 2023).

76. Ostrander (2013).

77. Lytle (2006).

Chapter 13. Radioactive Reaction: Anger, Trauma, and Self-Control

1. *Spider-Man: No Way Home* (2021 motion picture).

2. Ambrose (2005).

3. *Peter Parker: The Spectacular Spider-Man* #301 (2018).

4. American Psychological Association (n.d.).

5. Osgood & Muraven (2018); Norström & Pape (2010); Palmore (2019); Walters et al. (2018).

6. Baumeister et al. (1998).

7. Suarez & Krishan (2006).

8. *Friendly Neighborhood Spider-Man* #5 (2019).

9. *Ultimate Spider-Man* #74 (2005).

10. *The Amazing Spider-Man Annual* #5 (1968); *The Amazing Spider-Man 2* (2014 motion picture).

11. *Amazing Fantasy* #15 (1962).

12. *The Amazing Spider-Man* #121 (1973).

13. Bryant (2019).

14. Castillo et al. (2014).

15. Lewis et al. (2018).

16. *The Amazing Spider-Man* #7 (1963).

17. Lewis et al. (2018).

18. Asgeirdottir et al. (2011); Consolini et al. (2022); Di Giunta et al. (2018); du Pont et al. (2018).

19. *The Amazing Spider-Man* #136–137 (1974); *Spider-Man 3* (2007 motion picture).

20. Marson (2022).

21. *Son of M* #1 (2006).

22. *The Incredible Hulk* (1977 TV movie).

23. Bratko et al. (2017).

24. Bandura (1977).

25. Marcus-Newhall et al. (2000).

26. *The Amazing Spider-Man* #21 (1964).
27. *The Amazing Spider-Man* #31 (1965).
28. *The Amazing Spider-Man* #8 (1963).
29. *The Amazing Spider-Man Annual* #5 (1968).
30. DeWall et al. (2010).
31. *Amazing Fantasy* #15 (1962).
32. DeWall et al. (2009).
33. *The Amazing Spider-Man* #82 (1970).
34. Pedersen et al. (2011).
35. *The Amazing Spider-Man* #33 (1966).
36. *Spider-Man: No Way Home* (2021 motion picture).
37. *The Amazing Spider-Man* #542 (2007).
38. *The Amazing Spider-Man* #65.
39. *Peter Parker, the Spectacular Spider-Man* #110 (1985).
40. Respectively, *Spider-Man 2* (2004 motion picture); *Spider-Man 3* (2007 motion picture).
41. Anderson et al. (2012).
42. Graham & Livingston (2011).
43. *The Amazing Spider-Man* #23 (2017).
44. Chiang et al. (2019).
45. Ventegodt et al. (2016).
46. *Silk* #4 (2015). Cindy soon visits Sinclair in *Silk* #7 (2015).
47. *Silk* #3 (2016).
48. Freud (1940); Leahy (2001).
49. Mueller & McCullough (2017).
50. *The Amazing Spider-Man* #9 (2014).
51. *Spider-Gwen: Ghost Spider* #4 (2019).
52. Wheeler (2015).
53. Malchiodi (2006).
54. *The Amazing Spider-Man* #327 (1989).
55. *The Amazing Spider-Man* #60 (2021).
56. Germer et al. (2013).
57. Kellermann (1992).
58. *The Avengers* (2012 motion picture).
59. *Spider-Man: Homecoming* (2017 motion picture).
60. *The Amazing Spider-Man* #17 (1963).

Web File IV. Across Generations: How Miles Morales Sees Teen Peter Parker

1.   During Langley et al. (2021).
2.   *Generations: Miles Morales & Peter Parker Spider-Man* (2017).
3.   In fact, Peter attributes the future-superhero's visit to a stress- and fatigue-induced hallucination.

V. The Upswing

Chapter 14. Spidery Strengths and Virtues: From Radioactive Bite to Values-Driven Life

1.   Quoted by Vman (2012).
2.   *Spider-Man Annual* #1 (2018).
3.   A dozen times, starting with Langley et al. (2016).
4.   In Fingeroth et al. (2022). Paraphrased from memory, used here with Semper's approval.
5.   Personal communication (September 29, 2022).
6.   Seligman's 1998 address appeared in print as Seligman (1999).
7.   Peterson & Seligman (2004), p. 4.
8.   Peterson & Seligman (2004), p. 3.
9.   Littman-Ovadia & Niemiec (2016).
10.   American Psychiatric Association (2000—DSM-IV-TR at the time).
11.   Peterson & Seligman (2004).
12.   *The Amazing Spider-Man* #130 (1974).
13.   Cropley (2006); Guilford (1955, 1956).
14.   Web fluid—*Amazing Fantasy* #15 (1962); spider-tracers—*The Amazing Spider-Man* #11 (1964).
15.   Peterson & Seligman (2004), p. 199.
16.   For example, *The Amazing Spider-Man* #9–14 (2015), part of the first Spider-Verse crossover; most famously in *Spider-Man: No Way Home* (2021 motion picture).
17.   *Peter Parker: The Spectacular Spider-Man* #307 (2018).
18.   *The Amazing Spider-Man* #10 (2022).
19.   *Peter Parker: The Spectacular Spider-Man* #6 (2018).
20.   Niemiec & Wedding (2014).
21.   *Spider-Geddon* #3 (2019).
22.   *The Amazing Spider-Man* #656 (2011).
23.   *The Amazing Spider-Man* #89 (2022), borrowing from *The Avengers* (2012 motion picture).

24. *The Amazing Spider-Man* #700 (2012).

25. *Superior Spider-Man Team-Up* #6 (2013).

26. *The Amazing Spider-Man* #2 (2014). Later, her clone becomes the next Electro—*The Amazing Spider-Man* #17 (2016).

27. Peterson & Seligman (2004), p. 519.

28. Benner (2011); McEntee et al. (2013); Smigelsky (2013).

29. *The Amazing Spider-Man* #4 (1962).

30. Kabir (2015), pp. 80–81.

31. *Amazing Fantasy* #15 (1962).

32. *Peter Parker: The Spectacular Spider-Man* #6 (2018).

33. Park et al. (2004).

34. Paraphrased from Wood (2017).

35. Corrêa et al. (2019); Miller et al. (2021).

36. *The Amazing Spider-Man* #141 (1975).

37. *Spider-Man: No Way Home* (2021 motion picture), regarding the path his character has followed since *The Amazing Spider-Man 2* (2014 motion picture).

38. *Ultimate Comics Spider-Man* #1 (2011).

39. Hare (1999).

40. *X-Men* #60 (1969), borrowing from Tolkien (1937, etc.). See Polo (2020).

41. *Spider-Man and the X-Men* #2 (2015), reminiscent of the Lizard's goal in *The Amazing Spider-Man* (2012 motion picture).

42. Lerner (1980); Lerner & Miller (1978).

43. Lipkus et al. (1996); Stroebe (2013).

44. Dawtry et al. (2020); Lipkus (1991).

45. Elmore (2018).

46. Coetzee (2020); Orjiakor et al. (2022); Pettigrew (2020); Stacer & Solinas-Saunders (2018).

47. Fischer et al. (2022).

48. Johnstone (2003); Scriven (2018); Umbreif (1989); Zdaniuk & Bobocel (2012).

49. *Marvel Preview* #2 (1975).

50. Maffly-Kipp et al. (2022); Umbreit (1989).

51. Greenberger (2006).

52. *Peter Parker, the Spectacular Spider-Man* #100 (1985).

53. *Spider-Man: No Way Home* (2021 motion picture).

54. *Amazing Fantasy* #15 (1962).

55. VIA Institute on Character (n.d.).

56. Blanchard et al. (2020); Niemiec (2013); Stichter & Saunders (2019).

57. Debut: *Marvel Tails Starring Peter Porker, the Spectacular Spider-Ham* #1 (1984). Origin: *Peter Porker, the Spectacular Spider-Ham* #15 (1987).

58. *Edge of Spider-Verse* #4 (2022).

59. Dunn & Bolt (2016); Niemiec & McGrath (2019).

60. Herbert (2015); Schultz & Thompson (2017); Quinn et al. (2021).

61. Burke (2014); Ekong (2021); Fournier (2021).

62. *Amazing Fantasy* #15 (1962).

63. *Spider-Man/Deadpool* #1 (2016).

64. *Spider-Man 2* (2004 motion picture); *The Amazing Spider-Man 2* (2014 motion picture).

65. *Stanley* (2015/2018), p. 89.

66. Years ago, the academic professional side of my life and creative nerdy side of my life seemed unconnected. Once those tracks merged into one, though, I told people it felt "the truest to myself I've ever been."

67. *Spider-Man: No Way Home* (2021 motion picture).

68. Peterson & Park (2008), p. 8.

69. *Spider-Man: No Way Home* (2021 motion picture).

70. T. Kashdan, interviewed by K. Britton (2015/2018), p. 37.

71. Mulheron (2021).

72. Quoted by Vman (2012).

Chapter 15. Daring to Dream the Myth Onward: The Persistence of Archetypal Themes in Spider-Man

1. *The Amazing Spider-Man* #527 (2006).

2. Jung (1939).

3. *Edge of Spider-Verse* #1–5 (2014); *Edge of Spider-Verse* #1–5 (2022); *Spider-Man* #1 (2022).

4. Ezekiel first makes this assertion in *The Amazing Spider-Man* #30 (2001). Deception revelation and subsequent redemption—*The Amazing Spider-Man* #508 (2004).

5. Chevalier & Gheerbrant (1969/1996).

6. *The Amazing Spider-Man* #32 (2001).

7. Jung (1931/1960).

8. Klopfer (1955).

9. Jung (2009); Lu (2018).

10. For deliberate uses of Jung in comics, see *Arkham Asylum* (1989) and *Amazing Spider-Man* #130 (1974).

11. *The Amazing Spider-Man* #527 (2006).

12. *The Amazing Spider-Man* #33–35 (2001).

13. Campbell (1949/1973).

14. *The Amazing Spider-Man* #506 (2004).

15. *The Amazing Spider-Man* #528 (2006).

16. Turner (1974).

17. *The Amazing Spider-Man* #33 (2001).

18. *The Amazing Spider-Man* #35 (2001).

19. *The Amazing Spider-Man* #46 (2002).

20. Jung (1937/1960).

21. Jung (1948/1989).

22. Jung (1954/1960).

23. Campbell (1949/1973)—Editors.

24. *The Amazing Spider-Man* #504 (2004).

25. Jung (1936/1991).

26. *The Amazing Spider-Man* #527 (2006).

27. Jung (1916/1953).

28. Jung (1916/1953).

29. *The Amazing Spider-Man* #527 (2006).

30. Jung (1956/1976).

31. *The Amazing Spider-Man* #32 (2001).

Chapter 16. You'd Think Having Superpowers Would Make Life Easier

1.   *The Amazing Spider-Man* #18 (1964).

2.   Hochman (2014).

3.   Smith (2018).

4.   Carlson & Lester (1980).

5.   Zuckerman (1979, 1983).

6.   Sarshar et al. (2022).

7.   Kopetz et al. (2019).

8.   *Amazing Fantasy* #15 (1962).

9.   Lue (2021).

10. Davis (2007); Hegde (2022); Nurmohamed et al. (201).

11. Michniewicz & Vandello (2013).

12. Quesque et al. (2021); Tan et al. (2009).

13. DeLara (2016); Smith (2018).

14. *The Amazing Spider-Man* #7 (1963).

15. *The Amazing Spider-Man* #8 (1964).

16. *The Amazing Spider-Man* #25 (1965).

17. Pavri (2015).

18. Steele (n.d.).

19. Clark (2019).

20. Pavri (2015).

21. Baylor College of Medicine (2018).

22. Nuwer (2013)—Editors.

23. Concepcion (2018).

24. Bridson (2016).

25. *The Amazing Spider-Man* #4 (1963).

26. *The Amazing Spider-Man* #25 (1965).

27. *Daredevil* #17 (1966).

28. *The Amazing Spider-Man* #6 (1963).

29. *The Amazing Spider-Man* #33 (1966).

30. *The Amazing Spider-Man* #24 (1965).

31. *The Amazing Spider-Man* #4 (1963).

32. *The Amazing Spider-Man* #32–33 (1966), as noted by Watt-Evans (2006).

33. Morman (2021).

34. Middleearthnj (2019).

35. *Amazing Fantasy* #15 (1962).

36. *Amazing Fantasy* #15 (1962).

37. Cherry (2022).

38. *Amazing Fantasy* #15 (1962).

39. *The Amazing Spider-Man* #1 (1963).

40. *The Amazing Spider-Man* #20 (1965).

41. *The Amazing Spider-Man* #18 (1964).

42. *The Amazing Spider-Man* #121 (1973).

43. *The Amazing Spider-Man* #90 (1970).

44. *The Amazing Spider-Man* #122 (1973). Editor's Note: Yes, he later returns as explained in *Spider-Man: The Osborn Journal* #1 (1996), but for three decades in our time, the character stays dead.

45. *The Amazing Spider-Man* #10 (1964); Castro (2006).

46. *The Amazing Spider-Man* #10 (1964).

47. *Marvel Two-In-One Annual* #2 (1977).

48. *The Amazing Spider-Man* #252 (1984).

49. *The Amazing Spider-Man* #10 (1964).

Chapter 17. The "Cure" For Spider-Man: Therapy Offers an Alternate Way Home

1. *The Amazing Spider-Man* #8 (2014).

2. Phillips (2021), p. 20.

3. *The Spectacular Spider-Man* #203 (1993)

4. Wizard Magazine staff (1998), p. 57.

5. e.g., *The Amazing Spider-Man* #6 (1963), #79 (1969); *Civil War II: Amazing Spider-Man* #1 (2016); *Spider-Man* #26 (1992).

6. *Spider-Man Unlimited* #2 (1993).

7. *Spider-Man: No Way Home* (2021 motion picture).

8. Phillips (2019), p. 23.

9. Saunders (2022), p. xxviii.

10. e.g., *The Amazing Spider-Man* #50 (1967); *The Amazing Spider-Man* #100 (1971); *The Amazing Spider-Man* #341 (1990); *Spider-Man 2* (2004 motion picture).

11. Phillips (2021), p. 135.

12. *Spider-Man: No Way Home* (2021 motion picture).

13. *The Amazing Spider-Man* #6 (1963).

14. *The Amazing Spider-Man* #102 (1971); *Morbius* (2022 motion picture).

15. Knaus (2014); Sokol & Fox (2019); Tolin (2016). Also Morrow & Spencer (2018); Resick et al. (2016).

16. Frankl (1969).

17. *Spider-Man: No Way Home* (2021 motion picture); Freud (1924); Vaillant (1977).

18. Phillips (2019), p. 103.

19. *The Amazing Spider-Man* #380 (1993); *Spider-Man Unlimited* #2 (1993).

20. *The Sensational Spider-Man* #34 (2007).

21. *Spider-Man: No Way Home* (2021 motion picture).

22. Phillips (2021), p. 145, writing on William James's (1907) book *Pragmatism*.

23. Phillips (2019), p. 225.

24. Freud (1912), p. 111.

25. Kahr (2020).

26. *Spider-Man: No Way Home* (2021 motion picture).

27. *Spider-Man: No Way Home* (2021 motion picture).

28. *The Amazing Spider-Man* (2012 motion picture). Not an exact quote.

29. *Spider-Man: No Way Home* (2021 motion picture).

30. Freud (1937), p. 393. See also Margolis (1986).

31. *Spider-Man: No Way Home* (2021 motion picture).

32. Dorsey (2011), p. 205

33. *Amazing Fantasy* #15 (1962); *Strange Tales* #110 (1963). In the MCU, this Spider-Man's origin is not depicted, and Stephen Strange debuts in *Doctor Strange* (2016 motion picture).

34. *Spider-Man: No Way Home* (2021 motion picture).

35. *Spider-Man: No Way Home* (2021 motion picture).

36. Phillips (2021), p. 23.

37. Freud (1937), p. 377.

38. *Spider-Man: No Way Home* (2021 motion picture).

39. Phillips (2021), p. 97.

Web File V. Life Lessons from the Hero Overhead: The Unsung Hero with the Famous Song

1. *Amazing Fantasy* #15 (1962). See also *Spider-Man* #4 (2023).

2. Allison & Goethals (2011), p. 171. For some examples who eventually received some recognition but deserve to be better known, see Randolph (2021).

3. *Spider-Man* (1967 animated series), theme song composed by P. F. Webster & B. Harris.

4. Comics example—*Spider-Man: Renew Your Vows* #5 (2015). Ring-tone, also whistled—*The Amazing Spider-Man 2* (2014 motion picture). Raimi—*Spider-Man, Spider-Man 2, Spider-Man 3* (2002, 2004, 2007 motion pictures).

5. *Peter Parker, the Spectacular Spider-Man* #87 (1983).

6. *The Amazing Spider-Man* #538 (2007); *Spider-Man: No Way Home* (2021 motion picture).

7. *Spider-Man: No Way Home* (2021 motion picture).

8. *Ant-Man and the Wasp: Quantumania* (2023 motion picture).

9. Babula (2013); Herzog (2019); Oliner & Oliner (1988); Ricard (2015).

10. *Peter Parker: The Spectacular Spider-Man* #306 (2018).

Final Word: choices

1. *What If?* #19 (1979).

2. Pope (1711).

3. *The Amazing Spider-Man* #500 (2003).

4. *Spider-Man 2* (2004 motion picture).

5. Paraphrasing *Spider-Man: Into the Spider-Verse* (2018 animated motion picture).

6. *Peter Parker: The Spectacular Spider-Man* #310 (2018).

References

Comic Books and Graphic Novels

Regarding credits: Except where uncredited Golden Age creators have been identified, names listed here come from the original publications. They do not fully reflect artists' critical roles in "Marvel method" storytelling. To keep production flowing while **Stan Lee** worked on all their series as writer/editor, Marvel Comics developed its house style: Instead of starting with full script as was common practice at other companies, the writer provided a plot—sometimes in page-by-page detail, sometimes on a single sheet, sometimes as a rough idea. Each artist then planned and illustrated the full story. Lee (or, later, other writers) then added narrative and dialogue. Artists **Jack Kirby and Steve Ditko,** in particular, merit praise not only for plotting stories but also for weaving much of the fabric of the Marvel Universe. After Kirby and Ditko left their Marvel titles, the stories changed. Among other things, the growth of Spidey's colorful rogue's gallery slowed after Ditko's final issue, *The Amazing Spider-Man* #38. **John Romita** worked on the remainder of Lee's run (through issue #110) and beyond in multiple artistic capacities. They and others illustrating under the Marvel method contributed more than we may ever confirm.

Regarding issue numbers: Marvel and DC do not normally number their series' volumes in the indicia when retitling or relaunching a series with a new #1 issue. Comics listed here appear in alphabetical order by title. Within each title, they're in chronological order by cover dates first, then issue numbers within each year. Because of subtitles, title changes, numbering changes, and resumption of old numbering, only the date places a story in historical context.

Action Comics #1 (1938). "Superman! Champion of the Oppressed." Script: J. Siegel. Art: J. Shuster. National Allied.

All-New Captain America Special #1 (2015). "Inhuman Error: Part 3." Script: J. Loveness. Art: A. Morgan.

Amazing Fantasy #15 (1962). "Spider-Man!" Script: S. Lee. Art: S. Ditko.

The Amazing Spider-Man

> #1 (1963). (a) "Spider-Man." Script: S. Lee. Art: S. Ditko. (b) "Spider-Man vs. the Chameleon!" Script: S. Lee. Art: S. Ditko.
>
> #2 (1963). (a) "Duel to the Death with the Vulture!" Script: S. Lee. Art: S. Ditko. (b) "The Uncanny Threat of the Terrible Tinkerer!" Script: S. Lee. Art: S. Ditko.
>
> #3 (1963). "Spider-Man versus Doctor Octopus." Script: S. Lee. Art: S. Ditko.
>
> #4 (1963). "Nothing Can Stop . . . the Sandman!" Script: S. Lee. Art: S. Ditko.
>
> #6 (1963). "Face-To-Face with . . . the Lizard!" Script: S. Lee. Art: S. Ditko.
>
> #7 (1963). "The Vulture's Return!" Script: S. Lee. Art: S. Ditko.
>
> #8 (1964). "The Living Brain!" Script: S. Lee. Art: S. Ditko.
>
> #9 (1964). "The Man Called Electro!" Script: S. Lee. Art: S. Ditko.
>
> #10 (1964). "The Enforcers!" Script: S. Lee. Art: S. Ditko.
>
> #11 (1964). "Turning Point." Script: S. Lee. Art: S. Ditko.
>
> #13 (1964). "The Menace of Mysterio!" Script: S. Lee. Art: S. Ditko.
>
> #14 (1964). "The Green Goblin." Script: S. Lee. Art: S. Ditko.
>
> #15 (1964). "Kraven the Hunter!" Script: S. Lee. Art: S. Ditko.
>
> #17 (1964). "The Return of the Green Goblin!" Script: S. Lee. Art: S. Ditko.
>
> #18 (1964). "The End of Spider-Man!" Script: S. Lee. Art: S. Ditko.
>
> #20 (1964). "The Coming of the Scorpion! Or: Spidey Battles Scorpey!" Script: S. Lee. Art: S. Ditko.
>
> #21 (1965). "Where Flies the Beetle . . . !" Script: S. Lee. Art: S. Ditko.
>
> #24 (1965). "Spider-Man Goes Mad!" Script: S. Lee. Art: S. Ditko.
>
> #25 (1965). "Captured by J. Jonah Jameson!" Script: S. Lee. Plot & Art: S. Ditko.
>
> #26 (1965). "The Man in the Crime-Master's Mask!" Script: S. Lee. Plot & Art: S. Ditko.
>
> #30 (1965). "The Claws of the Cat!" Script: S. Lee. Plot & Art: S. Ditko.
>
> #31 (1965). "If This Be My Destiny . . . !" Script: S. Lee. Art: S. Ditko.

#32 (1966). "Man on a Rampage!" Script: S. Lee. Plot & Art: S. Ditko.

#33 (1966). "The Final Chapter!" Script: S. Lee. Plot & Art: S. Ditko.

#37 (1966). "Once Upon a Time, There Was a Robot!" Script: S. Lee. Plot & Art: S. Ditko.

#38 (1966). "Just a Guy Named Joe!" Script: S. Lee. Plot & Art: S. Ditko.

#39 (1966). "How Green Was My Goblin!" Script: S. Lee. Art: J. Romita & M. Demeo [M. Esposito].

#40 (1966). "Spidey Saves the Day!" Script: S. Lee. Art: J. Romita & M. Demeo.

#41 (1966). "The Horns of the Rhino!" Script: S. Lee. Art: J. Romita.

#46 (1967). "The Sinister Shocker!" Storytelling: S. Lee & J. Romita.

#50 (1967). "Spider-Man No More!" Storytelling: S. Lee & J. Romita. Finished Art: M. Dimeo (sic).

#53 (1967). "Enter: Dr. Octopus." Storytelling: S. Lee & J. Romita. Finished Art: M. Demeo. [Mickey Demeo was a pseudonym for long-time Spider-Man inker Mike Esposito.]

#54 (1967). "The Tentacles and the Trap!" Storytelling: S. Lee & J. Romita. Finished Art: M. Demeo.

#59 (1968). "The Brand of the Brainwasher!" Storytelling: S. Lee & J. Romita. Finished Art: D. Heck & M. Demeo.

#65 (1968). "The Impossible Escape!" Script: S. Lee. Art: J. Romita & J. Mooney.

#70 (1969). "Spider-Man Wanted!" Script: S. Lee. Plot: J. Romita. Art: J. Mooney.

#71 (1969). "The Speedster and The Spider" Script: S. Lee. Plot & Art: J. Romita. Finished Art: J. Mooney.

#78 (1969). "The Night of the Prowler!" Script: S. Lee. Art: J. Buscema & J. Mooney.

#79 (1969). "To Prowl No More!" Script: S. Lee. Plot & Art: J. Buscema. Finished Art: J. Mooney.

#82 (1970). "And Then Came . . . Electro!" Script: S. Lee. Art: J. Romita & J. Mooney.

#90 (1970). "And Death Shall Come!" Script: S. Lee. Art: G. Kane & J. Romita.

#91 (1970). "To Smash the Spider!" Script: S. Lee. Art: G. Kane & J. Romita.

#96 (1971). "And Now, the Goblin!" Script: S. Lee: Art. G. Kane & J. Romita.

#98 (1971). "The Goblin's Last Gasp!" Script: S. Lee. Art: G. Kane & F. Giacoia.

#100 (1971). "The Spider or the Man?" Script: S. Lee. Art: G. Kane & F. Giacoia.

#101 (1971). "A Monster Called . . . Morbius!" Script: R. Thomas. Art: G. Kane & F. Giacoia.

#102 (1971). "Vampire at Large!" Script: R. Thomas. Art: G. Kane.

#110 (1972). "The Birth of . . . the Gibbon!" Storytelling: S. Lee & J. Romita.

#113 (1972). "They Call the Doctor . . . Octopus!" Script: G. Conway. Art: J. Romita, T. Mortellaro, & J. Starlin.

#114 (1972). "Gang War, Schmang War! What I Want to Know is . . . Who the Heck is Hammerhead?" Script: G. Conway. Art: J. Romita, T. Mortellaro, & J. Starlin.

#115 (1972). "The Last Battle!" Script: G. Conway. Art: J. Romita, T. Mortellaro, & J. Starlin.

#121 (1973). "The Night Gwen Stacy Died!" Script: G. Conway. Art: G. Kane, J. Romita, & T. Mortellaro.

#122 (1973). "The Goblin's Last Stand!" Script: G. Conway. Art: G. Kane, J. Romita, & T. Mortellaro.

#123 (1973). ". . . Just a Man Called Cage!" Script: G. Conway. Art: G. Kane, J. Romita, & T. Mortellaro.

#130 (1974). "Betrayed!" Script: G. Conway. Art: R. Andru, F. Giacoia, & D. Hunt.

#136 (1974). "The Green Goblin Lives Again!" Script: G. Conway. Art: R. Andru, F. Giacoia, & D. Hunt.

#137 (1974). "The Green Goblin Strikes!" Script: G. Conway. Art: R. Andru, F. Giacoia, & D. Hunt.

#141 (1975). "The Man's Name Appears to Be . . . Mysterio!" Script: G. Conway. Art: R. Andru, F. Giacoia, & D. Hunt.

#146 (1975). "Scorpion . . . Where is Thy Sting?" Script: G. Conway. Art: R. Andru, J. Romita, & the gang.

#149 (1975). "Even if I Live, I Die!" Script: G. Conway. Art: R. Andru & M. Esposito.

#150 (1975). "Spider-Man . . . or Spider-Clone!" Script: A. Goodwin. Art: G. Kane, M. Esposito, & F. Giacoia.

#153 (1975). "The Longest Hundred Yards!" Script: L. Wein. Art: R. Andru & M. Esposito.

#159 (1976). "Arm-in-Arm-in-Arm-in-Arm-in-Arm-in-Arm with Doctor Octopus." Script: L. Wein. Art: R. Andru & M. Esposito.

#161 (1976). ". . . And the Nightcrawler Came Prowling, Prowling." Script: L. Wein. Art: R. Andru & M. Esposito.

#175 (1977). "Big Apple Battleground!" Script: L. Wein. Art: R. Andru & J. Mooney.

#194 (1979). "Never Let the Black Cat Cross Your Path!" Script: M. Wolfman. Art: K. Pollard & F. Giacoia.

#195 (1979). "Nine Lives Has the Black Cat!" Script: M. Wolfman. Art: K. Pollard, J. Mooney, M. Esposito, & A. Milgrom.

#196 (1979). "Requiem!" Script: M. Wolfman. Art: A. Milgrom, J. Mooney, & F. Giocoia.

#199 (1979). "Now You See Me! Now You Die!" Script: M. Wolfman. Art: S. Buscema & J. Mooney.

#200 (1980). "The Spider and the Burglar . . . a Sequel." Script: M. Wolfman & S. Lee. Art: K. Pollard & J. Mooney.

#248 (1984). "And He Strikes Like a Thunderball." Script: R. Stern. Art: J. Romita Jr. & B. Breeding.

#252 (1984). "Where are They?!? Still No Word on Missing Heroes!" Plot: R. Stern. Script: T. DeFalco. Art: R. Frenz & B. Breeding.

#257 (1984). "Beware the Claws of Puma!" Script: T. DeFalco. Art: R. Frenz & J. Rubinstein.

#259 (1984). "All My Pasts Remembered!" Script: T. DeFalco. Art: R. Frenz & J. Rubinstein.

#300 (1988). "Venom." Script: D. Michelinie. Art: T. McFarlane.

#327 (1989). "Cunning Attractions!" Script: D. Michelinie. Art: E. Larsen & A. Gordon.

#341 (1990). "With(out) Great Power . . ." Script: D. Michelinie. Art: E. Larsen & R. Emberlin.

#365 (1992). "Fathers and Sins." Script: D. Michelinie. Art: M. Bagley & R. Emberlin.

#377 (1993). "Dust to Dust." Plot: D. Michelinie. Script: S. Grant. Art: J. Johnson & R. Emberlin.

#378 (1993). "Maximum Carnage, Chapter III: Demons on Broadway." Script: D. Michelinie. Art: M. Bagley & R. Emberlin.

#379 (1993). "Maximum Carnage, Chapter VII: The Gathering Storm." Script: D. Michelinie. Art: M. Bagley & R. Emberlin.

#380 (1993). "Maximum Carnage Chapter XI: Soldiers of Hope." Script: D. Michelinie. Art: M. Bagley & R. Emberlin.

#381 (1993). "Samson Unleashed!" Script: D. Michelinie. Art: M. Bagley, R. Emberlin, & A. Milgrom.

#396 (1994). "Deadmen." Script: J. M. DeMatteis. Art: M. Bagley & L. Mahlstedt.

#400 (1995). "The Gift." Script: J. M. DeMatteis. Art: M. Bagley, L. Mahlstedt, & R. Emberlin.

#425 (1997). "The Chump, the Challenge, and the Champion!" Script: T. De-Falco. Art: S. Skroce & B. LaRosa.

#28 (2001). "Distractions." Script: H. Mackie. Art: J. Bennett & S. Florea.

#30 (2001). "Transformations, Literal & Otherwise." Script: J. M. Straczynski. Art: J. Romita Jr. & S. Hanna.

#31 (2001). "Coming Home." Script: J. Straczynski. Art: J. Romita Jr. & S. Hanna.

#32 (2001). "The Long, Dark Pizza of the Soul." Script: J. M. Straczynski. Art: J. Romita Jr. & S. Hanna.

#33 (2001). "All Fall Down." Script: J. M. Straczynski. Art: J. Romita Jr. & S. Hanna.

#34 (2001). "Meltdown." Script: J. M. Straczynski. Art: J. Romita Jr. & S. Hanna.

#35 (2001). "Coming Out." Script: J. M. Straczynski. Art: J. Romita Jr. & S. Hanna.

#38 (2002). "The Conversation." Script: J. M. Straczynski. Art: J. Romita Jr. & S. Hanna.

#46 (2002). "Unnatural Enemies." Script: J. M. Straczynski. Art: J. Romita Jr. & S. Hanna.

#49 (2003). "Bad Connections." Script: J. M. Straczynski. Art: J. Romita Jr. & S. Hanna.

#500 (2003). "Happy Birthday, Part Three." Script: J. M. Straczynski. Art: J. Romita Jr., J. Romita, & S. Hanna.

#504 (2004). "The Coming of Chaos." Script: J. M. Straczynski. Art: J. Romita Jr. & S. Hanna.

#506 (2004). "The Book of Ezekiel: Chapter One." Script: J. M. Straczynski. Art: J. Romita Jr. & S. Hanna.

#508 (2004). "The Book of Ezekiel: Chapter Three." Script: J. M. Straczynski. Art: J. Romita Jr. & S. Hanna.

#527 (2006). "Evolution." Script: J. M. Straczynski. Art: M. Deodato Jr. & J. Pimentel.

#528 (2006). "Spider-Man the Other—Evolve or Die, Part Twelve: Post Mortem." Script: J. M. Straczynski. Art: M. Deodato Jr. & J. Pimentel.

#529 (2006). "Mr. Parker Goes to Washington: Part One of Three." Script: J. M. Straczynski. Art: R. Garney & B. Reinhold.

#532 (2006). "The War at Home: Part One." Script: J. M. Straczynski. Art: R. Garney & B. Reinhold.

#533 (2006). "The War at Home: Part Two." Script: J. M. Straczynski. Art: R. Garney & B. Reinhold.

#536 (2006). "The War at Home: Part Five." Script: J. M. Straczynski. Art: R. Garney & B. Reinhold.

#538 (2007). "The War at Home: Part Seven." Script: J. M. Straczynski. Art: R. Garney & B. Reinhold.

#542 (2007). "Back in Black: Part Four of Five." Script: J. M. Straczynski. Art: R. Garney & B. Reinhold.

#544 (2007). "Spider-Man: One More Day, Part One." Script: J. M. Straczynski. Art: J. Quesada & D. Miki.

#641 (2010). "One Moment in Time, Chapter Four: Something Blue." Script: J. Quesada. Art: P. Rivera, J. Quesada, & D. Miki.

#655 (2011). "No One Dies, Part One of Two: Awakening." Script: D. Slott. Art: M. Martin.

#656 (2011). "No One Dies, Part Two of Two: Resolve." Script: D. Slott. Art: M. Martin.

#673 (2011). "Spider-Island Epilogue: The Naked City." Script: D. Slott. Art: S. Caselli.

#700 (2012). "Dying Wish: Suicide Run." Script: D. Slott. Art: H. Ramos & V. Olazaba.

#1 (2014). "Lucky to Be Alive." Script: D. Slot. Art: H. Ramos & V. Olazaba.

#1.5 (2014). "Learning to Crawl: Part Five." Script: D. Slott. Art: R. Pérez.

#2 (2014). [Untitled]. Script: D. Slott. Art: H. Ramos & V. Olazaba.

#4 (2014). [Untitled]. Script: D. Slott. Art: H. Ramos & E. Delgado.

#7 (2014). "Ms. Marvel Team-Up." Script: D. Slott & C. N. Gage. Art: G. Camuncoli & C. Smith.

#8 (2014). "Ms. Adventures in Babysitting." Script: D. Slott & C. N. Gage. Art: G. Camuncoli & C. Smith.

#9 (2014). "Spider-Verse, Part One: The Gathering." Script: D. Slott. Art: O. Coipel & J. Ponsor.

#11 (2014). "Spider-Verse, Part Three: Higher Ground." Script: D. Slott. Art: O. Coipel, W. V. Grawbadger, J. Livesay, V. Olazaba, & M. Morales.

#14 (2015). "Spider-Verse, Part Six: Web Warriors." Script: D. Slott. Art: G. Camuncoli, O. Coipel, W. V. Grawbadger, C. Smith, & Livesay.

#15 (2016). "The New Iron Spider?!" Script: C. Gage & D. Slott. Art: G. Camuncoli & C. Smith.

#17 (2016). "Before Dead No More—Part Two: Spark of Life." Script: D. Slott. Art: R. B. Silva & A. Di Benedetto.

#19 (2016). "Before Dead No More—Part 4: 'Change of Heart.'" Script: D. Slott & C. N. Gage. Art: G. Camuncoli.

#23 (2017). "The Moment You Know." Script: D. Slott & C. N. Gage. Art: G. Camuncoli & Cam Smith.

#28 (2017). "The Osborn Identity—Part Four: One-on-One." Script: D. Slott. Art: S. Immonen & W. V. Grawbadger.

#60 (2021). "No Exit." Script: N. Spencer. Art: M. Bagley, J. Dell, A. Hennessy.

#68 (2021). "Chameleon Conspiracy: Part 2." Script: N. Spencer & E. Brisson. Art: M. Ferreira, C. Gómez, & Z. Carlos.

#75 (2021). [Untitled]. Script: Z. Wells. Art: P. Gleason.

#88 (2022). [Untitled]. Script: Z. Wells. Art: M. Dowling.

#89 (2022). [Untitled]. Script: P. Gleason. Art: M. Bagley, A. Hennessey, & J. Dell.

#8 (2022). [Untitled]. Script: Z. Wells. Art: J. Romita Jr. & S. Hanna.

#10 (2022). [Untitled]. Script: Z. Wells. Art: N. Dragotta.

#14 (2023). [Untitled *Dark Web* tie-in]. Script: Z. Wells. Art: M. Dowling, K. Hotz, T. Dodson, R. Stegman, T. Townsend, & J. P. Mayer.

Annual #1 (1964). "The Sinister Six!" Script: S. Lee & S. Ditko. Art: S. Ditko.

Annual #5 (1968). "The Parents of Peter Parker." Script: S. Lee & L. Lieber. Art: M. Demeo & J. Romita.

Annual #9 (1973). "The Goblin Lives!" Storytelling: S. Lee & J. Romita. Finished Art: J. Mooney.

Annual #15 (1981). "Spider-Man: Threat or Menace?" Script: D. O'Neil. Art: F. Miller & K. Jansen.

Annual #37 (2010). "The Spider and the Shield." Script: K. Kesel. Art: P. Siqueira.

The Amazing Spider-Man: Extra #1 (2008). "Birthday Boy." Script: Z. Wells. Art: P. Rivera.

The Amazing Spider-Man: Soul of the Hunter (1992). Script: J. M. DeMatteis. Art: M. Zeck & B. McLeod.

Arkham Asylum: A Serious House on Serious Earth (1989). Script: G. Morrison. Art: D. McKean. DC Comics.

Civil War #2 (2006). "Part Two." Script: M. Millar. Art: S. McNiven & D. Vines.

Civil War II: Amazing Spider-Man #1 (2016). [Untitled]. Script: C. Gage. Art: T. Foreman.

Daredevil

#17 (1966). "None Are So Blind . . . !" Script: S. Lee. Art: J. Romita & F. Ray [F. Giacoia].

#8 (1998). "Guardian Devil, Part Eight: The Devil's Deliverance." Script: K. Smith. Art: J. Quesada & J. Palmiotti.

#1 (2022). "The Red Fist Saga—Part 1." Script: C. Zdarsky. Art: M. Checchetto.

Dark Web Finale #1 (2023). "Dawn." Script: Z. Wells. Art: A. Kubert & F. Mortarino with S. Hanna.

Detective Comics #33 (1939). "Legend of the Batman—Who He Is and How He Came to Be!" Script: [B. Finger]. Art: B. Kane. National Comics.

Edge of Spider-Verse #1–5 (2014). Scripts: Various. Art: Various.

Edge of Spider-Verse #1–5 (2022) Scripts; Various. Art: Various.

Fantastic Four

#1 (1961). "The Fantastic Four." Script: S. Lee. Art: J. Kirby, G. Klein, & C. Rule.

#4 (1962). "The Coming of . . . Sub-Mariner!" Script: S. Lee. Art: J. Kirby & S. Brodsky.

FF #1 (2011) "The Club." Script: J. Hickman. Art: S. Epting & R. Magyar.

Free Comic Book Day (Secret Empire) (2017). "Time Flies." Script: C. Zdarsky. Art: Various.

Friendly Neighborhood Spider-Man

#5 (2019). "Not Running." Script: T. Taylor. Art: Y. Cinar

Annual #1 (2007). "Sandman: Year One." Script: P. David. Art: R. Cliquet & R. Stull.

Generations: Miles Morales & Peter Parker Spider-Man #1 (2017). "The Vanishing Point." Script: B. M. Bendis. Art: R. Pérez after S. Ditko.

Incoming #1 (2019). "Incoming!" Script: Various. Art: Various.

M. Bagley, A. Thibert, & D. Panosian.

Marvel Comics #1000 (2019). "We're Calling Him Ben." Script: B. Meltzer. Art: J. T. Tedesco.

Marvel Graphic Novel #46 (1989). "The Amazing Spider-Man: Parallel Lives." Script: G. Conway. Art: A. Saviuk & A. Mushynsky.

Marvel Preview #2 (1975). "Death Sentence." Script: G. Conway. Art: T. DeZuniga.

Marvel Tails Starring Peter Porker, the Spectacular Spider-Ham #1 (1984). "If He Should Punch Me!" Script: T. DeFalco. Art: M. Armstrong & J. Albelo.

Marvel Team-Up

#1 (1972). "Have Yourself a Sandman Little Christmas!" Script: R. Thomas. Art: R. Andru & M. Esposito.

#102 (1981). "Samson and Delilah!" Script: M. W. Barr. Art: F. Springer & M. Esposito.

Marvel Two-In-One Annual #2 (1977). "Death Watch!" Story & Art: J. Starlin. Finished Art: J. Rubinstein.

Miles Morales: Spider-Man

> #1–3 (2019). [Untitled]. Script: S. Ahmed. Art: J. Garrón.

> #11 (2020). [Untitled]. Script: S. Ahmed. Art: Z. Carlos & I. Guara.

> #17 (2021). [Untitled]. Script: S. Ahmed. Art: C. Carmero.

Miles Morales: The Ultimate Spider-Man Ultimate Collection

> #1 (2015). [Untitled]. Script: B. M. Bendis. Art: S. Pichelli, C. Samnee, & D. Marquez.

> #10 (2015). [Untitled]. Script: B. M. Bendis. Art: S. Pichelli, C. Samnee, & D. Marquez.

Miles Morales: Ultimate Spider-Man #1–3 (2014). [Untitled]. Script: B. M. Bendis. Art: D. Marquez.

The New Avengers #5 (2005). "Breakout! Part 5." Script: B. M. Bendis. Art: P. Finch & D. Miki.

Peter Parker, the Spectacular Spider-Man

> #87 (1983). "Mistaken Identities." Script: B. Mantlo. Art: A. Milgrom & J. Mooney.

> #100 (1985). "Breakin'!" Script & Pencils: A. Milgrom. Finished Art: G. Isherwood & V. Colletta.

> #107 (1985). "Original Sin." Script: P. David. Art: R. Buckler & B. Breeding.

> #110 (1986). "All My Sins Remembered." Writer: P. David. Art: R. Buckler & M. Hands.

Peter Parker: The Spectacular Spider-Man

> #300 (2018). "Showdown." Script: C. Zdarsky. Art: A. Kubert & J. Frigeri.

> #301 (2018). "Amazing Fantasy, Part One." Script: C. Zdarsky. Art: J. Quinones & J. Rivera.

> #304 (2018). "No More—Part One." Script: C. Zdarsky. Art: A. Kubert.

> #306 (2018). "Coming Home—Part One." Script: C. Zdarsky. A. Kubert & J. Frigeri.

> #307 (2018). "No More—Part Four." Script: C. Zdarsky. Art: A. Kubert & J. Frigeri.

> #310 (2018). "Finale." Script & Art: C. Zdarsky.

> #6 (2018). "My Dinner with Jonah." Script: C. Zdarsky. Art: M. Walsh.

> *Annual* #1 (1979). "And Men Shall Call Him . . . Octopus!" Script: B. Mantlo. Art: R. Buckler & J. Mooney.

Peter Porker, the Spectacular Spider-Ham #15 (1987). "To Oink or Not to Oink" or "The Days of Swing and Roses." Script: S. Mellor. Art: J. Albelo & P. Fornier.

The Pulse #5 (2004). "Thin Air (Part 5 of 5)." Script: B. M. Bendis. Art: M. Bagley & S. Hanna.

Sandman (1989). "Preludes and Nocturnes." Script: N. Gaiman. Art: S. Kieth, M. Dringenberg, M. Jones II, & D. McKean. DC Comics.

Savage Wolverine #6 (2013). [Untitled]. Script: Z. Wells. Art: J. Maduriera.

The Sensational Spider-Man #34 (2007). "Nothing Can Stop the Rhino." Script: R. Aguirre-Sacasa. Art: S. Chen & S. Hanna.

She-Hulk #4 (2004). "Web of Lies." Script: D. Slott. Art: J. Bobilo & M. Sosa.

Silk

    #1 (2015). [Untitled]. Script: R. Thompson. Art: S. Lee.

    #4 (2015). [Untitled]. Script: R. Thompson. Art: D. Johnson.

    #7 (2015). [Untitled]. Script: R. Thompson. Art: T. Ford.

    #3 (2016). [Untitled]. Script: R. Thompson. Art: T. Ford.

    #1–2 (2022). [Untitled]. Script: E. Kim. Art: T. Miyazawa.

Son of M #1 (2006). "One Day in the Life of Pietro Maximoff—Homo Sapiens." Script: D. Hine. Art: R. A. Martinez.

The Spectacular Spider-Man

    #189 (1992). "The Osborn Legacy." Script: J. M. DeMatteis. Art: S. Buscema.

    #200 (1993). "Best of Enemies." Script: J. M. DeMatteis. Art: S. Buscema.

    #201 (1993). "To Kill the Cat!" Script: J. M. DeMatteis. Art: S. Buscema.

    #202 (1993). "Chapter IX: The Turning Point!" Script: J. M. DeMatteis. Art: S. Buscema.

    #203 (1993). "Maximum Carnage Chapter XIII: War of the Heart!" Script: J. M. DeMatteis. Art: S. Buscema.

    #206 (1993). "Death by Tombstone: Conclusion: Fatal Desire!" Script: S. Grant. Art: S. Buscema.

    #211 (1994). "Pursuit, Part 2: Face Value." Script: M. Lackey. Art: S. Buscema.

    #220 (1995). "Web of Death, Part 2: A Time to Live!" Script: T. DeFalco. Art: S. Buscema & B. Sienkiewicz.

    #21 (2005). "Read 'Em an' Weep." Script: P. Jenkins. Art: T. Caldwell & R. Campanella.

    Magazine (1968). "Lo, This Monster!" Script: S. Lee. Art: J. Romita.

Spider-Geddon

    #1 (2018). [Untitled]. Script: C. N. Gage & D. Slott. Art: J. Molina.

#3 (2019). [Untitled]. Script: C. N. Gage & D. Slott. Art: C. Barberi, T. Nauck, & J. Marzan Jr.

Spider-Gwen #34 (2018). "The Life of Gwen Stacy. Conclusion." Script: J. Latour. Art: R. Rodriguez.

Spider-Gwen: Ghost Spider

> #1 (2018). "Spider-Geddon Part 1: Uncharted." Script: S. McGuire. Art: R. Kampe.
>
> #4 (2019). "Spider-Geddon Part 4: Like Stars from the Sky." Script: S. McGuire. Art: R. Kampe & T. Miyazawa.
>
> #10 (2019). "You Can't Stop the Beat." Script: S. McGuire. Art: T. Miyazawa & R. Kämpe.

Spider-Man

> #1–2 (2016). Script: B. M. Bendis. Art: S. Pichelli.
>
> #26 (1992). "With Great Responsibility!" Script: T. DeFalco, & R. Frenz. Art: M. Bagley, K. Janson, A. Milgrom, K. Williams, M. Texeira, J. Rubinstein, & T. Palmer.
>
> #1–5 (2020). "Bloodline." Script: J. J. Abrams & H. Abrams. Art: S. Pichelli & E. D'Amico.
>
> #1 (2022). "End of the Spider-Verse, Part One: The One and Only-ish." Script: D. Slott. Art: M. Bagley & J. Dell.
>
> #2 (2023). "End of the Spider-Verse, Part Two: The Last Spider-Man Standing." Script: D. Slott. Art by M. Bagley & J. Dell.
>
> #4 (2023). "End of the Spider-Verse, Part Four: The Unraveling." Script: D. Slott. Art: M. Bagley, J. Dell, & A. Hennessy.
>
> *Annual* #1 (2018). "Youngblood." Script: B. E. Hill. Art: M. Bagley, N. Blake II, A. Martinez, & R. Poggi.

Spider-Man and the X-Men #1–2 (2015). [Untitled]. Script: E. Kalan. Art: M. Failla.

Spider-Man Special: Black & Blue & Read All Over #1 (2006). "Black & Blue & Read All Over." Script: J. Krueger. Art: D. Johnson & T. Palmer.

Spider-Man Unlimited

> #1 (1993). "Maximum Carnage, Chapter I: Carnage Rising!" Script: T. DeFalco. Art: R. Lim & J. Sanders III.
>
> #2 (1993). "Maximum Carnage, Chapter XIV: The Hatred, the Horror, and the Hero!" Script: T. DeFalco. Art: M. Bagley, R. Lim, S. de la Rosa, & J. Sanders III.

Spider-Man/Deadpool #1 (2016). "Isn't It Bromantic? Part One." Script: J. Kelly. Art: E. McGuinness & M. Morales.

Spider-Man: Bloodline (2019). Script: J. J. Abrams & H. Abrams. Art: S. Pichelli & E. D'Amico.

Spider-Man: Hobgoblin Lives #2 (1997). "Back in Business." Script: R. Stern. Art: R. Frenz, J. Moore, & S. Hanna.

Spider-Man: The Osborn Journal #1 (1996). "Spider-Man: The Osborn Journals." Script: D. Greenberg. Art: K. Hotz, J. Moore, & A. Milgrom.

Spider-Man: Renew Your Vows #5 (2015). "I'll Always Be There for You." Script: D. Slott. Art: A. Kubert & S. Hanna.

Spider-Man's Tangled Web #20 (2003). "Behind the Mustache." Script: Z. Wells. Art: D. Haspiel.

Spider-Men #1–5 (2012). [Untitled]. Script: B. M. Bendis. Art: S. Pichelli.

Spider-Woman

> #1 (1978). ". . . A Future Uncertain!" Script: M. Wolfman. Art: C. Infantino & T. DeZuniga.

> #5 (2020). [Untitled]. Script: K. Pacheco. Art: P. Pérez.

Spidey: School's Out #1 (2018). [Untitled]. Script: J. Barber. Art: T. Nauck.

Strange Tales #110 (1963). "Doctor Strange, Master of Black Magic!" Script: S. Lee. Art: S. Ditko.

Superior Spider-Man

> #4 (2014). "The Aggressive Approach." Script: D. Slott. Art: G. Camuncoli & J. Dell.

> #9 (2019). "Troubled Mind, Part Three: Gray Matters." Script: C. Gage. Art: M. Hawthorne & W. V. Grawbadger.

> #10 (2013). "Independence Day." Script: D. Slott. Art: R. Stegman & C. Smith.

> #15 (2013). "Run, Goblin, Run, Part 1- The Tinkerer's Apprentice." Script: D. Slott. Art: H. Ramos & V. Olazaba.

> #20 (2013). "Still Standing." Script: D. Slott. Art: G. Camuncoli & J. Dell.

Superior Spider-Man Team-Up #6 (2013). [Untitled]. Script: C. Yost. Art: M. Checchetto.

Ultimate Avengers vs. New Ultimates #4 (2011). "Ultimate Avengers vs. New Ultimates (Part IV)." Script: M. Millar. Art: L. Yu, S. Segovia, G. Alanguilan, J. Paz, & J. Huet.

Ultimate Comics Spider-Man

> #1 (2011). "All-New Ultimate Spider-Man." Script: B. M. Bendis. Art: S. Pichelli.

> #2 (2011). "Who is Miles Morales?" Script: B. M. Bendis. Art: S. Pichelli.

#3 (2011). "To Be or Not to Be . . . Spider-Man!" Script: B. M. Bendis. Art: S. Pichelli.

#14 (2012). "Divided We Fall (Part Two)." Script: B. M. Bendis. D. Marquez.

Ultimate Fallout #4 (2011). "Spider-Man No More (Part IV)." Script: B. M. Bendis, J. Hickman, & N. Spencer. Art: S. Pichelli, S. Larroca, & S. Crain.

Ultimate Spider-Man

#1 (2000). "Powerless." Story: B. M. Bendis & B. Jemas. Script: B. M. Bendis. Art: M. Bagley & M. Thibert.

#4 (2001). "With Great Power." Script: B. M. Bendis & B. Jemas. Art: M. Bagley.

#6 (2001). "Big Time Super Hero." Story: B. M. Bendis & B. Jemas. Script: B. M. Bendis. Art: M. Bagley & A. Thibert.

#66 (2004). "Even We Don't Believe This." Script: B. M. Bendis. Art: M. Bagley & S. Hanna.

#74 (2005). "Hobgoblins, Part 3." Script: B. M. Bendis Art: M. Bagley & S. Hanna

Super Special #1 (2002). "Ultimate Spider-Man Super Special." Script: B. M. Bendis. Art: Various.

Untold Tales of Spider-Man #16 (1996). "The Boy Next Door." Script: K. Busiek. Art: P. Olliffe & D. Giordano.

Web of Spider-Man

#31 (1985). "Part 1: The Coffin." Script: J. M. DeMatteis. Art: M. Zeck & B. McLeod.

#102 (1993). "Maximum Carnage Chapter VI: Sinking Fast." Script: T. Kavanagh. Art: A. Saviuk & D. Hudson.

Web Warriors #1 (2015). "Electroverse, Part One: Static." Script: M. Costa. Art: D. Baldeon & S. Hanna.

Webspinners: Tales of Spider-Man

#10 (1999). "The Show Must Go On." Script: P. Jenkins. Art: S. Phillips.

#11 (1999). "Off the Deep End." Script: P. Jenkins. Art: S. Phillips.

#12 (1999). "Perchance to Dream." Script: P. Jenkins. Art: J. G. Jones & J. Palmiotti.

What If...? #19 (1979). "What If Spider-Man Had Stopped the Burglar Who Killed His Uncle?" Script: P. Gillis. Art: P. Broderick & M. Esposito.

What If...? Miles Morales #4 (2022). "What If . . . Miles Morales . . . Became Thor?" Script: Y. Mercado. Art: L. Zagaria.

X-Men #60 (1969). "In The Shadow of . . . Sauron!" Script: R. Thomas. Art: N. Adams & T. Palmer.

Not Comics or Graphic Novels

Acevedo, A. (2018). A personalistic appraisal of Maslow's needs theory of motivation: From "humanistic" psychology to integral humanism. *Journal of Business Ethics*, *148*(4), 741–763.

Adame, J. L., Lo, C. C., & Cheng, T. C. (2022). Ethnicity and self-reported depression among Hispanic immigrants in the U.S. *Community Mental Health*, *58*(1), 121–135.

Allison, S. T. (2016). The initiation of heroism science. *Heroism Science*, *1*(1), Artl 1. https://scholarship.richmond.edu/heroism-science/vol1/iss1/1

Allison, S. T., & Goethals, G. R. (2011). *Heroes: What they do and why we need them.* Oxford University Press.

Allison, S. T., & Goethals, G. R. (2016). Hero worship: The elevation of the human spirit. *Journal for the Theory of Social Behaviour*, *46*(2), 187–210.

Alvarado, S. (2019). *The science of Marvel: From Infinity Stones to Iron Man's armor, the real science behind the MCU revealed!* Adams Media.

Ambrose of Milan (2010). *Ambrose of Milan: Political letters and speeches* (J. H. W. G. Liebeschuetz, Trans.). Liverpool University Press.

American Psychiatric Association (1952). *Diagnostic and statistical manual of mental disorders* [DSM-I]. American Psychiatric Association.

American Psychiatric Association (1968). *Diagnostic and statistical manual of mental disorders* (2nd ed.) [DSM-II]. American Psychiatric Association.

American Psychiatric Association (1980). *Diagnostic and statistical manual of mental disorders* (3rd ed.) [DSM-III]. American Psychiatric Association.

American Psychiatric Association (2000). *Diagnostic and statistical manual of mental disorders* (4th ed., text rev.) [DSM-IV-TR]. American Psychiatric Association.

American Psychiatric Association (2013). *Diagnostic and statistical manual of mental disorders* (5th ed.) [DSM-5]. American Psychiatric Association.

American Psychiatric Association (2022). *Diagnostic and statistical manual of mental disorders* (5th ed., text rev.) [DSM-5-TR]. American Psychiatric Association.

American Psychological Association (n.d.). *Self-control.* APA Dictionary of Psychology. https://dictionary.apa.org/self-control

Anderson, P. D., Bokor, G. (2012). Forensic aspects of drug-induced violence. *Journal of Pharmacy Practice*, *25*(1), 41–9.

Arain, M., Haque, M., Johal, L., Mathur, P., Nel, W., Rais, A., Sandhu, R., & Sharma, S. (2013). Maturation of the adolescent brain. *Neuropsychiatric Disease & Treatment*, *9*, 449–461.

Arciniega, G. M., Anderson, T. C., Tovar-Blank, Z. G., & Tracey, T. J. (2008). Toward a fuller conception of Machismo: Development of a traditional Machismo and Caballerismo scale. *Journal of Counseling Psychology*, *55*(1), 19.

Arkes, H. (1979). Competence and the overjustification effect. *Motivation & Emotion* *3*(2), 143–150.

Armstrong-Carter, E., Do, K. T., Guassi Moreira, J. F., Prinstein, M. J., & Telzer, E. H. (2021). Examining a new prosocial risk-taking scale in a longitudinal sample of ethnically diverse adolescents. *Journal of Adolescence*, *93*, 222–233.

Armstrong-Carter, E., Do, K. T., Duell, N., Kwon, S., Lindquist, K. A., Prinstein, M. J., & Telzer, E. H. (2022). Adolescents' perceptions of social risk and prosocial tendencies: Developmental change and individual differences. *Social Development*, 1–16. Advance online publication. https://onlinelibrary.wiley.com/toc/14679507/0/0

Arnett, J. J. (2000). Emerging adulthood: A theory of development from the late teens through the twenties. *American Psychologist*, *55*(5), 469–480.

Aron, A., & Aron, E. N. (1986). *Love and the expansion of self: Understanding attraction and satisfaction*. Hemisphere.

Aron, A., McLaughlin-Volpe, T., Mashek, D., Lewandowski, G., Wright, S. C., & Aron, E. N. (2004). Including others in the self. *European Review of Social Psychology*, *15*(1), 101–132.

Asaro, M.R. (2001). Working with adult homicide survivors, part II: Helping family members cope with murder. *Perspectives in Psychiatric Care*, *37*(4), 115–124, 136.

Asgeirsdottir, B. B., Sigfusdottir, I. D., Gudjonsson, G. H., & Sigurdsson, J. F. (2011). Associations between sexual abuse and family conflict/violence, self-injurious behavior, and substance use: The mediating role of depressed mood and anger. *Child Abuse & Neglect*, *35*(3), 210–219.

Averill, J. R. (1968). Grief: Its nature and significance. *Psychological Bulletin*, *70*(6), 721–748.

Babula, M. (2013). *Motivation, altruism, personality, and social psychology*. Palgrave Macmillan.

Bach, P., Frischknecht, U., Bungert, M., Karl, D., Karl, D., Vollmert, C., Vollstädt-Klein, S., Lis, S., Kiefer, F. & Hermann, D. (2019). Effects of social exclusion and physical pain in chronic opioid maintenance treatment: fMRI correlates. *European Neuropsychopharmacology*, *29*(2), 291–305.

Ballard, P. J. (2016). Longitudinal links between discrimination and civic development among Latino and Asian adolescents. *Journal of Research on Adolescence*, *26*(4), 723–737.

Bandura, A. (1977). *Social learning theory.* Prentice-Hall.

Barash, D. P., & Lipton, J. E. (2011). *Payback: Why we retaliate, redirect aggression, and take revenge.* Oxford University Press.

Barber, L. (2018). Exploring forgiveness of self and others using integrative methodologies. *Dissertation Abstracts International Section C: Worldwide, 75*(4-C).

Bareket-Bojmel, L., Moran, S., and Shahar, G. (2016). Strategic self-presentation on Facebook: Personal motives and audience response to online behavior. *Computers in Human Behavior, 55*(Pt. B), 788–795.

Barlé, N., Wortman, C. B., & Latack, J. A. (2017). Traumatic bereavement: Basic research and clinical implications. *Journal of Psychotherapy Integration, 27*(2), 127–139.

Barnes, R. D., Ickes, W., & Kidd, R. F. (1979). Effects of the perceived intentionality and stability of another's dependency on helping behavior. *Personality & Social Psychology Bulletin, 5*(3), 367–372.

Barrett, S. (2020, December 25). *Nick Spencer's new Spider-Man twist literally demonizes the mentally ill.* The Mary Sue. https://www.themarysue.com/spider-man-comics-harry-mental-illness

Barrie, J. M. (1904). *Peter Pan or the boy who wouldn't grow up* [theatrical play]. Project Gutenberg. http://gutenberg.net.au/ebooks03/0300081h.html

Bartholomaeus, C. (2012). "I'm not allowed wrestling stuff": Hegemonic masculinity and primary school boys. *Journal of Sociology, 48*(3), 227–247.

Bartolomé, Y. (2021). *Radical ecstasy: The passionate compassion of sacred altruism.* Pacifica Graduate Institute Dissertations Publishing. https://www.proquest.com/docview/2479077556

Barton, A., McLaney, S., & Stephens, D. (2020). Targeted interventions for violence among Latinx youth: A systematic review. *Aggression & Violent Behavior, 53*(3), 101434.

Batchelor, B. (2017). *Stan Lee: The man behind Marvel.* Rowman & Littlefield.

Batson, C. D., Batson, J. G., Griffit, C. A., Barrientos, S., Brandt, J. R., Sprengelmeyer, P. (1989). Negative-state relief and the empathy-altruism hypothesis. *Journal of Personality & Social Psychology, 56*(6), 922–933.

Batson, C. D., Batson, J. G., Slingsby, J. K., Harrell, K. L., Peekna, H. M., & Todd, R. M. (1991). Empathic joy and the empathy-altruism hypothesis. *Journal of Personality & Social Psychology, 61*(3), 413–426.

Batson, C. D., Lishner, D. A., & Stocks, E. L. (2014). The empathy-altruism hypothesis. In D. A. Schroeder & W. G. Graziano (Eds.), *The Oxford handbook of prosocial behavior* (pp. 259–281). Oxford University Press.

Baumeister R.F., Bratslavsky, E., Muraven, M., Tice, D.M. (1998). Ego depletion: Is the active self a limited resource? *Journal of Personality & Social Psychology, 74*(5), 1252–65.

Baumeister, R. F. (Ed.) (1999). *The self in social psychology.* Psychology Press, Taylor & Francis.

Baumeister, R. F., & Vohs, K. D. (2007). Belief perseverance. In R. F. Baumeister & K. D. Vohs (Eds.), *Encyclopedia of social psychology* (Vol. 1), 110.

Baylor College of Medicine (2018). *Why do we root for the underdog?* Baylor College of Medicine. https://www.bcm.edu/news/why-we-root-for-underdog

Becker, S. W., & Eagly, A. H. (2004). The heroism of women and men. *American Psychologist, 59*(3), 163–178.

Benner, D. G. (2011). *Soulful spirituality: Being fully alive and deeply human.* Brazos.

Bergman, A. S., Axberg, U., & Hanson, E. (2017). When a parent dies–a systematic review of the effects of support programs for parentally bereaved children and their caregivers. *BMC Palliative Care, 16*(1), 1–15.

Berzoff, J. (2011). The transformative nature of grief and bereavement. *Clinical Social Work Journal, 39*(3), 262–269.

Besharat, M. A., & Shahidi, S. (2010). Perfectionism, anger, and anger rumination. *International Journal of Psychology, 45*(6), 427–434.

Bettencourt, B.A., Talley, A., Benjamin, A.J., & Valentine, J. (2006). Personality and aggressive behavior under provoking and neutral conditions: A meta-analytic review. *Psychology Bulletin, 132*(5), 751–77.

Beutel, M. E., Klein, E. M., Brähler, E. (2017). Loneliness in the general population: Prevalence, determinants and relations to mental health. *BMC Psychiatry,* 17, Artl 97.

Biswas, S., & Visell, Y. (2021). Haptic perception, mechanics, and material technologies for virtual reality. *Advanced Functional Materials, 31*(39), Artl 2008186.

Blanchard, T., Kerbeykian, T., & McGrath, R. E. (2020). Why are signature strengths and well-being related? Tests of multiple hypotheses. *Journal of Happiness Studies, 21*(6), 2095–2114.

Bo, S., Abu-Akel, A., Kongerslev, M., & Simonsen, E. (2021). Predictors of criminal offending in a clinical sample of patients diagnosed with schizophrenia: A 6-year follow-up study. *Personality Disorders: Theory, Research, & Treatment, 12*(3), 216–227.

Bogner, J., Corrigan, J. D., Yi, H., Singichetti, B., Manchester, K., Huang, L., & Yang, J. (2020). Lifetime history of traumatic brain injury and behavioral health problems in a population-based sample. *Journal of Head Trauma Rehabilitation, 35*(1), E43–E50.

Bolt, M., & Dunn, D. S. (2016). *Pursuing human strengths: A positive psychology guide* (2nd ed.). Worth.

Bonow, R. H., Wang, J., Zatzick, D. F., Rivara, F. P., & Rowhani-Rahbar, A. (2019). Traumatic brain injury and the risk for subsequent crime perpetration. *Journal of Head Trauma Rehabilitation, 34*(1), E61–E69.

Borawski, D., & Nowak, A. (2022). As long as you are self-compassionate, you will never walk alone: The interplay between self-compassion and rejection sensitivity in predicting loneliness. *International Journal of Psychology, 57*(5), 621–628.

Bowlby, J., & Ainsworth, M. (2013). The origins of attachment theory. *Attachment Theory: Social, Developmental, & Clinical Perspectives, 45*(28), 759–775.

Boyd-Franklin, N. (2003). *Black families in therapy: Understanding the African-American experience.* Guilford.

Bozeman, B., & Feeney, M. K. (2008). Mentor matching: A "goodness of fit" model. *Administration & Society, 40*(5), 465–482.

Bratko D., Butković A., Vukasović T. (2017). Heritability of personality. *Psychological Topics, 26*(1), 1–24.

Bretherton, I. (1992). The origins of attachment theory: John Bowlby and Mary Ainsworth. *Developmental Psychology, 28*(5), 759–775. https://doi.org/10.1037/0012-1649.28.5.759

Brewer-Smyth, K., Cornelius, M. E., & Pickelsimer, E. E. (2015). Childhood adversity, mental health, and violent crime. *Journal of Forensic Nursing, 11*(1), 4–14.

Bridson, S. (2016, December 19). *Peter Parker: The relatable one.* Anfield Index. https://anfieldindex.com/geek/comics/peter-parker-relatable-one

Britton, K. (2015/2018). Curiosity as the engine of well-being. In S. Polly & K. H. Britton (Eds.), *Character strengths matter: How to live a full life* (pp. 37–43). Positive Psychology News. https://read.amazon.com/?asin=B010965J5A

Bronfenbrenner, U. (1978). The social role of the child in ecological perspective/die soziale rolle des kindes in ökologischer perspektive. *Zeitschrift für Soziologie, 7*(1), 4–20.

Brophy, B. (1989, March 6). It doesn't hurt to be alone. *U.S. News & World Report, 106*, 54–55.

Brown, A. S. (2004). *The déjà vu experience.* Psychology Press.

Brown, B. (2015). *Daring greatly: How the courage to be vulnerable transforms the way we live, love, parent, and lead.* Penguin.

Brown, B. (2021). *Atlas of the heart: Mapping meaningful connection and the language of human experience.* Random House.

Bryant, A. (2019a, October 30). *Analyzing race-bending in comic book media*. Cinema Debate. https://cinemadebate.com/2019/10/30/analyzing-race-bending-in-comic-book-media

Bryant, R. A. (2019b). Post-traumatic stress disorder: A state-of-the-art review of evidence and challenges. *World Psychiatry, 18*(3), 259–269.

Budiarto, Y., Helmi A.F, (2021). Shame and self-esteem: A meta-analysis. *European Journal of Psychology, 17*(2), 131–145.

Bull, B. (2021). Parents of non-binary children: Stories of understanding and support. *Dissertation Abstracts International: Section B: The Sciences & Engineering, 82*(12-B).

Burke, C. (2014). An exploration of the effects of mindfulness training and practice in association with enhanced wellbeing for children and adolescents: Theory, research, and practice. In F. A. Huppert & C. L. Cooper (Eds.), *Interventions and policies to enhance wellbeing* (pp. 141–184). Wiley Blackwell.

Burstein, M. (2006). The friendly neighborhood of Peter Parker. In G. Conway (Ed.), *Webslinger: Unauthorized essays on your friendly neighborhood Spider-Man* (pp. 87–104). BenBella.

Burton, L. (2007). Childhood adultification in economically disadvantaged families: A conceptual model. *Family Relations, 56*(4), 329–345.

Byrne, D., Clore, G. L., & Worchel, P. (1966). Effect of economic similarity-dissimilarity on interpersonal attraction. *Journal of Personality & Social Psychology, 4*(2), 220–224.

Cacioppo, S., Capitanio, J. P., & Cacioppo, J. T. (2014). Toward a neurology of loneliness. *Psychological Bulletin, 140*(6), 1464–1504.

Campbell, J. (1949/1973). *The hero with a thousand faces*. Princeton University Press.

Cardoza, K. (2016, May 23). *Feeling 'invisible'—how mental illness often goes unnoticed in the classroom*. WAMU. https://wamu.org/story/16/05/23/feeling_invisible_how_mental_illness_often_goes_unnoticed_in_the_classroom

Carlson, L. D., & Lester, D. (1980). *Thrill seeking in police officers. Psychological Reports, 47*(3, pt. 2), 1102.

Carveth, D. L. (2006). Self-punishment as guilt evasion: Theoretical issues. *Canadian Journal of Psychoanalysis/Revue Canadienne de Psychanalyse, 14*(2), 174–196.

Casey, B. J., & Galván, A. (2016). The teen brain: "Arrested development" in resisting temptation. In T. S. Braver (Ed.), *Motivation and cognitive control* (pp. 263–282). Routledge/Taylor & Francis.

Cassell, W. A., Charles, T., Dubey, B. L., & Janssen, H. (2014). SIS incites long term PTSD combat memories and survivor guilt. *Journal of Projective Psychology & Mental Health, 21*(2), 68–80.

Castillo, D. T., Joseph, J. S., Tharp, A. T., C'de Baca, J., Torres-Sena, L. M., Qualls, C., & Miller, M. W. (2014). Externalizing and internalizing subtypes of posttraumatic psychopathology and anger expression. *Journal of Traumatic Stress, 27*(1), 108–111.

Castro, A. T. (2006). J. Jonah Jameson: Just what the heck is that guy's major malfunction anyway? In G. Conway (Ed.), *Webslinger: Unauthorized essays on your friendly neighborhood Spider-Man* (pp. 165-174). BenBella.

Cattell, R. B. (1943). The description of personality: Basic traits resolved into clusters. *Journal of Abnormal & Social Psychology, 38*(4), 476–506.

Center for Victim Research. (2019). *Losing a loved one to homicide: What we know about homicide co-victims from research and practice evidence.* Center for Victim Research.

Chen, C.-K., & Murray, R. M. (2004). How does drug abuse interact with familial and developmental factors in the etiology of schizophrenia? In M. S. Keshavan, J. L. Kennedy, & R. M. Murray (Eds.), *Neurodevelopment and schizophrenia* (pp. 248–269). Cambridge University Press.

Cherry, K. (2022, August). *What is a guilt complex?* Very Well Mind. https://www.verywellmind.com/guilt-complex-definition-symptoms-traits-causes-treatment-5115946

Cheung, I., Jakovcevski, M., & Akbarian, S. (2012). The epigenetics of schizophrenia. In A. S. Brown & P. H. Patterson (Eds.), *The origins of schizophrenia* (pp. 227–252). Columbia University Press.

Chevalier, J., & Gheerbrant, A. (1969/1996). *The Penguin dictionary of symbols* (2nd ed.). Penguin.

Chiang, M., Reid-Varley, W. B., & Fan, X. (2019). Creative art therapy for mental illness. *Psychiatry Research, 275*, 129–136.

Chin, B., Murphy, M. L. M., Janicki-Deverts, D., Cohen, S. (2017). Marital status as a predictor of diurnal salivary cortisol levels and slopes in a community sample of healthy adults. *Psychoneuroendocrinology, 78*, 68–75.

Chu, C. (2017). Role of oxytocin: Social exclusion and suicidal behavior. *Electronic Theses, Treatises, & Dissertations.* Florida State University Libraries.

Clark, C. (2019). *How to protect yourself from an emotional bully.* Courtney Clark. https://www.courtneyclark.com/stress/how-to-protect-yourself-from-an-emotional-bully

Clark, C. B., Martinez, K. A., Moroney, K., & Schroeder, R. W. (2020). The impact of traumatic brain injury on criminal justice involvement. *North American Journal of Psychology, 22*(3), 483–498.

Clark, M. S., & Mills, J. (1979). Interpersonal attraction in exchange and communal relationships. *Journal of Personality & Social Psychology, 37*(1), 12–24.

Clevenger, S., Navarro, J. N., Marcum, C. D., & Higgins, G. E. (2018). *Understanding victimology: An active learning approach*. Routledge.

Clyman, J. (2012). *The Amazing Spider-Man:* Growth over grief [Review of the film *The Amazing Spider-Man*, by M. Webb, Dir.]. *PsycCRITIQUES, 57*(36). http://dx.doi .org/10.1037/a0029762

Coan, J. A., Schaefer, H. S., & Davidson, R. J. (2006). Lending a hand: Social regulation of the neural response to threat. *Psychological Science, 17*(12), 1032–1039.

Coetzee, L. (2020). Victim empathy in young sex offenders in the emergent adulthood developmental phase. *Journal of Sexual Aggression, 26*(2), 251–262.

Colantonio, A., Kim, H., Allen, S., Asbridge, M., Pergrave, J., & Brochu, S. (2014). Traumatic brain injury and early life experiences among men and women in a prison population. *Journal of Correctional Health Care, 20*(4), 271–279.

Coleman, J. (2021). *The teacher and the teenage brain*. Routledge/Taylor & Francis.

Collins, N. L., & Feeney, B. C. (2000). A safe haven: An attachment theory perspective on support seeking and caregiving in intimate relationships. *Journal of Personality & Social Psychology, 78*(6), 1053–1073.

Concepcion, J. (2018, November). *Stan Lee gave us relatable superheroes*. The Ringer. https://www.theringer.com/movies/2018/11/14/18094480/stan-lee-gave-us-relat- able-superheroes

Connell, R. W. (2005). *Masculinities* (2nd ed.). University of California Press.

Consolini, J., Sorella, S., & Grecucci, A. (2022). Evidence for lateralized functional con- nectivity patterns at rest related to the tendency of externalizing or internalizing anger. *Cognitive, Affective, & Behavioral Neuroscience, 22*(4), 788–802.

Contino, J. M. (2002). A view to a kill. *Wizard's Spider-Man Special*, 6–11.

Contreras, I. M., Kosiak, K., Hardin, K. M., & Novaco, R. W. (2020). Anger rumination in the context of high anger and forgiveness. *Personality & Individual Differences, 171*. Advance online publication. https://doi.org/10.1016/j.paid.2020.110531

Cornelius, M. E. (2013). PTSD and substance use disorders among offenders: Ex- amining the effects of TBI, gender and interpersonal violence victimization. *Dissertation Abstracts International Section A: Humanities & Social Sciences, 73*(11- A(E)).

Corr, C. A. (2020). Elisabeth Kübler-Ross and the "five stages" model in a sampling of recent American textbooks. *Omega: Journal of Death & Dying, 82*(2), 294–322.

Corrêa, J. C., Ávila, M. P. W., Lucchetti, A. L. G., & Lucchetti, G. (2019). Altruis- tic behaviour, but not volunteering, has been associated with cognitive perfor- mance in community-dwelling older persons. *Psychogeriatrics, 19*(2), 117–125.

Di Silvestro, R. (2020, January 24). *Spider-Man vs the real deal: Spider powers.* National Wildlife Federation. https://blog.nwf.org/2012/06/spiderman-vs-the-real-deal-spider-powers

Diemer, M. A., & Blustein, D. L. (2006). Critical consciousness and career development among urban youth. *Journal of Vocational Behavior, 68*(2), 220–232.

Do, K. T., Guassi Moreira, J. F., & Telzer, E. H. (2017). "But is helping you worth the risk?" Defining prosocial risk taking in adolescence. *Developmental Cognitive Neuroscience, 25*, 260–271.

Dorsey, E. (2011). Dilemmas in search of a code. *Modern Psychoanalysis, 36*(2), 176–211.

Doumas, D. M., Russo, G. M., Miller, R., Esp, S., Mastroleo, N. R., & Turrisi, R. (2022). Sensation seeking and adolescent drinking: Do protective behavioral strategies lower risk? *Journal of Counseling & Development, 100*(4), 352–363.

Dovidio, J. F., Piliavin, J. A., Schroeder, D. A., & Penner, L. A. (2006). *The social psychology of prosocial behavior.* Erlbaum.

Draven, D. (2021, March 7). *10 most iconic one-liners from Marvel superheroes.* Comic Book Resources. https://www.cbr.com/most-iconic-quotes-marvel-superheroes

Du Bois, W. E. B. (1969). *The souls of Black folk.* New American Library.

du Pont, A., Rhee, S. H., Corley, R. P., Hewitt, J. K., & Friedman, N. P. (2018). Rumination and psychopathology: Are anger and depressive rumination differentially associated with internalizing and externalizing psychopathology? *Clinical Psychological Science, 6*(1), 18–31.

Duck, S., & Wright, P. (1993). Reexamining gender differences in same-gender friendships. *Sex Roles, 28*, 709–727.

Duell, N., & Steinberg, L. (2020). Differential correlates of positive and negative risk taking in adolescence. *Journal of Youth & Adolescence, 49*(6), 1162–1178.

Dutton, D. G., & Aron, A. P. (1974). Some evidence for heightened sexual attraction under conditions of high anxiety. *Journal of Personality & Social Psychology, 30*(4), 510–517.

Earnshaw, E. (2021). *The Four Horsemen of the Apocalypse: Four relationship habits that predict divorce.* Mind Body Green Relationships. https://www.mindbodygreen.com/articles/four-horsemen-gottman-research

Ebstein, R. P., Israel, S., Chew, S. H., Zhong. S., Knafo, A. (2010) Genetics of human social behavior. *Neuron, 65*(6), 831–44.

Eby, L. T. (1997). Alternative forms of mentoring in changing organizational environments: A conceptual extension of the mentoring literature. *Journal of Vocational Behavior, 51*(1), 125–144.

Edwards, B. G. (2019, February 16). *I'm neurotic, you're neurotic.* Psychology Today. https://www.psychologytoday.com/us/blog/progress-notes/201902/im-neurotic-youre-neurotic

Eigen, J. P. (1995). *Witnessing insanity.* Yale University Press.

Eisenberger, N. I. (2012). The pain of social disconnection: Examining the shared neural underpinnings of physical and social pain. *Nature Reviews Neuroscience, 13*(6), 421–434.

Ekong, R. O. (2021). The effectiveness of using mindfulness exercises in the treatment of women veterans suffering from depression. *Dissertation Abstracts International: Section B: The Sciences & Engineering, 82*(10-B).

Elbogen, E. B., Wolfe, J. R., Cueva, M., Sullivan, C., & Johnson, J. (2015). Longitudinal predictors of criminal arrest after traumatic brain injury: Results from the Traumatic Brain Injury Model System National Database. *Journal of Head Trauma Rehabilitation, 30*(5), E3–E13.

Ellison, R. (1952). *Invisible man.* Vintage.

Elmore, J. D. (2018). Rationalizing undeserved outcomes: Effects of random positive events on reactions to victims. *Dissertation Abstracts International: Section B: The Sciences & Engineering, 79*(4-B(E)).

Emoto, M. (2011). *The hidden messages in water.* Simon & Schuster.

Engel, M. (2010). *I'm here: Compassionate communication in patient care.* Phillips Press.

Engelstad, K. N., Rund, B. R., Lau, B., Vaskinn, A., & Torgalsbøen, A. K. (2019). Increased prevalence of psychopathy and childhood trauma in homicide offenders with schizophrenia compared to nonviolent individuals with schizophrenia. *Nordic Journal of Psychiatry, 73*(8), 501–508.

Epel, E. S., & Lithgow, G. J. (2014). Stress biology and aging mechanisms: Toward understanding the deep connection between adaptation to stress and longevity. *Journals of Gerontology Series A: Biomedical Sciences & Medical Sciences, 69*, S10–S16.

Epstein, R., Blake, J. J., & Gonzalez, T. (2017). *Girlhood interrupted: The erasure of Black girls' childhood.* Center on Poverty and Inequality, Georgetown Law. https://genderjusticeandopportunity.georgetown.edu/wp-content/uploads/2020/06/girlhood-interrupted.pdf

Erb, S. R., Barata, P. C., Yi, S., McLachlan, K., & Powell, D. (2022). The shame and guilt distinction: Addressing the (mal)adaptive nature of guilt. *Traumatology.* Advance online publication. https://doi.org/10.1037/trm0000388

Erikson, E. H. (1956). The problem of ego identity. *Journal of the American Psychoanalytic Association, 4*(1), 56–121.

Erikson, E. H. (1959). Identity and the life cycle: Selected papers. *Psychological Issues, 1* (Monograph 1).

Erikson, E. H. (1968). *Identity, youth, and crisis.* Norton.

Erikson, E. H., & Erikson, J. M. (1998). *The life cycle completed* (extended version). Norton.

Eriksson, Å. (2022). Schizophrenia and criminal offending: Risk factors and the role of treatment. *Dissertation Abstracts International: Section B: The Sciences & Engineering, 83*(3-B).

Etemesi, P. (2022, February 6). *Spider-Man: Aunt May's most controversial comic book moments.* ScreenRant. https://screenrant.com/spider-man-aunt-may-controversial-moments-marvel-comics

Exline, J. J., & Geyer, A. L. (2004). Perceptions of humility: A preliminary study. *Self & Identity, 3*(2), 95–114.

Fell, L. C., with Downs, B., & Downs, J. (2016). *Grief diaries: Loss by impaired drive.* AlyBlue Media.

Fergus, E., & Noguera, P. (2009). *Latino males, masculinity, and marginalization: A summary report on research and policy forum.* Metropolitan Center for Urban Education.

Fernandez-Kranz, D., & Nollenberger, N. (2022). The impact of equal parenting time laws on family outcomes and risky behavior by teenagers: Evidence from Spain. *Journal of Economic Behavior & Organization, 195*(2), 303–325.

Ferradás, M. d. M., Freire, C., Núñez, J. C., Piñeiro, I., & Rosário, P. (2017). Motivational profiles in university students. Its relationship with self-handicapping and defensive pessimism strategies. *Learning & Individual Differences, 56*, 128–135.

Ferris, C., & O'Brien, K. (2022). The ins and outs of posttraumatic growth in children and adolescents: A systematic review of factors that matter. *Journal of Traumatic Stress.* Advance online publication. https://doi.org/10.1002/jts.22845

Fersch, E. L. (Ed.) (2005). *Thinking about the insanity defense.* iUniverse.

Fettinger, J. R. (2006). The absent father and Spider-Man's unfulfilled potential. In G. Conway (Ed.), *Webslinger: Unauthorized essays on your friendly neighborhood Spider-Man* (pp. 149–163). BenBella.

Fimiani, R., Gazzillo, F., Dazzi, N., & Bush, M. (2021). Survivor guilt: Theoretical, empirical, and clinical features. *International Forum of Psychoanalysis.* Advance online publication. https://psycnet.apa.org/doi/10.1080/0803706X.2021.1941246

Fingeroth, D. (2004). *Superman on the couch: What superheroes really tell us about ourselves and our society.* Continuum.

Fingeroth, D. (2007). *Disguised as Clark Kent: Jews, comics, and the creation of the superhero.* Bloomsbury Academic.

Fingeroth, D. (2011). *The Stan Lee Universe*. TwoMorrows.

Fingeroth, D. (2019). *A marvelous life: The amazing story of Stan Lee*. St. Martin's.

Fingeroth, D., Langley, T., Chu, A., Semper, J., Jr., Parris, L., & Dandridge, V., Jr. (2022, July). *Who's the most neurotic superhero now?* Panel presented at San Diego Comic-Con International, San Diego, CA.

Fischer, M., Twardawski, M., Strelan, P., & Gollwitzer, M. (2022). Victims need more than power: Empowerment and moral change independently predict victims' satisfaction and willingness to reconcile. *Journal of Personality & Social Psychology, 123*(3), 518–536.

Fisher, J. (2017). *Healing the fragmented selves of trauma survivors: Overcoming internal self-alienation*. Routledge.

Fisher, J. (2021). *Transforming the living legacy of trauma*. PESI.

Fiske, S. T., & Linville, P. W. (1980). What does the schema concept buy us? *Personality & Social Psychology Bulletin, 6*(4), 543–557.

Folgey, B. (2019, May 30). *7 most common phobias & how they affect patients*. Psychiatry Associates of Baton Rouge. https://www.psychiatryassociatesofbatonrouge.com/blog/7-most-common-phobias-how-they-affect-patients

Foster, J. D., & Campbell, W. K. (2005). Narcissism and resistance to doubts about romantic partners. *Journal of Research in Personality, 39*(5), 550–557.

Fournier, J. (2021). Mindfulness and mental preparation. In M. Bertollo, E. Filho, & P. C. Terry (Eds.), *Advancements in mental skills training* (pp. 57–69). Routledge/Taylor & Francis.

Franco, Z. E., & Zimbardo, P. G. (2006). The banality of heroism. *Greater Good, 3*(2), 30–35.

Frankl, V. E. (1956/2006). *Man's search for meaning* (I. Lasch, Trans.). Pocket.

Frankl, V. E. (1969). *The will to meaning: Foundations and applications of logotherapy*. New American Library.

Freud, A. (1936). *The ego and mechanisms of defense*. International Universities Press.

Freud, S. (1905). Three essays on the theory of sexuality. *The standard edition of the complete psychological works of Sigmund Freud* (Vol. 7, pp. 123–246). Hogarth.

Freud, S. (1905/1960). *De Witz und seiner Beziehung zum Unbewußten* [Jokes and their relation to the unconscious] (J. Trachey, Trans.). Norton.

Freud, S. (1912). Recommendations to physicians practicing psychoanalysis. In J. Strachey (Ed., Trans.), *The standard edition of the complete psychological works of Sigmund Freud* (Vol. 12, pp. 109–120). Hogarth.

Freud, S. (1917/1920). *A general introduction to psychoanalysis* (G. S. Hall, Trans.). Boni & Liveright.

Freud, S. (1924). Neurosis and psychosis. (J. Riviere, Trans.). In P. Rieff (Ed.), *General psychological theory (The collected papers of Sigmund Freud*, Vol. BS 190V, pp. 185–189). Collier.

Freud, S. (1928). Humor. *International Journal of Psychoanalysis, 9*(1), 1–6.

Freud, S. (1937). Analysis terminable and interminable. *International Journal of Psychoanalysis 18*(4), 373–405.

Freud, S. (1940). *An outline of psychoanalysis.* Hogarth.

Friedmann, E., Thomas, S. A., Liu, F., Morton, P. G., Chapa, D., & Gottlieb, S. S. (2006). Relationship of depression, anxiety, and social isolation to chronic heart failure outpatient mortality. *American Heart Journal, 152*(5), 940.e1–940.e8.

Frimer, J. A. (2016). Groups create moral superheroes to defend sacred values. In J. P. Forgas, L. Jussim, & P. A. M. Van Lange (Eds.), *The social psychology of morality* (pp. 304–315). Routledge.

Fry, C. L. (2019). *Primal roots of horror cinema: Evolutionary psychology and narratives of fear.* McFarland.

Fuller, B., & García Coll, C. (2010). Learning from Latinos: Context, families, and child development in motion. *Developmental Psychology, 46*(3), 559–565.

Gaab, E. (2012). Altruism in families facing the death of a child: How do they do it? *Journal of Pediatrics & Child Health, 48*(12), 1056–1057.

Gaiman, N. (2016). Some reflections on myth (with several digressions onto gardening, comics and fairy tales). *The view from the cheap seats: Selected nonfiction* (pp. 59–68). William Morrow.

Galovski, T. E., Smith, B. N., Micol, R. L., & Resick, P. A. (2021). Interpersonal violence and head injury: The effects on treatment for PTSD. *Psychological Trauma: Theory, Research, Practice, & Policy, 13*(3), 376–384.

Gandhi, M. (1993). *An autobiography: The story of my experiments with the truth.* Beacon.

García, F. E., Cova, F., Vázquez, C., & Páez, D. (2022). Posttraumatic growth in people affected by an occupational accident: A longitudinal multilevel model of change. *Applied Psychology: Health & Well-Being.* Advance online publication. https://doi.org/10.1111/aphw.12386

Geller, L. (1982). The failure of self-actualization theory: A critique of Carl Rogers and Abraham Maslow. *Journal of Humanistic Psychology, 22*(2), 56–73.

Germer, C. K., Siegel, R. D., & Fulton, P. R. (Eds.). (2013). *Mindfulness and psychotherapy.* Guilford.

Gibson, J. J. (1979). *The ecological approach to visual perception.* Houghton Mifflin.

Gilbert, P., & Irons, C. (2009). Shame, self-criticism, and self-compassion in adolescence. In N. Allen & L. Sheeber (Eds.), *Adolescent emotional development and the emergence of depressive disorders* (pp. 195–214). Cambridge University Press.

Goldstein, K. (1939). *The organism: a holistic approach to biology derived from pathological data in man.* American.

Gonzales, E. (2021, May 21). *Racebending in superhero adaptations, 2001–2021.* Book Riot. https://bookriot.com/racebending-in-superhero-adaptations

Gordon, W. A., Spielman, L. A., Hahn-Ketter, A. E., & Sy, K. T. L. (2017). The relationship between traumatic brain injury and criminality in juvenile offenders. *Journal of Head Trauma Rehabilitation, 32*(6), 393–403.

Gottman, J. M. (1993). A theory of marital dissolution and stability. *Journal of Family Psychology, 7*(1), 57–75.

Graham, K. & Livingston, M. (2011) The relationship between alcohol and violence: Population, contextual and individual research approaches. *Drug Alcohol Review, 30*(5), 453–457.

Graham, M. A., Border, J., Decaluwe, G., Foemmel, J., & McGraw, K. (2001). Adolescents' hero identification and self-perception. *Perceptual & Motor Skills, 93*(1), 71–72.

Green, J. D., Van Tongeren, D. R., Cairo, A. H., & Hagiwara, N. (2016). Heroism and the pursuit of meaning. In S. T. Allison, G. R. Goethals, & R. M. Kramer (Eds.), *Handbook of heroism and heroic leadership* (pp. 529–546). Routledge.

Greenberg, J., & Arndt, J. (2012). Terror management theory. In P. A. M. Van Lange, A. W. Kruglanski, & E. T. Higgins (Eds.), *Handbook of theories of social psychology* (pp. 398–415). Sage.

Greenberger, R. (2006). Spider-Man: Ultimate loner—ultimate partner. In G. Conway (Ed.), *Webslinger: Unauthorized essays on your friendly neighborhood Spider-Man* (pp. 117–127). BenBella.

Greenfield, D. (2019, July 1). *The Spider's Web: The days of Ditko to the reign of Romita.* 13th Dimension. https://13thdimension.com/the-spiders-web-the-days-of-ditko-to-the-reign-of-romita

Gresh, L., & Weinberg, R. (2002). *The science of superheroes.* Wiley.

Griffin, B. J., Purcell, N., Burkman, K., Litz, B. T., Bryan, C. J., Schmitz, M., Villierme, C., Walsh, J., & Maguen, S. (2019). Moral injury: An integrative review. *Journal of Traumatic Stress, 32*(3), 350–362.

Guilford, J. P. (1955). *Les dimensions de l'intellect. Deliberations, Colloque internaternationale de l'analyse factorielle et ses applications.* Centre National Recherche Scientifique.

Guilford, J. P. (1956). The structure of intellect. *Psychological Bulletin, 53*(4), 267–293.

Hale, A. E., Chertow, S. Y., Weng, Y., Tabuenca, A., & Aye, T. (2021). Perceptions of support among transgender and gender-expansive adolescents and their parents. *Journal of Adolescent Health, 68*(6), 1075–1081.

Halnon, E. (2022). *Romantic partners can influence each other's beliefs and behaviors on climate change.* ScienceDaily. https://www.sciencedaily.com/releases/2022/06/220629161100.htm

Hare, R. D. (1999). *Without conscience: The disturbing world of the psychopaths among us.* Guilford.

Harlow, H. F. (1959). Love in infant monkeys. *Scientific American, 200*(6), 68–75.

Harris, B., McCredie, M. N., Truong, T., Regan, T., Thompson, C. G., Leach, W., & Fields, S. A. (2022). Relations between adolescent sensation seeking and risky sexual behaviors across sex, race, and age: A meta-analysis. *Archives of Sexual Behavior.* Advance online publication. https://doi.org/10.1007/s10508-022-02384-7

Hart, C. (1943). The Hawthorne experiments. *Canadian Journal of Economics & Political Science, 9*(2), 150–163.

Harvard T. H. Chan School of Public Health (2002, January 13). *Who mentored you: Oprah Winfrey.* https://sites.sph.harvard.edu/wmy/celebrities/oprah-winfrey

Hatfield, C. (2012). *Hand of fire: The comics art of Jack Kirby.* University Press of Mississippi.

Hawkley, L. C., & Cacioppo, J. T. (2003). Loneliness and pathways to disease. *Brain, Behavior, & Immunity, 17*(1), 98–105.

Hays-Grudo, J., & Morris, A. S. (2020). *Adverse and protective childhood experiences: A developmental perspective.* American Psychological Association.

Hazan, C., & Shaver, P. (1987). Romantic love conceptualized as an attachment process. *Journal of Personality & Social Psychology, 52*(3), 511–524.

Hegde, S. (2022, January 22). *Why do we root for the underdog?* Science ABC. https://www.scienceabc.com/social-science/why-do-we-root-for-the-underdog.html

Henschel, S., Nandrino, J. L., & Doba, K. (2020). Emotion regulation and empathic abilities in young adults: The role of attachment styles. *Personality & Individual Differences, 156*, 109763.

Herbert, C. P. (2015). Perspectives in primary care: Values-driven leadership is essential in health care [Editorial]. *Annals of Family Medicine, 13*(6), 512–513.

Herzog, P. S. (2019). *The science of generosity: Causes, manifestations, and consequences.* Palgrave Macmillan.

Hick, D. H. (2006). Horror in long underwear. In G. Conway (Ed.), *Webslinger: Unauthorized essays on your friendly neighborhood Spider-Man* (pp. 5–15). BenBella.

Hill, C. A. (1987). Affiliation motivation: People who need people . . . but in different ways. *Journal of Personality & Social Psychology, 52*(5), 1008–1018.

Ho, R. (2004, December). Stand and deliver. *Wizard Magazine* (158), 38–44.

Hochman, D. (2014, April). The Playboy interview with Stan Lee. *Playboy.* https://www.playboy.com/read/stan-lee-playboy-interview

Hoggard, L. S., Byrd, C. M., & Sellers, R. M. (2015). The lagged effect of racial discrimination on depressive symptomatology and interactions with racial identity. *Journal of Counseling Psychology, 62*(2), 216–225.

Holbeche, L. (1996). Peer mentoring: The challenges and opportunities. *Career Development International, 7*(1), 24–27.

Hope, E. C. (2016). Preparing to participate: The role of youth social responsibility and political efficacy on civic engagement for Black early adolescents. *Child Indicators Research, 9*(3), 609–630.

Hope, E. C., Cryer-Coupet, Q. R., & Stokes, M. N. (2020). Race-related stress, racial identity, and activism among young Black men: A person-centered approach. *Developmental Psychology, 56*(8), 1484–1495.

Horwitz, A. V., & Wakefield, J. C. (2007). *The loss of sadness: How psychiatry transformed normal sorrow into depressive disorder.* Oxford University Press.

Howze, T. (2016, April 30). *Does Spider-Man have superhuman healing abilities?* Medium. https://medium.com/panel-frame/does-spider-man-have-superhuman-healing-abilities-like-wolverine-or-deadpool-c97bd4a3b85d

Hu, C., Kumar, S., Huang, J., & Ratnavelu, K. (2017). Disinhibition of negative true self for identity reconstructions in cyberspace: advancing self-discrepancy theory for virtual setting. *PLoS One, 12*(4), Artl e0175623.

Hu, C., Zhao, L., & Huang, J. (2015). Achieving self-congruency? Examining why individuals reconstruct their virtual identity in communities of interest established within social network platforms. *Computers in Human Behavior, 50*, 465–475.

Huerta, A. H. (2018). Educational persistence in the face of violence. *Boyhood Studies.*

Humphrey, A., & Bliuc, A. M. (2021). Western individualism and the psychological wellbeing of young people: A systematic review of their associations. *Youth, 2*(1), 1–11.

Hurych, A. (2020, May 6). *Spider-Man: 10 worst things Aunt May ever did, ranked.* Comic Book Resources. https://www.cbr.com/spider-man-aunt-may-worst-actions

Hutson, S. P., Hall, J. M., & Pack, F. L. (2015). Survivor guilt analyzing the concept and its contexts. *Advances in Nursing Science, 38*(1), 20–33.

Hysi, G. (2015). *Conflict resolution styles and health outcome in married couples: A systematic literature review.* Paper presented at the International Conference on Research and Education, Rome, Italy.

Ineson, K. M., Erlangsen, A., Nordentoft, M., Benros, M. E., & Madsen, T. (2022). Traumatic brain injury and risk of subsequent attempted suicide and violent crime. *Psychological Medicine.* Advance online publication. https://doi.org/10.1017/S0033291722000769

Izadi, E. (2015). This hero has been dressing up as Spider-Man to feed the homeless. The Washington Post. https://www.washingtonpost.com/news/inspired-life/wp/2015/03/16/this-hero-has-been-dressing-up-as-spider-man-to-feed-the-homeless

James, W. (1907). *Pragmatism: A new name for some old ways of thinking.* Hackett.

Jansen, J. (2020). Traumatic brain injury and its relationship to previous convictions, aggression, and psychological functioning in Dutch detainees. *Journal of Forensic Psychology Research & Practice, 20*(5), 395–412.

Jaye, L (2022). *Why race matters when it comes to mental health.* BBC. https://www.bbc.com/future/article/20200804-black-lives-matter-protests-race-mental-health-therapy

Jewers, C. (2021). *Spider-Man meets the Pope! Real-life hero who dresses as the webslinger while visiting sick children holds the pontiff's hand as they meet at the Vatican.* The Daily Mail. https://www.dailymail.co.uk/news/article-9717965/Spider-Man-meets-Pope-Real-life-hero-holds-pontiffs-hand-meet-Vatican.html

Jinkerson, J. D. (2016). Defining and assessing moral injury: A syndrome perspective. *Traumatology, 22*(2), 112–130.

Johannesdottir, G. B., Bjarnason T., Stockdale, A., & Haartson, T. (2021). What's love got to do with it? Love-life gossip and migration intentions in rural Iceland. *Journal of Rural Studies, 87,* 236–242.

Johnson, K. C., LeBlanc, A. J., Sterzing, P. R., Deardorff, J., Antin, T., & Bockting, W. O. (2020). Trans adolescents' perceptions and experiences of their parents' supportive and rejecting behaviors. *Journal of Counseling Psychology, 67*(2), 156–170.

Johnson, R. E., Silverman, S. B., Shyamsunder, A., Swee, H., Rodopman, O. B., Cho, E., & Bauer, J. (2010). Acting superior but actually inferior? Correlates and consequences of workplace arrogance. *Human Performance, 23*(5), 403–427.

Johnston, R. (2022, June 23). *Yehudi Mercado apologizes for "Miles Thor-ales" portrayal in What If?* Bleeding Cool. https://bleedingcool.com/comics/yehudi-mercado-apologises-for-miles-thor-ales-portrayal-in-what-if

Johnstone, G. (2003). [Review of the book *Repair or revenge: Victims and restorative justice,* by H. Strang]. *International Review of Victimology, 10*(2), 178–180.

Jung, C. G. (1915). *The theory of psychoanalysis* (Nervous and mental disease monograph series, Vol. 19). Journal of Nervous & Mental Disease Publishing.

Jung, C. G. (1916/1953). The relations between the ego and the unconscious. In *Two essays on analytical psychology* (CW7, pp. 123–1241). Routledge & Kegan Paul.

Jung, C. G. (1931/1960). The stages of life. In *The structure and dynamics of the psyche* (CW8, pp. 37-43). Routledge & Kegan Paul.

Jung, C. G. (1936/1991). Wotan. In *Civilization in transition* (CW10, pp. 179–193). Routledge & Kegan Paul.

Jung, C. G. (1937/1960). Psychological factors determining human behaviour. In *The structure and dynamics of the psyche.* (CW8, pp. 114–125). Routledge & Kegan Paul.

Jung, C. G. (1939/1959). Conscious, unconscious, and individuation. In *The archetypes and the collective unconscious.* (CW9, pp. 275–289). Routledge & Kegan Paul.

Jung, C. G. (1948/1989). A psychological approach to the dogma of the trinity. In *Psychology and religion: West and east.* (CW11, pp. 107–200). Princeton University Press.

Jung, C. G. (1953/1959). The relations between the ego and the unconscious. In V. S. de Laszlo (Ed.), *The basic writings of C. G. Jung* (pp. 105–182). Modern Library.

Jung, C. G. (1954/1960). On the nature of the psyche. In *The structure and dynamics of the psyche.* (CW8, pp. 61–66). Routledge & Kegan Paul.

Jung, C. G. (1956/1976). *Symbols of transformation* (CW5). Princeton University Press.

Jung, C. G. (2009). *The red book: Liber novus.* Norton.

Juni, S. (2016). Survivor guilt: A critical review from the lens of the Holocaust. *International Review of Victimology, 22*(3), 321–337.

Juvonen, J., & Gross, E. F. (2005). The Rejected and the Bullied: Lessons About Social Misfits from Developmental Psychology. In K. D. Williams, J. P. Forgas, & W. von Hippel (Eds.), *The Social Outcast: Ostracism, social exclusion, rejection, and bullying* (pp. 155–170). Psychology Press.

Kabir, H. (2015). The lighter side of life. In S. Polly & K. Britton (Eds.), *Character strengths matter: How to live a full life* (pp. 80–84). Positive Psychology News.

Kahr, B. (2020). *Bombs in the consulting room: Surviving psychological shrapnel.* Routledge.

Kakalios, J. (2009). *The physics of superheroes.* Gotham.

Karatekin, C., Mason, S. M., Riegelman, A., Bakker, C., Hunt, S., Gresham, B., Corcoran, F., & Barnes, A. (2022). Adverse childhood experiences: A scoping review of measures and methods. *Children & Youth Services Review, 136,* 1–26.

Karimi, R., Bakhtiyari, M., Arani, A. M. (2019). Protective factors of marital stability in long-term marriage globally: A systematic review. *Epidemiol Health, 41,* e2019023.

Karns, C. M., Moore, W.E., Mayr, U. (2017). The cultivation of pure altruism via gratitude: A functional MRI study of change with gratitude practice. *Frontiers in Human Neuroscience, 11,* 599.

Kassin, S. (2003). *Psychology.* Prentice-Hall.

Kaufman, S. B. (2011, March 16). *Psychotic is not the same as psychopathic.* Psychology Today. https://www.psychologytoday.com/us/blog/beautiful-minds/201103/psychotic-is-not-the-same-psychopathic

Keat, L. H. (2012, July). *Of bats and spiders: An examination of the appeal of comics* [Conference session]. International Conference on Language, Literature & Linguistics, Medan, Indonesia.

Keller, H. (1929). *We bereaved.* Fulenwider.

Kellermann, P. F. (1992). *Focus on psychodrama: The therapeutic aspects of psychodrama.* Kingsley.

Kelly, S. (2021, December 14). *No Way Home: An arachnologist critiques Spider-Man's powers.* Science Focus. https://www.sciencefocus.com/nature/spider-man-powers

Kentor, R. A., & Kaplow, J. B. (2021). Using superheroes in grief counseling with children. In J. A. Harrington & R. A. Neimeyer (Eds.), *Superhero grief: The transformative power of loss* (pp. 214–220). Routledge.

Kesavelu, D., Sheela, K., & Abraham, P. (2021). Stages of psychological development of child: An overview. *International Journal of Current Research & Review, 13*(13), 131320.

Kessler, D. (2019). *Finding meaning: The sixth stage of grief.* Scribner.

Ki, J. (2022). When the brain plays a game: Neural responses to visual dynamics during naturalistic visual tasks. *Dissertation Abstracts International: Section B: The Sciences & Engineering, 83*(2-B).

Kim, J., & Lee, J. E. (2011). The Facebook paths to happiness: Effects of the number of Facebook friends and self-presentation on subjective well-being. *Cyberpsychology, Behavior, & Social Networking, 14*(6), 359–64.

King, S., St-Hilaire, A., & Heidkamp, D. (2010). Prenatal factors in schizophrenia. *Current Directions in Psychological Science, 19*(4), 209–213.

Kinsella, E. L., Igou, E. R., & Ritchie, T. D. (2019). Heroism and the pursuit of a meaningful life. *Journal of Humanistic Psychology, 59*(4), 474–498.

Kinsella, E. L., Ritchie, T. D., & Igou, E. R. (2015a). Lay perspectives on the social and psychological functions of heroes. *Frontiers in Psychology, 6,* 130.

Kinsella, E. L., Ritchie, T. D., & Igou, E. R. (2015b). Zeroing in on heroes: A prototype analysis of hero features. *Journal of Personality & Social Psychology, 108*(1), 114-127.

Klapp, O. E. (1954). Heroes, villains and fools, as agents of social control. *American Sociological Review, 19*(1), 56–62.

Knaus, W. J. (2014). *The cognitive behavioral workbook for anxiety: A step-by-step program.* New Harbinger.

Knight, Z. G. (2017). A proposed model of psychodynamic psychotherapy linked to Erik Erikson's eight stages of psychosocial development. *Clinical Psychology & Psychotherapy, 24*(5), 1047–1058.

Kohlberg, L. & Kramer, R. (1969). Continuities and discontinuities in child and adult moral development. *Human Development, 12*(2), 93–120.

Kohlberg, L. (1971). Stages of moral development. *Moral Education, 1*(51), 23–92.

Kohlberg, L. (1976). Moral stages and moralization: The cognitive-development approach. In T. Lickona (Ed.), *Moral development and behavior: Theory and research and social issues* (pp. 31–53). Holt, Rienhart, & Winston.

Komarovskaya, I. A., Booker, A. L., Warren, J., & Jackson, S. (2011). Exploring gender differences in trauma exposure and the emergence of symptoms of PTSD among incarcerated men and women. *Journal of Forensic Psychiatry & Psychology, 22*(3), 395–410.

Kopetz, C., Woerner, J. L., MacPherson, L., Lejeuz, C. W., Nelson, C. A., Zeanah, C. H., & Fox, N. A. (2019). Early psychological deprivation and adolescent risk-taking: The role of motivation and executive control. *Journal of Experimental Psychology: General, 148*(2), 388–399.

Kopfler, B. (1955). C. G. Jung and projective techniques: A testimonial to Dr. Jung's 80th birthday on July 25th, 1955. *Journal of Projective Techniques, 19*(3), 225.

Krakowski, M. I., & Czobor, P. (2018). Distinctive profiles of traits predisposing to violence in schizophrenia and in the general population. *Schizophrenia Research, 202*, 267–273.

Kram, K. E., & Isabella, L. A. (1985). Mentoring alternatives: The role of peer relationships in career development. *Academy of Management Journal, 28*(1), 110–132.

Kreitler, S., Barak, F., & Siegelman-Danieli, N. (2013). Coping with bereavement: Survivor's guilt. In S. Kreitler & H. Shanun-Klein (Eds.), *Studies of grief and bereavement* (pp. 67–81). Nova Science.

Kübler-Ross, E. (1969). *On death and dying.* Macmillan.

Kuiper, N. A., & Leite, C. (2010). Personality impressions associated with four distinct humor styles. *Scandinavian Journal of Psychology, 51*(2), 115–122.

Kwan J., Sparrow, K., Facer-Irwin, E., Thandi, G., Fear, N. T., & MacManus, D. (2020). Prevalence of intimate partner violence perpetration among military populations: A systematic review and meta-analysis. *Aggressive & Violent Behavior, 53*, Artl 101419.

LaBouff, J. P., Rowatt, W. C., Johnson, M. K., Tsang, J. A., & Willerton, G. M. (2012). Humble persons are more helpful than less humble persons: Evidence from three studies. *Journal of Positive Psychology, 7*(1), 16–29.

LaFleur, A. K., & White, B. J. (2010). Appreciating mentorship: The benefits of being a mentor. *Professional case management, 15*(6), 305–311.

Laird, M. J. (2017, December 15). *Spider-Man! The horrors of puberty.* Mikayla J. Laird. https://mikaylajlaird.wordpress.com/2017/12/15/spider-man-the-horrors-of-puberty

Langley, T. (2017, July 2). *Heroes' origins: Must superheroes suffer parental loss?* Psychology Today. https://www.psychologytoday.com/us/blog/beyond-heroes-and-villains/201707/heroes-origins-must-superheroes-suffer-parental-loss

Langley, T. (2022). *Batman and psychology: A dark and stormy knight* (2nd ed.). Wiley.

Langley, T., Fingeroth, D., Bendis, B. M., Miller, B. Q., Simonson, L, & Wolfman, M. (2021, July). *Neurotic superheroes and the writers who love them.* Panel presented at San Diego Comic-Con @Home. https://www.youtube.com/watch?v=ECQzTdBJMyg

Langley, T., Sedelmaier, J. J., Langley, A., & Fingeroth, D. (2016, August). *Who's the most neurotic superhero? Inside the minds of Batman, Spider-Man, Captain America, Jessica Jones, and more.* Wizard World Chicago Comic-Con, Rosemont, IL.

Lankau, M. J., & Scandura, T. A. (2002). An investigation of personal learning in mentoring relationships: Content, antecedents, and consequences. *Academy of Management Journal, 45*(4), 779–790.

LaRocca, M. A., & Avery, T. J. (2020). Combat experiences link with posttraumatic growth among veterans across conflicts: The influence of PTSD and depression. *Journal of Nervous & Mental Disease, 208*(6), 445–451.

Latané, B., & Walton, D. (1972). Effects of social deprivation and familiarity with the environment on social attraction in rats. *Psychonomic Science, 27*(1), 9–11.

Laurie, A., & Neimeyer, R. A. (2008). African-Americans in bereavement: Grief as a function of ethnicity. *Omega: Journal of Death & Dying, 57*(2), 173–193.

Laursen, B. (2017). Making and keeping friends: The importance of being similar. *Child Development Perspectives, 11*(3), 282–289.

Leahy, R. L. (2001). *Overcoming resistance in cognitive therapy.* Guilford.

Lee, H. (1960). *To kill a mockingbird.* Lippincott.

Lee, S. (2016). Foreword: The head! The heart! The heroes! In T. Langley (Ed.), *Captain America vs. Iron Man: Freedom, security, psychology* (pp. xiii–xv). Sterling.

Lee, S. (2018). Foreword: The devil you know. In T. Langley (Ed.), *Daredevil psychology: The devil you know* (pp. xii–xiii). Sterling.

Leidenfrost, B., Strassnig, B., Schütz, M., Carbon, C.-C., & Schabmann, A. (2014). The impact of peer mentoring on mentee academic performance: Is any mentoring style better than no mentoring at all? *International Journal of Teaching & Learning in Higher Education, 26*(1), 102–111.

Leonhardt, D., & Quealy, K. (2015). How your hometown affects your chances of marriage. *The New York Times.* https://www.nytimes.com/interactive/2015/05/15/upshot/the-places-that-discourage-marriage-most.html

Lerner, B. H. (2011). *One for the road: Drunk driving since 1900.* Johns Hopkins University Press.

Levine, R. V., Reysen, S., & Ganz, E. (2008). The kindness of strangers revisited: A comparison of 24 US cities. *Social Indicators Research, 85*(3), 461–481.

Levy, D. A. (2019). The "self-esteem" enigma: A critical analysis. *North American Journal of Psychology, 21*(2), 305–338.

Lewis, M. (1995). *Shame: The exposed self.* Simon & Schuster.

Lewis-Schroeder, N. F., Kieran, K., Murphy, B. L., Wolff, J. D., Robinson, M. A., & Kaufman, M. L. (2018). Conceptualization, assessment, and treatment of traumatic stress in first responders: A review of critical issues. *Harvard Review of Psychiatry, 26*(4), 216.

Little, C. A., Kearney, K. L., & Britner, P. A. (2010). Students' self-concept and perceptions of mentoring relationships in a summer mentorship program for talented adolescents. *Roeper Review, 32*(3), 189–199.

Littman-Ovadia, H., & Niemiec, R. M. (2016). Character strengths and mindfulness as core pathways to meaning in life. In R. N. Pninit, S. E. Schulenberg, & A. Batthyany (Eds.), *Clinical perspectives on meaning: Positive and existential psychotherapy* (pp. 383–406). Springer.

Litz, B. T., Stein, N., Delaney, E., Lebowitz, L., Nash, W. P., Silva, C., & Maguen, S. (2009). Moral injury and moral repair in war veterans: A preliminary model and intervention strategy. *Clinical Psychology Review, 29*(8), 695–706.

Liu, P. J., Rim, S., Min, L., & Min, K. E. (2022). The surprise of reaching out: Appreciated more than we think. *Journal of Personality & Social Psychology.* Advance online publication. https://doi.org/10.1037/pspi0000402

Lu, K. (2018). Teaching Jung in the academy: The representation of comic book heroes on the big screen. In L. Hockley (Ed.), *The Routledge international handbook of Jungian film studies.* Routledge.

Lue, A. (2021, September 30). *Why Marvel's Spider-Man is the most popular superhero*. Inside the Magic. https://insidethemagic.net/2021/09/spider-man-most-popular-superhero-a11mmb

Lytle, P. (2006). Power, responsibility, and pain: The price of being Spider-Man. In G. Conway (Ed.), *Webslinger: Unauthorized essays on your friendly neighborhood Spider-Man* (pp. 175–187). BenBella.

Machluf, K., & Bjorklund, D. (2015) Understanding risk-taking: Insights from evolutionary psychology. In R. A. Scott, S. M. Kosslyn, & M. Buchmann (Eds.), *Emerging trends in the social and behavioral sciences* (pp. 1–15). Wiley.

Maffly-Kipp, J., Rivera, G. N., Schlegel, R. J., & Vess, M. (2022). The effect of true self-attributions on the endorsement of retributive and restorative justice. *Personality & Social Psychology Bulletin, 48*(8), 1284–1297.

Malchiodi, C. (2006). *Art therapy sourcebook* (2nd ed.). McGraw-Hill.

Malti, T. (2016). Toward an integrated clinical-developmental model of guilt. *Developmental Review, 39*, 16–36.

Malti, T., Galarneau, E., & Peplak, J. (2021). Moral development in adolescence. *Journal of Research on Adolescence, 31*(4), 1097–1113.

Marano, M. (2006). Inner demons, outer heroes, outer villains: A look at monstrosity in *Spider-Man* and *Spider-Man 2*. In G. Conway (Ed.), *Webslinger: Unauthorized essays on your friendly neighborhood Spider-Man* (pp. 215–229). BenBella.

Marcia, J. E. (1966). Development and validation of ego identity status. *Journal of Personality & Social Psychology, 3*(5), 551–558.

Marcus-Newhall, A., Pederson, M., Carlson, M., & Miller, N. (2000). Displaced aggression is alive and well: A meta-analytic review. *Journal of Personality & Social Psychology, 78*(4), 678–689.

Margolis, B. D. (1986). Joining, mirroring, psychological reflection: Terminology, definitions, theoretical considerations. *Modern Psychoanalysis, 11*(1-2), 19–35.

Marica, J. E. (1966). Development and validation of ego-identity status. *Journal of Personality & Social Psychology, 3*(5), 551–558.

Marson, G. (2022). *The negative impact of prolonged survival mode: What can you do?* Dr. Gia Marson. https://drgiamarson.com/the-negative-impact-of-prolonged-survival-mode-what-can-you-do-to-thrive

Martin, R. A., & Ford, T. (2018). *The psychology of humor: An integrative approach* (2nd ed.). Academic Press.

Maslow, A. H. (1943). A theory of human motivation. *Psychological Review, 50*(4), 370–396.

Maslow, A. H. (1971). *The farther reaches of human nature.* Viking.

Maslow, A. H. (1996). Critique of self-actualization theory. In E. Hoffman (Ed.), *Future visions: The unpublished papers of Abraham Maslow.* Sage.

MBK Alliance (n.d.). *About.* MBKA. https://www.obama.org/mbka/about-mbk

May, R. (2004, July 1). *Truth, justice and the Canadian way.* Superman Homepage. https://www.supermanhomepage.com/comics/comics.php?topic=articles/canadian-way

McAdams, D. P. (1989). *Intimacy: The need to be close.* Doubleday.

McCabe, J. (2006). Spinning a web of shame. In G. Conway (Ed.), *Webslinger: Unauthorized essays on your friendly neighborhood Spider-Man* (pp. 105–116). BenBella.

McCrae, R. R., & Costa, P. T. (1987). Validation of the five-factor model of personality across instruments and observers. *Journal of Personality & Social Psychology, 52*(1), 81–90.

McCullough, M. E., Bono, G., & Root, L. M. (2007). Rumination, emotion, and forgiveness: Three longitudinal studies. *Journal of Personality & Social Psychology, 92*(3), 490–505.

McEntee, M. L., Dy-Liacco, G. S., & Haskins, D. G. (2013). Human flourishing: A natural home for spirituality. *Journal of Spirituality in Mental Health, 15*(3), 141–159.

McGreal, C. (2012, June 9). *Robert Caro: A life with LBJ and the pursuit of power.* The Guardian. https://www.theguardian.com/world/2012/jun/10/lyndon-b-johnson-robert-caro-biography

McLeod, S. (2022). *Vygotsky's sociocultural theory of cognitive development.* Simply Psychology. www.simplypsychology.org/vygotsky.html

McNally, K. (2016). *A critical history of schizophrenia.* Palgrave Macmillan.

Meléndez Guevara, A. M., Lindstrom Johnson, S., Elam, K., Hilley, C., Mcintire, C., & Morris, K. (2021). Culturally responsive trauma-informed services: A multilevel perspective from practitioners serving Latinx children and families. *Community Mental Health, 57*(2), 325–339.

Menakem, R. (2021). *My grandmother's hands: Racialized trauma and the pathway to mending our hearts and bodies.* Penguin UK.

Mercado, Y. (2022, June 22). *I've taken the last few days to step back and listen . . .* [Tweet]. Twitter. https://twitter.com/ymercado/status/1539686044521611265

Michniewicz, K. S., & Vandello, J. A. (2013). The attractive underdog: When disadvantage bolsters attractiveness. *Journal of Social & Personal Relationships, 30*(7), 942–952.

Middleearthnj. (2017, July 31). *How to deal with a self-absorbed teen.* Middle Earth. https://middleearthnj.org/2017/07/31/how-to-deal-with-a-self-absorbed-teen

Milburn, M. A., & Liss, J. (2008). Emotion, affect displacement, conflict, and coopera-tion. In B. A. Sullivan, M. Snyder, & J. L. Sullivan (Eds.), *Cooperation: The political psychology of effective human interaction* (pp. 75–88). Blackwell.

Miller, D., Rees, J., & Pearson, A. (2021). "Masking is life": Experiences of masking in autistic and nonautistic adults. *Autism in Adulthood, 3*(4), 330–338.

Miller, L., Wickramaratne, P., Hao, X., McClintock, C. H., Pan, L., Svob, C., & Weissman, M. M. (2021). Altruism and "love of neighbor" offer neuro-anatomical protection against depression. *Psychiatry Research: Neuroimaging, 315,* Article 111326.

Miranda, A. O., Molina, B., & MacVane, S. L. (2003). Coping with the murder of a loved one: Counseling survivors of murder victims in groups. *Journal for Specialists in Group Work, 28*(1), 48–63.

Mischel, W. (2009). From personality and assessment (1968) to personality science, 2009. *Journal of Research in Personality, 43*(2), 282–290.

Mitchell, Eby, L. T., & Ragins, B. R. (2015). My mentor, my self: Antecedents and outcomes of perceived similarity in mentoring relationships. *Journal of Vocational Behavior, 89,* 1–9.

Miville, M. L., Mendez, N., & Louie, M. (2017). Latina/o gender roles: A content anal-ysis of empirical research from 1982 to 2013. *Journal of Latino/a Psychology, 5*(3), 173–194.

Moller-Roth, A. (2021). *The hidden consequences of touch starvation and how you can lever-age the healing power of positive touch.* The Maps Institute. https://themapsinstitute. com/the-hidden-consequences-of-touch-starvation-and-how-you-can-leverage-the-healing-power-of-positive-touch

Momi, D., Smeralda, C. L., Di Lorenzo, G., Neri, F., Rossi, S., Rossi, A., & Santarnec-chi, E. (2021). Long-lasting connectivity changes induced by intensive first-person shooter gaming. *Brain Imaging & Behavior, 15*(3), 1518–1532.

Momi, D., Smeralda, C., Sprugnoli, G., Neri, F., Rossi, S., Rossi, A., Di Lorenzo, G., & Santarnecchi, E. (2019). Thalamic morphometric changes induced by first-person action videogame training. *European Journal of Neuroscience, 49*(9), 1180–1195.

Monin, B., & Merritt, A. (2012). Moral hypocrisy, moral inconsistency, and the struggle for moral integrity. In M. Mikulincer & P. R. Shaver (Eds.), *The social psychology of morality: Exploring the causes of good and evil* (pp. 167–184). American Psychological Association.

Moore, M. (2013). When the body betrays. In S. Akhtar (Ed.), *Betrayal: Developmental, literary, and clinical realms* (pp. 61–80). Karnac.

Moore, M. M. (2021). Posttraumatic growth, superheroes, and the bereaved. In J. A. Harrington & R. A. Neimeyer (Eds.), *Superhero grief: The transformative power of loss* (pp. 157–162). Routledge.

Moran, R. (1981). *Knowing right from wrong: The insanity defense of Daniel McNaughtan.* Free Press.

Morman, E. (2021, December 10). *How to deal with self-absorbed teens.* Metro Parent. https://www.metroparent.com/parenting/tweens-teens/self-centered-teens-deal

Morrow, K., & Spencer, E. D. (2018). *CBT for anxiety: A step-by-step training manual for the treatment of fear, panic, worry, and OCD.* PESI.

Mothers Against Drunk Driving (n.d.). *Saving lives, serving people.* MADD. https://madd.org/our-history

Mueller, M. K., & McCullough, L. (2017). Effects of equine-facilitated psychotherapy on post-traumatic stress symptoms in youth. *Journal of Child & Family Studies, 26*(4), 1164–1172.

Mulheron, J. (2021). Parental grief and activism: On becoming your friendly neighborhood Spider-Man. In J. A. Harrington & R. A. Neimeyer (Eds.), *Superhero grief: The transformative power of loss* (pp. 191–195). Routledge.

Mulvey, E. P., & Fardella J. (2000). *Are the mentally ill really violent?* Psychology Today. https://www.psychologytoday.com/us/articles/200011/are-the-mentally-ill-really-violent

Murray, H., Pethania, Y., & Medin, E. (2021). Survivor guilt: A cognitive approach. *Cognitive Behavior Therapy, 14,* e28.

Murthy, V. H. (2020a). *Together.* Harper Collins.

Murthy, V. H. (2020b). Technology and social connection. In J. P. Steyer (Ed.), *Which side of history? How technology is reshaping democracy and our lives* (pp. 64–74). Chronicle Prism.

National Alliance on Mental Health (n.d.). *Mental health by the numbers.* NAMI. https://www.nami.org/mhstats

National Institute of Mental Health (n.d.). *Mental illness.* NIH. https://www.nimh.nih.gov/health/statistics/mental-illness

Nelson, J. S., Baud-Bovy, G., Smeets, J. B. J., & Brenner, E. (2019). Accuracy of intercepting moving tactile targets. *Perception, 48*(8), 685–701.

Nesseth, N. (2022). *Nightmare fuel: The science of horror films.* Tor Nightfire.

Newcomb, M. E., Feinstein, B. A., Matson, M., Macapagal, K., & Mustanski, B. (2018). "I have no idea what's going on out there:" Parents' perspectives on promoting sexual health in lesbian, gay, bisexual, and transgender adolescents. *Sexuality Research & Social Policy, 15*(2), 111–122.

Nezlek, J. B., Derks, P. L., & Simanski, J. (2021). Relationships between everyday use of humor and daily experience. *Humor: International Journal of Humor Research, 34*(1), 21–39.

Niemiec, R. M. (2013, June). *Signature strengths: Recent research informing best practices* [Conference session abstract]. Third World Congress on Positive Psychology, Los Angeles, CA.

Niemiec, R. M., & McGrath, R. E. (2019). *The power of character strengths.* VIA Institute on Character.

Niemiec, R. M., & Wedding, D. (2014). *Positive psychology at the movies: Using films to build character strengths and well-being* (2nd ed.). Hogrefe.

Nin, A. (1966). *The Diary of Anaïs Nin* (Vol. 1). Mariner.

Norem, J. K., & Cantor, N. (1986). Anticipatory and post hoc cushioning strategies: Optimism and defensive pessimism in "risky" situations. *Cognitive Therapy & Research, 10*(3), 347-362.

Norris, C. J. (2021). The negativity bias, revisited: Evidence from neuroscience measures and an individual differences approach. *Social Neuroscience, 16*(1), 68–82.

Norström, T., & Pape, H. (2010). Alcohol, suppressed anger and violence. Addiction, 105(9), 1580–1586.

Nurmohamed, S., Kundro, T. G., & Myers, C. G. (2021). Against the odds: Developing underdog versus favorite narratives to offset prior experiences of discrimination. *Organizational Behavior & Human Decision Processes, 167*, 206–221.

Nuwer, R. (2013, July 15). *The psychology of character bonding. Why we feel a real connection to actors.* Motion Pictures Association. https://www.motionpictures.org/2013/07/the-psychology-of-character-bonding-why-we-feel-a-real-connection-to-actors

Oliner, S. P., & Oliner, P. M. (1988). *The altruistic personality: Rescuers of Jews in Nazi Europe.* The Free Press.

Oosthuizen, R. M. (2021). Resilience as moderator between workplace humour and well-being, a positive psychology perspective. In E. Vanderheiden & C. H. Mayer (Eds.), *The Palgrave handbook of humour research* (pp. 263–287). Palgrave Macmillan/Springer Nature.

Orjiakor, C. T., Ndiwe, C. G., Anwanabasi, P., & Onyekachi, B. N. (2022). How do internet fraudsters think? A qualitative examination of pro-criminal attitudes and cognitions among internet fraudsters in Nigeria. *Journal of Forensic Psychiatry & Psychology. Advance online publication.* https://doi.org/10.1080/14789949.2022.2051583

Ortiz, F. A. (2020). Self-actualization in the Latino/Hispanic culture. *Journal of Humanistic Psychology, 60*(3), 418–435.

Osgood, J. M., & Muraven, M. (2018). Self-control and alcohol consumption. In D. de Ridder, M. Adriaanse, & K. Fujita (Eds.), *The Routledge international handbook of self-control in health and well-being* (pp. 251–263). Routledge/Taylor & Francis.

Ostrander, J. (2013, September 22). *John Ostrander: Realistic fantasy.* Comic Mix. https://www.comicmix.com/2013/09/22/john-ostrander-realistic-fantasy

Owens, B. C. (2017, February 6). *Racebending and representation in comic books.* Black Perspectives. https://www.aaihs.org/racebending-and-representation-in-comic-books

Page, K. (2011). *Attractions of Inspiration and Attractions of Deprivation.* Psychology Today. https://www.psychologytoday.com/us/blog/finding-love/201103/attractions-inspiration-and-attractions-deprivation

Palgi, Y., Dicker-Oren, S. D., & Greene, T. (2020). Evaluating a community fire as human-made vs. natural disaster moderates the relationship between peritraumatic distress and both PTSD symptoms and posttraumatic growth. *Anxiety, Stress & Coping: An International Journal, 33*(5), 569–580.

Palmore, C. (2019). The social context of crime: Self-control, alcohol use, and dispute-related violence. *Dissertation Abstracts International Section A: Humanities & Social Sciences, 80*(4-A(E)).

Park, N., Peterson, C., & Seligman, M. E. P. (2004). Strengths of character and well-being. *Journal of Social & Clinical Psychology, 23*(5), 603–619.

Patterson, R. C. (2006). Spider-Man no more: Moral responsibility, the morose hero, and his web of relationships. In G. Conway (Ed.), *Webslinger: Unauthorized essays on your friendly neighborhood Spider-Man* (pp. 129–148). BenBella.

Pavri, S. (2015). Loneliness: The cause or consequence of peer victimization in children and Youth. *The Open Psychology Journal, 8*(Suppl 2-M4) 78–84. https://openpsychologyjournal.com/contents/volumes/V8/TOPSYJ-8-78/TOPSYJ-8-78.pdf

Pedersen, W. C., Denson, T. F., Goss, R. J., Vasquez, E. A., Kelley, N. J., & Miller, N. (2011). The impact of rumination on aggressive thoughts, feelings, arousal, and behaviour. *British Journal of Social Psychology, 50*(Pt. 2), 281–301.

Peplau, L. A., & Perlman, D. (Eds.). (1982). *Loneliness: A sourcebook of current theory, research, and therapy.* Wiley.

Peterson, A.L., Luethcke, C.A., Borah, E.V., Borah, A.M., & Young-McCaughan, S. (2011). Assessment and treatment of anger in combat-related PTSD in returning war veterans. *Journal of Clinical Psychology in Medical Settings, 18*(2), 164–175.

Peterson, C., & Park, N. (2009). The positive psychology of superheroes. In R. S. Rosenberg, *The psychology of superheroes* (pp. 5–18). BenBella.

Petri, A. (2011, August 3). *Sorry, Peter Parker. The response to the black Spiderman shows why we need one*. The Washington Post. https://www.washingtonpost.com/blogs/compost/post/sorry-peter-parker-the-response-to-the-black-spiderman-shows-why-we-need-one/2011/08/03/gIQAViObsI_blog.html

Pettigrew, M. (2020). Confessions of a serial killer: A neutralisation analysis. *Homicide Studies, 24*(1), 69–84. https://doi.org/10.1177/1088767918793674

Pfattheicher, S., Nielsen, Y. A., & Thielmann, I. (2022). Prosocial behavior and altruism: A review of concepts and definitions. *Current Opinion in Psychology, 44*, 124–129.

Phillips, A. (2019). *The cure for psychoanalysis*. Wrong Way.

Phillips, A. (2021a). *On getting better*. Penguin.

Phillips, A. (2021b). *On wanting to change*. Picador.

Phinney, J. S. (1989). Stages of ethnic identity development in minority group adolescents. *Journal of Early Adolescence, 9*(1-2), 34–49.

Polák, J., Rádlová, S., Janovcová, M., Flegr, J., Landová, E., & Frynta, D. (2020). Scary and nasty beasts: Self-reported fear and disgust of common phobic animals. *British Journal of Psychology, 111*(2), 297–321.

Polo, S. (2020, August 13). *Spider-Man's weirdest meme only gets weirder with context: Why doesn't the pterodactyl man want to cure cancer?* Polygon. https://www.polygon.com/2020/4/13/21218971/spider-man-dinosaur-cancer-meme-panel-marvel-comics-sauron-pterodactyl

Pope, A. (1711). *An essay on criticism*. Project Gutenberg. https://gutenberg.org/ebooks/7409

Prokop, P., & Tunnicliffe, S. D. (2008). "Disgusting" animals: Primary school children's attitudes and myths of bats and spiders. *Eurasia Journal of Mathematics, Science & Technology Education, 4*(2), 87–97.

Quesque, F., Foncelle, A., Barat, E., Chabanat, E., Rossetti, Y., & Van der Henst, J.-B. (2021). Sympathy for the underdog: People are inclined to adopt the emotional perspective of powerless (versus powerful) others. *Cognition & Emotion*. Advance online publication. https://doi.org/10.1080/02699931.2021.1902282

Quinn, K., Mollet, N., & Dawson, F. (2021). The Compassionate Schools Framework: Exploring a values-driven, hope-filled, relational approach with school leaders. *Educational & Child Psychology, 38*(1), 24–36.

Raine, A. (2013). *The anatomy of violence: The biological roots of crime*. Vintage.

Rando, T. A. (1984). *Grief, dying, and death*. Research Press.

Randolph, Z. (2021, December 20). *20 unsung heroes from history*. Mental Floss. https://www.mentalfloss.com/article/653487/unsung-heroes-history

Reinhardt, V., & Rossell, M. (2001). Self-biting in caged macaques: Cause, effect, and treatment. *Journal of Applied Animal Welfare Science, 4*(4), 285–294.

Remedios, R. (2018). Nominal fallacy. *Encyclopedia of animal cognition and behavior* (pp. 1–2). Springer International.

Rendon, J. (2015). *Upside: The new science of post-traumatic growth.* Touchstone.

Resick, P. A., Monson, C. M., & Chard, K. M. (2016). *Cognitive processing therapy for PTSD: A comprehensive manual.* Guilford.

Retsinas, J. (1988). A theoretical reassessment of the applicability of Kübler-Ross's stages of dying. *Death Studies, 12*(3), 207–216.

Ricard, M. (2015). *Altruism: The power of compassion to change yourself and the world.* Little, Brown.

Richards, H. J., Benson, V., Donnelly, N., & Hadwin, J. A. (2014). Exploring the function of selective attention and hypervigilance for threat in anxiety. *Clinical Psychology Review, 34*(1), 1–13.

Roberts, E., Joinson, C., Gunnell, D., Fraser, A., & Mars, B. (2020). Pubertal timing and self-harm: A prospective cohort analysis of males and females. *Epidemiology & Psychiatric Sciences, 29,* Artl e170.

Roberts, J. (1996) *The importance of Oskar Schindler.* Lucent.

Rodriguez, M. C., Morrobel, D. (2004). A review of Latino youth development research and a call for an asset orientation. *Hispanic Journal of Behavioral Sciences, 26*(2), 107–127.

Rogers, C. R. (1959). A theory of therapy, personality and interpersonal relationships as developed in the client-centered framework. In S. Koch (Ed.), *Psychology: A study of a science* (Vol. 3, pp. 184–256). McGraw-Hill.

Ronay, R., Oostrom, J., Lehmann-Willenbrock, N., & Van Vugt, M. (2017). Pride before the fall: (Over)confidence predicts escalation of public commitment. *Journal of Experimental Social Psychology, 69,* 13–22.

Roos, S. (2013). The Kübler-Ross model: An esteemed relic. *Gestalt Review, 17*(3), 312–315.

Rosenberg, R. S. (2013). Our fascination with superheroes. In R. S. Rosenberg (Ed.), *Our superheroes, ourselves* (pp. 3-18). Oxford University Press.

Rosenhaft, A. (2020, July 12). *Mental illness adds value to our lives.* Psychology Today. https://www.psychologytoday.com/us/blog/both-sides-the-couch/202007/mental-illness-adds-value-our-lives

Roy, K., Messina, L., Smith, J., & Waters, D. (2014). Growing up as "man of the house": Adultification and transition into adulthood for young men in economically disadvantaged families. *New Directions for Child & Adolescents Development, 143,* 55–72.

Rubin, L. C. (2013). Are superhero stories good for us? Reflections from clinical practice. In R. S. Rosenberg (Ed.), *Our superheroes, ourselves* (pp. 37–52). Oxford University Press.

Rubin, L., & Livesay, H. (2006). Look, up in the sky! Using superheroes in play therapy. *International Journal of Play Therapy, 15*(1), 117–133.

Rutter, M. (2006). *Genes and behavior: Nature-nurture interplay explained.* Blackwell.

Ruyter, D. D., & Conroy, J. (2002). The formation of identity: The importance of ideals. *Oxford Review of Education, 28*(4), 509–522.

Sanchez, D., Whittaker, T. A., Hamilton, E., & Arango, S. (2017). Familial ethnic socialization, gender role attitudes, and ethnic identity development in Mexican-origin early adolescents. *Cultural Diversity & Ethnic Minority Psychology, 23*(3), 335–347.

Sandler, I., & Gaffney, D. (2021). Parents and caregivers: The everyday heroes behind superheroes. In J. A. Harrington & R. A. Neimeyer (Eds.), *Superhero grief: The transformative power of loss* (pp. 111–116). Routledge.

Sarshar, M., Farley, F., Fiorello, C. A., & DuCette, J. (2022). T behavior: Psychological implications of thrill-seeking/risk-taking. *Current Psychology, 41*(1), 200–207.

Sasse, J., Li, M., & Baumert, A. (2022). How prosocial is moral courage? *Current Opinion in Psychology, 44,* 146–150.

Saunders, B. (2022). Volume introduction. In B. Saunders (Ed.), *Stan Lee and Steve Ditko: The Amazing Spider-Man* (pp. xxiii–xxix). Penguin.

Scarlet, J. (2017). *Superhero therapy: Mindfulness skills to help teens and young adults deal with anxiety, depression, and trauma.* New Harbinger.

Scarlet, J. (2020). *Super-women: Superhero therapy for women battling anxiety, depression, and trauma.* Little, Brown.

Scarlet, J. (2021). *It shouldn't be this way: Learning to accept the things you just can't change.* Hachette UK.

Scarlet, J. (2023). *Unseen, unheard, and undervalued.* Hachette UK.

Schachter, S. (1959). *The psychology of affiliation: Experimental studies of the sources of gregariousness.* Stanford University Press.

Schall, S. A. (2021). Adaptive and maladaptive humor styles as predictors of quality of life in individuals diagnosed with a chronic disease. *Dissertation Abstracts International: Section B: The Sciences & Engineering, 82*(3-B).

Scheimer, D., & Chakrabarti, M. (2020). *Former surgeon general Vivek Murthy: Loneliness is a public health crisis.* WBUR. https://www.wbur.org/onpoint/2020/03/23/vivek-murthy-loneliness

Schermer, J. A., Papazova, E. B., Kwiatkowska, M. M., . . . & Krammer, G. (2021).

Predicting self-esteem using humor styles: A cross-cultural study. In E. Vanderheiden & C.-H. Mayer (Eds.), *The Palgrave handbook of humour research* (pp. 15–39). Palgrave Macmillan/Springer Nature.

Schouten, J. W. (1991). Selves in transition: Symbolic consumption in personal rites of passage and identity reconstruction. *Journal of Consumer Research, 17*(4), 412–425.

Scott, C., McKinlay, A., McLellan, T., Britt, E., Grace, R., & MacFarlane, M. (2015). A comparison of adult outcomes for males compared to females following pediatric traumatic brain injury. *Neuropsychology, 29*(4), 501–508.

Scriven, G. (2018). Restorative justice. In R. Woolley (Ed.), *Understanding inclusion: Core concepts, policy and practice* (pp. 172–184). Routledge/Taylor & Francis.

Seligman, M. E. P. (1999). The president's address. *American Psychologist, 54,* 559–562.

Sellers, R. M., Caldwell, C. H., Schmeelk-Cone, K. H., & Zimmerman, M. A. (2003). Racial identity, racial discrimination, perceived stress, and psychological distress among African American young adults. *Journal of Health & Social Behavior, 44*(3), 302–317.

Shakespeare, W. (1623/1982). *All's well that ends well.* In *The illustrated Stratford Shakespeare* (pp. 264–288). Chancellor.

Shapiro, F. (2001). *Eye movement desensitization and reprocessing: Basic principles, protocols, and procedures* (2nd ed.). Guilford.

Shaw, D. (2014). *Traumatic narcissism: Relational systems of subjugation.* Routledge/Taylor & Francis.

Shepela, S. T., Cook, J., Horlitz, E., Leal, R., Luciano, S., Lutfy, E., Miller, C., Mitchell, G., & Worden, E. (1999). Courageous resistance: A special case of altruism. *Theory & Psychology, 9*(6), 787–805.

Sherwin, A. (2014, April 16). *Oy vey! Spider-Man is Jewish, Andrew Garfield confirms.* The Independent. https://www.independent.co.uk/arts-entertainment/films/news/oy-vey-spiderman-is-jewish-andrew-garfield-confirms-9262205.html

Shevlin, M., McElroy, E., & Murphy, J. (2015). Loneliness mediates the relationship between childhood trauma and adult psychopathology: Evidence from the adult psychiatric morbidity survey. *Social Psychiatry & Psychiatric Epidemiology, 50*(4), 591–601.

Shi, Y., Kang, J., Xia, P., Tyagi, O., Mehta, R. K., & Du, J. (2021). Spatial knowledge and firefighters' wayfinding performance: A virtual reality search and rescue experiment. *Safety Science, 139,* Artl 105231.

Silverman, S. B., Johnson, R. E., McConnell, N., & Carr, A. (2012). Arrogance: A formula for leadership failure. *The Industrial-Organizational Psychologist, 50*(1), 21–28.

Singer, T., & Klimecki, O. M. (2014). Empathy and compassion. *Current Biology, 24*(18), R875–R878.

Sjöström, A., & Gollwitzer, M. (2015). Displaced revenge: Can revenge taste "sweet" if it aims at a different target? *Journal of Experimental Social Psychology, 56,* 191–202.

Skitka, L. J. (2012). Moral convictions and moral courage: Common denominators of good and evil. In M. Mikulincer & P. R. Shaver (Eds.), *The social psychology of morality: Exploring the causes of good and evil* (pp. 349–365). American Psychological Association.

Smigelsky, M. (2013). Becoming fully human: The promotion of meaning and spirituality in professional relationships and contexts. *Journal of Constructive Psychology, 26*(4), 316–318.

Smith, P. K. (2018). *The psychology of school bullying.* Routledge.

Smith, R. T. (2014). *Fighting for recognition: Identity, masculinity, and the act of violence in professional wrestling.* Duke University Press.

Smith, T. (2018, August 6). *What superheroes teach us about responsibility.* https://www.livehappy.com/practice/what-superheroes-teach-us-about-responsibility

Sochos, A., & Aleem, S. (2022). Parental attachment style and young persons' adjustment to bereavement. *Child & Youth Care Forum, 51*(1), 161–179.

Sokol, L., & Fox, M. (2019). *The comprehensive clinician's guide to cognitive behavior therapy.* PESI.

Soper, B., Milford, G. E., & Rosenthal, G. T. (1995). Belief when evidence does not support theory. *Psychology & Marketing, 12*(5), 415–422.

Soulliere, D. M. (2006). Wrestling with masculinity: Messages about manhood in the WWE. *Sex Roles, 55*(1-2), 1–11.

Spencer, M. B., & Spencer, T. R. (2014). Invited commentary: Exploring the promises, intricacies, and challenges of positive youth development. *Journal of Youth & Adolescence, 43*(6), 1027–1035.

Staats, S., Wallace, H., Anderson, T., Gresley, J., Hupp, J. M., & Weiss, E. (2009). The hero concept: Self, family, and friends who are brave, honest, and hopeful. *Psychological Reports, 104*(3), 820–832.

Stacer, M. J., & Solinas-Saunders, M. (2018). Criminal thinking among men beginning a batterer intervention program: The relevance of military background. *Journal of Aggression, Maltreatment & Trauma, 27*(2), 199–219.

Stanley, J. (2015/2018). Comfortable in your own skin. In S. Polly & K. H. Britton (Eds.), *Character strengths matter: How to live a full life* (pp. 87-91). Positive Psychology News. https://read.amazon.com/?asin=B010965J5A

Steele, A. (n.d.). *The psychological effects of bullying on kids & teens.* Masters in Psychology Guide. https://mastersinpsychologyguide.com/articles/psychological-effects-bullying-kids-teens

Steger, M.F. & Kashdan, T.B. (2009). Depression and everyday social activity, belonging, and well-being. *Journal of Counseling Psychology, 56*(2), 289–300.

Steinberg, L. (2009). Adolescent development and juvenile justice. *Annual Review of Clinical Psychology, 51*(1), 459–485.

Sternberg, R. J. (1986). A triangular theory of love. *Psychological Review, 93*(2), 119–135.

Sternberg, R. J. (1994). Experimental approaches to human intelligence. *European Journal of Psychological Assessment, 10*(2), 153–161.

Stevenson, R. L. (1886). *Strange case of Dr. Jekyll and Mr. Hyde.* Longmans, Green.

Stichter, M., & Saunders, L. (2019). Positive psychology and virtue: Values in action. *Journal of Positive Psychology, 14*(1), 1–5.

Stickley, A., & Koyanagi, A. (2016). Loneliness, common mental disorders and suicidal behavior: Findings from a general population survey. *Journal of Affective Disorders, 197*, 81–87.

Stretesky, P., Shelley, T., Hogan, M., & Unnithan, N. (2010). Sensemaking and secondary victimization among unsolved homicide co-victims. *Journal of Criminal Justice, 38*(5), 880–888.

Stroebe, K. (2013). Motivated inaction: When collective disadvantage does not induce collective action. *Journal of Applied Social Psychology, 43*(10), 1997–2006.

Su, Y. J., & Chow, C. C. (2020). PTSD, depression and posttraumatic growth in young adult burn survivors: Three-year follow-up of the 2015 Formosa Fun Coast Water Park explosion in Taiwan. *Journal of Affective Disorders, 274*, 239–246.

Suarez, E.C. (2008). Self-reported symptoms of sleep disturbance and inflammation, coagulation, insulin resistance and psychosocial distress: Evidence for gender disparity. *Brain, Behavior, & Immunity, 22*(6), 960–968.

Sue, D. W., Sue, D., Neville, H. A., & Smith, L. (2019). *Counseling the culturally diverse: theory and practice* (8th ed.). Wiley.

Sullivan, M. P., & Venter, A. (2005). The hero within: Inclusion of heroes into the self. *Self & Identity, 4*(2), 101–111.

Taihara, Q., & Malik, J. A. (2016). Is it adaptive or maladaptive? Elaborating conditional role of shame and guilt in development of psychopathologies. *Psychological Studies, 61*(4), 331–339.

Takeuchi, H., Taki, Y., Hashizume, H., Asano, K., Asano, M., Sassa, Y., Yokota, S.,

Kotozaki, Y., Nouchi, R., & Kawashima, R. (2016). Impact of videogame play on the brain's microstructural properties: Cross-sectional and longitudinal analyses. *Molecular Psychiatry, 21*(12), 1781–1789.

Tan, H. K., Jones, G. V., & Watson, D. G. (2009). Encouraging the perceptual underdog: Positive affective priming of nonpreferred local–global processes. *Emotion, 9*(2), 238–247.

Tangney, J. P. (1994). The mixed legacy of the superego: Adaptive and maladaptive aspects of shame and guilt. In J. M. Masling & R. F. Bornstein (Eds.), *Empirical perspectives on object relations theory* (pp. 1–28). American Psychological Association.

Tangney, J. P., & Dearing, R. L. (2002). *Shame and guilt.* Guilford.

Tanielian T., & Jaycox L.H. (Eds.). (2008). *Invisible wounds of war: Psychological and cognitive injuries, their consequences, and services to assist recovery.* RAND.

Tanner, J. L., & Arnett, J. J. (2016). The emergence of emerging adulthood: The new life stage between adolescence and young adulthood. In A. Furlong (Ed.), *Routledge handbook of youth and young adulthood* (pp. 50–56). Routledge.

Tate, N. (2018). *Loneliness rivals obesity, smoking as health risk.* WebMD Health News. https://www.webmd.com/balance/news/20180504/loneliness-rivals-obesity-smoking-as-health-risk

Tawwab, N. G. (2021). *Set boundaries, find peace: A guide to reclaiming yourself.* Penguin.

Taylor, F. W. (2003). *Scientific management.* Routledge.

Taylor, R. J., Chae, D. H., Lincoln, K. D., & Chatters, L. M. (2015). Extended family and friendship support networks are both protective and risk factors for major depressive disorder and depressive symptoms among African Americans and black Caribbeans. *Journal of Nervous & Mental Disease, 203*(2), 132–140.

Tedeschi, R.G., Calhoun, L.G. (1996). The posttraumatic growth inventory: Measuring the positive legacy of trauma. *Journal of Traumatic Stress, 9*(3), 455–71.

Tedeschi, R.G., Shakespeare-Finch, J., Taku, K., & Calhoun, L.G. (2018). *Posttraumatic growth: Theory, research, and applications.* Routledge.

The Take (2018, November 18). *Spider-Man: A metaphor for puberty* [Video]. YouTube. https://www.youtube.com/watch?v=lv3sRHmkqxo

Thomas, J. R. (2008). Genies & bottles: One more day for Spider-Man (afterword). In A. Alonso (Ed.), *One more day* trade paperback (unpaginated). Marvel.

Tignor, S. M. (2017). Distinguishing neurotic from prosocial "Guilt": Evidence for the conceptual distinctiveness of checklist and scenario measures. *Dissertation Abstracts International: Section B: The Sciences & Engineering, 78*(2-B(E)).

Tolin, D. F. (2016). *Doing CBT: A comprehensive guide to working with behaviors, thoughts, and emotions*. Guilford.

Tolkien, J. R. R. (1937). *The Hobbit, or there and back again*. George Allen & Unwin.

Tomich, P. L., & DiBlasio, A. M. (2022). Stress-related growth: An experimental approach to examine whether stressful events cause perceived growth. *Current Psychology: A Journal for Diverse Perspectives on Diverse Psychological Issues, 41*(4), 1976–1983.

Torvik, F. A., Flatø, M., McAdams, T. A., Colman, I., Silventoinen, K., & Stoltenberg, C. (2021). Early puberty is associated with higher academic achievement in boys and girls and partially explains academic sex differences. *Journal of Adolescent Health, 69*(3), 503–510.

Tucker, P. (1994). Substance abuse and psychosis: Chicken or the egg? *Australasian Psychiatry, 2*(6), 271–273.

Tucker, R. (2017). *Slugfest: Inside the 50-year battle between Marvel and DC*. Da Capo.

Turner, V. (1974). Liminal to liminoid in play, flow and ritual: An essay in comparative symbology. *Rice University Studies, 60*(3), 53–92.

Umbreit, M. S. (1989). Crime victims seeking fairness, not revenge. Toward restorative justice. *Federal Probation, 53*(3), 52–57.

Vaillant, G. E. (1977). *Adaptation to life*. Little, Brown.

Valent, P. (2010). Survivor guilt. In G. Fink (Ed.), *Stress of war, conflict and disaster* (pp. 623–625). Elsevier Academic Press.

Van der Kolk, B. (2014). *The body keeps the score: Mind, brain and body in the transformation of trauma*. Penguin UK.

Van Rens, F. E. C. A., & Heritage, B. (2021). Mental health of circus artists: Psychological resilience, circus factors, and demographics predict depression, anxiety, stress, and flourishing. *53*, Artl 101850.

Van Tongeren, D. R., Hibbard, R., Edwards, M., Johnson, E., Diepholz, K., Newbound, H., Shay, A., Houpt, R., Cairo, A., & Green, J. D. (2018). Heroic helping: The effects of priming superhero images on prosociality. *Frontiers in Psychology, 9*, 2243.

Vashi, N. A. (2015). Evolutionary basis of attraction. *Beauty and body dysmorphic disorder: A clinician's guide*. Springer International.

Velez, G., & Spencer, M. B. (2018). Phenomenology and intersectionality: Using PVEST as a frame for adolescent identity formation amid intersecting ecological systems of inequality. In C. E. Santos & R. B. Toomey (Eds.). *Envisioning the integration of an intersectional lens in developmental science* (pp. 75–90). Wiley.

Ventegodt, S., Kandel, I., Ervin, D. A., & Merrick, J. (2016). Concepts of holistic care. In I. L. Rubin, J. Merrick, D. E. Greydanus, & D. R. Patel (Eds.), *Health care for people with intellectual and developmental disabilities across the lifespan* (pp. 1935–1941). Springer.

Verhaeghe J, Gheysen R, Enzlin P. (2013). Pheromones and their effect on women's mood and sexuality. *Facts Views & Vision in ObGyn 5*(3), 189–95.

VIA Institute on Character (n.d.). [Homepage]. VIA Institute on Character. https://viacharacter.org

Vman (2012, May). *The amazing Andrew Garfield*. Vman. https://vman.com/article/the-amazing-andrew-garfield

Wahl, O. F. (1995). *Media madness: Public images of mental illness*. Rutgers University Press.

Waldinger, R. J., & Schulz, M. S. (2010). What's love got to do with it? Social functioning, perceived health, and daily happiness in married octogenarians. *Psychology & Aging, 25*(2), 422-431.

Walker, D. (2018). *Complex PTSD: From surviving to thriving*. Azure Coyote.

Wall, K., & Ferguson, G. (1998). *Rites of passage: Celebrating life's changes*. Beyond Words.

Walsh, J., & Schindehette, S. (1997). *Tears of rage—From grieving father to crusader for justice: The untold story of the Adam Walsh case*. Pocket.

Walters, K. J., Simons, J. S., & Simons, R. M. (2018). Self-control demands and alcohol-related problems: Within- and between-person associations. *Psychology of Addictive Behaviors, 32*(6), 573–582.

Wassertheil-Smoller, S. et al. (2014). Depression, anxiety, antidepressant use, and cardiovascular disease among Hispanic men and women of different national backgrounds: Results from the Hispanic Community Health Study/Study of Latinos. *Annals of Epidemiology, 24*(11), 822–830.

Watt-Evans, L. (2006). Superman vs. the amazing Spider-Man. In G. Conway with L. Wilson (Eds.), *Webslinger: Unauthorized essays on your friendly neighborhood Spider-Man* (pp. 17-24). BenBella.

Weber, M. C., & Schulenberg, S. E. (2022). The curvilinear relationships between posttraumatic growth and posttraumatic stress, depression, and anxiety. *Traumatology*. Advance online publication. https://doi.org/10.1037/trm0000398

Wedding, D., Boyd, M. A, & Niemiec, R. M. (2010). *Movies and mental illness: Using films to understand psychopathology* (3rd ed.). Hogrefe.

Wegner, D. M. (1994). Ironic processes of mental control. *Psychological Review, 101*(1), 34–52.

Weiston-Serdan, T. (2017). *Critical mentoring: A practical guide.* Stylus.

Weiten, W. (1998). Personality: Theory, research, and assessment. *Psychology: Themes and variations.* Brooks/Cole.

Western, B., & Pettit, B. (2010). Incarceration and social inequality. *Daedalus, 139*(3), 8–19.

Wheeler, B. L. (Ed.). (2015). *Music therapy handbook.* Guilford.

Williams, M. (2016). *When clients confess to crimes they did not commit.* Psychology Today. https://www.psychologytoday.com/us/blog/culturally-speaking/201606/when-clients-confess-to-crimes-they-did-not-commit

Williams, W. H., Chitsabesan, P., Fazel, S., McMillan, T., Hughes, N., Parsonage, M., & Tonks, J. (2018). Traumatic brain injury: A potential cause of violent crime? *The Lancet Psychiatry, 5*(10), 836–844.

Wilson, K. G., & Murrell, A. R. (2004). Values work in acceptance and commitment therapy. In S. C. Hayes, V. M. Follette, & M. Linehan (Eds.) *Mindfulness and acceptance: Expanding the cognitive-behavioral tradition* (pp. 120–151). Guilford.

Wilson, M. (1993). DSM-III and the transformation of American psychiatry: A history. *American Journal of Psychiatry, 150*(3), 399–410.

Wilson, R. S., Krueger, K. R., Arnold, S. E., Schneider, J. A., Kelly, J. F., Barnes, L. L., Tang, Y., & Bennett, D. A. (2007). Loneliness and risk of Alzheimer disease. *Archives of General Psychiatry, 64*(2), 234–240.

Wizard Magazine staff. (1998, February). Sticky situation. *Wizard Magazine, 1*(78), 52–57.

World Health Organization (2022). *International classification of diseases* (11th ed.) [ICD-11]. World Health Organization.

Worthington, E. L. Jr., & Allison, S. T. (2018). *Heroic humility: What the science of humility can say to people raised on self-focus.* American Psychological Association.

Xu, J., & Roberts, R. E. (2010). The power of positive emotions: It's a matter of life or death—subjective well-being and longevity over 28 years in a general population. *Health Psychology, 29*(1), 919.

Yerkes, R. M., & Dodson, J. D. (1908). The relation of strength of stimulus to rapidity of habit formation. *Journal of Comparative Neurology & Psychology, 18*, 459–482.

Zaikova, A. V. (2022). "Betrayed by my body." The views of women with polycystic ovarian syndrome on their experiences in their intimate partner relationships. *Dissertation Abstracts International: Section B: The Sciences & Engineering, 83*(5-B).

Zajonc, R. B. (1968). Attitudinal effects of mere exposure. *Journal of Personality & Social Psychology, 9*(2), 1–27.

Zarrett, N., & Eccles, J. (2006). The passage to adulthood: Challenges of late adolescence. *New Directions for Youth Development, 2006*(111), 13–28.

Zdaniuk, A., & Bobocel, D. R. (2012). Vertical individualism and injustice: The self-restorative function of revenge. *European Journal of Social Psychology, 42*(5), 640–651.

Zhang, Y., & Chen, Z. (1990). An experimental study of the sensation-seeking trait of special teenagers. *Acta Psychologica Sinica, 22*(4), 368–376.

Zuckerman, M. (1979). *Sensation seeking: Beyond the optimum level of arousal*. Erlbaum.

Zuckerman, M. (1983). *Biological cases of sensation seeking, impulsivity, and anxiety*. Erlbaum.

Index

Page numbers in *italics* indicate photographs.

knowledge. *See* wisdom and knowledge
Kohlberg, Lawrence, 62, 66
Kübler-Ross, Elisabeth, 108–9

Latinx, 49–60, 65–66
leadership, 173
learning
  love of, 72, 165
  social, 150
  See also education; wisdom and
    knowledge
Lee, Stan, xxii, xxv, xxvi, xxvii–xxviii,
  xxviii, xix, 133, 160, 191, 196, 247
Lieber, Larry, xxii
Lightner, Candace, 83
liminality, 182
listening, 43, 45, 46, 58, 60, 101, 102–3
  See also communication
logotherapy, 106
loneliness, 34, 97–103, 170
losses, xxvi, 33, 34, 73, 114, 115, 125–28, 197
  processing of/learning from, 105–6,
    109–13, 115–16, 125, 197
  See also death; grief; murders: co-
    victims of
love, xxvii, 43, 87–95, 169–70, 177, 201
  familial, 170, 171, 196
  intimate, 94
  passionate, 94
  See also families; relationships
LSD, 141

machismo, 54–55
Maguire, Tobey (self or as Spider-Man),
  14–15, 26, 97, 109–10, 133, 171,
  173, 176, 203, 210

masculinity, 31, 54–55, 57, 66, 76
Maslow, Abraham, 3, 74–78
megalomania, 208
memory and memories, 7, 106, 185, 219
  note 26
  network, 111
mental health, xxiv, xxv, xxvi–xxvi, 27,
  97–103, 134–39, 163–64
  persons of color and, 57–60
mental illnesses, 136–39, 145, 164, 207
  See also disorders; *and individual
    conditions*
mentors and mentorship, 37–46, 57–58,
  213
Mercado, Yehudi, 66
mercy, 166–67
  See also compassion; forgiveness
mere exposure effect, 89
mesosystemic level, 52
metamorphoses, 139–44
microsystemic level, 52
Milner, Marion, 209
mindfulness, 156–57, 174–75
modesty. *See* humility
money, xxvii, 6, 13, 31, 33, 87, 140, 195
moral injury, 63
moral development. *See* values:
  development of
morality. *See* values
mortality. *See* death
motivations, 4–10, 74–78, 83, 170,
  173–74, 192–93, 195, 199
multicultural counseling and therapy
  (MCT), 59
multiculturalism, 49
multilingualism, 55